BRAVE NEW PLAY RITES

Praise for the Brave New Play Rites Festival

The Brave New Play Rites Festival is a place where anything can happen. It's a celebration of the courage of creative writers who write for performance. They're a special group. As a director I'm always amazed by writers who dare to let me catch sight of their artistic vision, shape it in the physical world, and put it on display, downstage centre. The collaborative process of theatre is a ritual of creation that has been reinventing itself for more than two thousand years. But in my mind it starts here. With the brave new playwrights.

—RICHARD WOLFE, *Co-Artistic Director,*
Western Theatre Conspiracy

Without question, the underlying spirit of Brave New Play Rites was the absolute fearlessness with which everything was approached. First-time playwrights (often) paired with first-time directors with new scripts with ink still wet from the latest rewrite. Each festival was a testament to our faith in live theatre: "it will all work if we can get it up on its feet", and whether it did or didn't, it was the most extraordinary learning experience for playwrights and directors.

—KATHLEEN WEISS, *Assistant Professor, Drama Dept.,*
University of Alberta, Edmonton

Almost ten years ago, I wrote a one-act play for Brave New Play Rites. For hours I sat on a saggy couch listening, as the script was read and re-read, blocked, then finally performed. It was like watching a magic trick, a sleight of hand. The script, as a script, seemed to disappear and the play, performed in the moment, became the thing. It was intimate and wonderful and terrifying all at the same time.

—MADELEINE THIEN,
author of Simple Recipes *and* Certainty

Brave New Play Rites

20 YEARS OF DRAMATIC ENGAGEMENT FROM UBC'S CREATIVE WRITING PROGRAM

Edited by Bryan Wade

ANVIL PRESS | 2006

LIBRARY AND ARCHIVES CANADA CATALOGUING IN PUBLICATION

Brave New Play Rites : 20 years of dramatic engagement / Bryan Wade, editor.

ISBN 1-895636-75-2

1. Canadian drama (English)--21st century. 2. One-act plays, Canadian (English)--British Columbia. I. Wade, Bryan, 1950- II. University of British Columbia. Creative Writing Program

PS8315.5.B7B73 2006   C812'.041089711   C2006-901388-8

Printed and bound in Canada
Cover design: Typesmith Design
Typesetting: HeimatHouse
Photo of Bryan Wade: Kevin Minney

Represented in Canada by the Literary Press Group
Distributed by the University of Toronto Press

The publisher gratefully acknowledges the financial assistance of the B.C. Arts Council, the Canada Council for the Arts, and the Book Publishing Industry Development Program (BPIDP) for their support of our publishing program.

Anvil Press Inc.
P.O. Box 3008, Main Post Office
Vancouver, B.C. V6B 3X5 CANADA
www.anvilpress.com

TABLE OF CONTENTS

Introduction

A toilet bowl. A piano. A chair. Three pools of light on a bare stage. A Volkswagen Beetle. A table. A section of rope. A ladder. A fridge. A flashlight pointed up from below someone's chin. A talking tree. The outline of moonlight through a window on the floor.

All of the above were sets for plays produced in the Brave New Play Rites festival.

Twenty years is a long time. It's a lot of plays.

We've had musicals, comedies, sketches, excerpts from full-length plays, docu-dramas, one-person shows, self-indulgent rants, and dramas.

Three hundred and twenty plays have been produced at the festival.

We've had full-frontal nudity, foul language, gunshots, cigarettes being smoked, meals being eaten, illegal substances being inhaled. No children though. No animals either.

One year we produced twenty-four plays with three performances for each play over the course of six days. This year we will produce a much more manageable twelve plays.

We've had directors quit and run off to Japan. We've had actors drop out at the last moment (and I mean, the last moment, just a few hours before show time) when they landed a well-paying gig in a television show. We've had other actors perform in three plays, along with directing a play.

Venues have ranged from the Vancouver Little Theatre to late night shows at the Waterfront Theatre for the New Play Centre's New Play Festival to the original Dorothy Somerset Studio (a low ceiling black box theatre), to the ballroom at the Graduate Student Centre to Presentation House in North Vancouver, to the auditorium of the Asian Centre (where several 'Best Of' runs were staged), to the Telus Theatre at the Chan Centre. This year Brave New Play Rites is being presented on the stage of the Frederic Wood Theatre at UBC.

Until this year the festival has always had students who produced it for themselves. Even though the budget was minimal (small honourariums for the producers and stage manager plus a bit for advertising and basic costs like paint) they managed to co-ordinate, scheme, plan and hold the hands of stressed out playwrights as they witnessed their "babies being born." In other words, their plays were transformed from words on a page to lines of dialogue performed by actors on a stage lit by stage lights with SFX. Even more nerve-wracking for the playwrights, their plays were performed in front of a live audience.

Brave New Play Rites started out as a simple idea soon after I started teaching in the Creative Writing Department in 1986. Have your playwriting students write plays as part of their coursework. Find a space. Get actors. Get directors. Produce them and have the folks come. There is no better learning experience for a student who has written a play then to see it produced in front of a live audience. To actually have people laugh, cry or recognize a glimpse of themselves when they witness a student's work is a transforming experience for that writer and one that cannot be easily quantified. Plus, there is another more intrinsic learning experience for a student who has written a play. He or she gets to see firsthand the process involved for the theatre artists who collaborate together in the production of their play. Starting with the open auditions we would hold, the playwrights got to know how an actor approaches their craft in creating a character through rehearsal, how a director translates their words into a believable world on the stage, and how a stage manager, lighting, sound and costume designers all make significant contributions. Theatre is ultimately a collaborative art form.

For the following decade, Brave New Play Rites was supported and produced by the Creative Writing Department. Producers and stage managers were usually drawn from amongst a pool of Creative Writing students with some theatre training/experience. Actors and directors for the plays came from all walks of life, drawn by ads in Vancouver's *Georgia Straight*. These volunteers ranged from the experienced professional theatre artist to the "I always wanted to try my hand at . . ." type person. Sometimes the results were startlingly original and innovative; sometimes they were unmitigated disasters involving myself and the producers as arbitration counsellors.

In this last decade (after 1995 when the Creative Writing Department was merged and we became the Department of Theatre, Film and Creative Writing), the festival of Brave New Play Rites has come to represent what a department like this should be doing. Theatre technical students design the lighting and stage manage the shows, costume students create costumes for the many characters, and finally, directing students direct the plays that creative writing students write. Brave New Play Rites has become a much more integrated festival through the commitment of my colleagues in theatre. Kate Weiss, in particular, should be mentioned. She was instrumental in working together with me to shape the festival's current integration.

ABOUT THE BRAVE NEW PLAY RITES ANTHOLOGY

Faced with the daunting task of looking at approximately three hundred and twenty plays, I decided to develop first a long shortlist of plays. The criteria was simple: if the play had a significant impact when it was first produced it would be considered for the anthology. Then the real fun began. How does one find someone from twenty years ago—especially if he or she hasn't kept in touch with Creative Writing? Fortunately, many alumni have kept in touch with each other, so that was one way to find the writers. I was also fortunate to get a lot of cyber space detective work from Daniel Hershfield, who was able to find and contact several writers.

Of course, another interesting dilemma faced the playwrights before they could submit their plays. First, they had to find them. Many of them had written them on typewriters (I know it is hard to imagine a time without the personal computer, but in the late 1980s they weren't in common use) and stored the hard copies in an attic, crawl space or storage locker. Secondly, if they had written the play on a computer, it had long ago given up the ghost (remember floppy disks?) and the problem was to transpose them from one retrieval system to another. Still, if there is a will, often one finds a way and soon enough I was swimming in a sea of play scripts.

After reading the plays, it became apparent that there should be three main categories for the anthology: monologues, comedy, and drama. For an interested student from Creative Writing, Theatre, or English, that seems to be a useful way to categorize the collection of plays. That way if you're looking for a monologue to perform or study, you can directly go to that specific section.

The other reason I categorized the plays this way (even though I was loathe to do so since some of the monologues, for example, are remarkable dramas) was to give the reader a sense of the festival's make-up. Over the years there has been a significant number of monologues presented, thus it made sense to show this as a definite characteristic of the festival. Every year there would also be an abundance of comedy, ranging from quirky black comedies to more middle of the road sketches and situational pieces (heavily influenced by TV) to sophisticated well-constructed plays with well-developed characters. Finally, there were the dramatic plays. Usually they weren't as plentiful as the comedies since it was more problematic in a twenty minute timeframe to create an insightful piece of drama. But I think the plays in the drama category in this anthology are superb examples of what can be done with a short timeframe, small cast and simple setting.

My aim for this anthology was to present a balanced collection of plays, which range in the comedic spectrum from black comedy to satire to knee-slapping funny, and in the dramatic spectrum from naturalistic drama to highly stylized explorations which freely borrow elements from surrealism, expressionism, the theatre of alienation and of the absurd. My hope is that many of these plays will be produced again in the future (a few have already had several stage productions and one has been produced as a film).

Another key element I have aimed for in the make-up of this anthology is with the writers themselves. I tried to strike a balance between relatively young writers (i.e., rookies) who demonstrated a keen comedic or dramatic eye in their first plays and more experienced writers who have gone on to be successfully published and produced in poetry, fiction, non-fiction, film and television and won major awards like the Governor General's. I thought it was crucial in terms of the development of their careers as playwrights at this time that the following "young" writers be included in the anthology: Craig Barron, Kathy Friedman, Daniel Hershfield, Tim Kennaley, Tsering Lama, Kuei-ming Lin, Sherry Mac-Donald, Meah Martin and Andrew Westoll. For example, Craig Barron's work needs to be more widely known for its compact polished yet ironic style. The same reasoning applies to Kuei-ming Lin's work, whose *The Last Prayer* is emblematic of her ability to combine large themes that explore death and sacrifice and present them in what appears to be a simple fable. And of course, what would the balance be in the end if several of the plays in this anthology weren't from successful working playwrights such as Aaron Bushkowsky, Tim Carlson, Corrina Hodgson, Jaan Kolk, and Jason Patrick Rothery?

Brave New Play Rites has also been fortunate to have had some of Vancouver's theatrical visionaries participate in the festival: Richard Wolfe, co-artistic director of the Western Theatre Conspiracy, and Katrina Dunn, artistic director of Touchstone Theatre, directed plays in the festival. David Mackay, John Murphy, Annabel Kershaw, Joy Coghill (as a voiceover), and Dean Haglund, one of the members of the "Smoking Gun" team in the *X-Files* series, have also participated as performers.

Finally, I would like to say a few words about the plays that didn't make it into this anthology. Many of them are of stellar quality and should be published in the near future. (Yes, it's true, a shameless plug for volume two of *Brave New Play Rites*.) The editorial process is difficult and complex as one tries to juggle so many plays in terms of length, style, subject matter and themes into a balanced whole.

I also feel I should make note of several of the notable writers who didn't make it into the anthology for various reasons. Lynn Coady, Steven Galloway, Zsuzsi Gartner and Madeleine Thien couldn't find their Brave New play scripts. C.E. Gatchchalian's play, *Motifs & Repetitions*, which is a stunning meditation on sex and love, was finally unconsidered for the anthology because of its recent publication in an anthology of his own plays, *Motifs & Repetitions & Other Plays*. And finally there is the ironic turn of events involving Frank Borg, a writer who now works in film and television, and Sara Graefe, who works in television and stage. Neither of them ended up having their plays produced in the festival, thus their work couldn't be considered for the anthology. Frank's play was left out of the festival program because an actor in the cast dropped out at the last moment; and in Sara's case, she had another play, *Scribbles*, being produced at the National Arts Centre, English Theatre, in Ottawa around the same time as the Brave New Play Rites Festival.

In closing I would like to say that, in spite of the chaos of the early years of the festival when we often moved like gypsies from venue to venue, it has been a truly glorious ride. Any time one can be involved in a process where young writers' stage plays are presented to a live audience, one feels a certain level of accomplishment.

I hope you too get to experience the awe that I felt about these plays when I first witnessed them and still feel now.

Start reading.

Enjoy.

Bryan Wade, Editor

February, 2006

Vancouver, B.C.

MONOLOGUES

Mrs. Frank

A MONOLOGUE BY

MEAH MARTIN

Mrs. Frank was first produced for the Brave New Play Rites Festival in Vancouver in 1997 with the following cast and crew:

CLARA: Sarah Eeckout
        Cheryl McNamara
        Edel Strassmann★

Directed by Jan Selman
Costumes: Nancy Mizinski
Set Painter: Alan Connelly

(★Appeared courtesy of Canadian Actors' Equity Association.)

NOTE: *Mrs. Frank* was initially written as a monologue, but for this production the director interpreted the play utilizing three performers.

SETTING: *A woman,* **CLARA***, sits on a chair. Behind her is a screen, with three panels arched like church stained glass windows, with recipes for cake and cookies and cinnamon buns on the panels, rather than saints.*

CLARA: My father painted our house pink one summer—salmon pink. He made a fence to match. We have two trees in our front yard and a verandah on the front of the house. My father hates the house. My mother picked it out when he was away on the road. So he says, "All right, we'll live here but don't ever let me see that verandah in a mess." So every Thursday night before my father arrives home from his travels Friday, Mother sends us out to the verandah to make sure it is tidy. It is important that everything be nice for Daddy. He doesn't like to see people be mad or fight so we do all that during the week, when he is gone.

My father always arrives home late Friday afternoon, except when he has a short week, in which case he arrives home Thursday afternoon. But we always know if he is having a short week because when he leaves he says, as he is going out the door, "Remember, it's a short week." So my mother sends my two sisters and me out to the verandah to clean it up on Wednesday. That is always good because it is never as messy as if we have to clean it up on Thursdays being one day less.

Friday night after supper my father cleans out his car and all of his sample bags. He gives us the boxes of broken cookies, and crushed chocolate bars that he can't sell because they are broken. All those crumbled tea biscuits, smashed chocolate puffs, and rolled out Fig Newton's that no one else wants. Sometimes we try to put them together like a jigsaw but mostly we just eat them. We eat those and all go to bed early. Later Friday night I hear strange noises coming from the heat ventilator between my bedroom and my parents' room. I call out, "What's going on, what's that noise, is there something wrong?" My mother calls back, "Go to sleep, everything's fine."

Saturday morning after breakfast my father and mother bathe and dress, then go out to shop for groceries and other things. My two sisters and I clean the house while they are gone. My mother divides the house into three sections, one for each of us girls. There is the upstairs, which has three bedrooms, a bathroom, long hallway, and my father's office; the downstairs which includes a living-room, a piano room, and a dining-room and the verandah, which doesn't really count because it has already been cleaned, and the kitchen which includes the fridge, stove, cupboards, and floor. We rotate every week. If you get the kitchen you have to clean the oven, defrost the fridge, wash down the cupboards, wash and wax the floor. When you are done all of that you bake a Devil's food chocolate cake from the Watkins cook book, and cinnamon buns from my grandma's recipe book. If you get the downstairs you have to first wipe up all of the hardwood floors around the rug with a rag, then with a mop. Then you dust all of the furniture. Finally you take a vacuum to it all. If you have the upstairs you have to clean the bathroom first, Dutch Cleanser to the bathtub, bleach to the toilet, and the sink. Then you have to sweep the floor and wash and wax it. Then you have to make sure all of the beds are made and pick up things off the floors. Then you take a rag and wipe up all of the floors. This is harder than downstairs because there are no carpets upstairs. Finally you take a mop and mop all the floors, then vacuum, same as downstairs. The upstairs is the hardest. My mother is very fastidious about how the cleaning is done.

I never saw my mother's breast until this year when I was putting her to bed after her bath. She is going into a nursing home the next day. She stands in front of the mirror and holds her breast. She says, "I love my boobies, they are beautiful." I hate mine. I try to nurse my baby like Mrs. Reulinski but it doesn't work. So I bind my chest up real tight to dry them out and when I take the bandages off my breasts are long, flat and empty. Breasts are a lot of trouble, always looking for lumps, sore, having to have them tested. I had a mammogram last week and the technician is so mad at my right breast because it won't cooperate and do what she wants. I want to say to her, "would you like me to cut it off and leave it?" I don't, but I think there should be a Midas Mammogram Centre, where you drive in, leave it and pick it up later.

She phones the ultra sound people because she finds something. She says, "Can you do a breast at two o'clock?" Then she tells me to pick up my clothes and I follow her down the hall wearing my blue gown. I imagine that I had this huge mask, this breast mask with an elastic band that went around my body and my two legs were sticking out the bottom. I imagine that this breast has two time hands on them indicating two o'clock. And I am right because when we get to the counter she says, "Your two o'clock breast is here."

Just as we are finishing all the cleaning my mother and father arrive home with the groceries. My sisters and I unpack the groceries while my parents have a nap because they are going dancing at the church hall tonight. After supper my mother goes upstairs to get dressed up. She takes one of her dancing dresses out of the plastic cover and puts it on. My father always wears a suit and tie except when he wears a bow tie. His shoes are always shined. My father and mother talk about whose table they are going to sit at tonight. My father is allowed to dance with other women but not too long or too close and the last dance is definitely always to be with my mother.

After my parents leave for the dance my sisters and I make popcorn, watch television, and eat some of the baking. When there is only one channel it is boring as there is only hockey. We all always go to bed at ten o'clock except when we babysit. In that case we are at other people's houses and stay up as late as they do because the people are usually at the same dance as my parents. I like babysitting especially if they leave good food. I cut the cake in long strips so the people won't know I had a piece. If I babysit I always get home later than my parents because the people go to other people's houses after the dance for coffee. Then when they come home they pay me and the husband walks me home, leaves me at the verandah door. If I'm not baby-sitting and am in bed I always wake up when my parents come home. I hear the slamming of the car door and their voices as they come up the stairs. Then it is quiet. Then those noises start up again from their room. I don't call out.

Sunday morning we all go to Mass. We always have to go to High Mass because my father is an usher and shows people where to sit; except when he isn't an usher, then we go to Low Mass which I like better because it is shorter. Sometimes my sisters and I go to Low Mass and my parents go to High Mass. Most people sit in the same place every week. People who sit way in the back of the church are not considered to be strong Catholics. Those who sit in the choir loft are worse. I like sitting in the choir loft. There are big windows and you can see outside. We are definitely not allowed to sit in the loft. Today I sit up there anyway and Mrs. Reulinski sees me and she phones my mother when she and Mr. Reulinski get home from Mass which is sooner than I do because they have a car and I have to walk. When I get home my mother asks me where I sat for Mass and I say, "On the right side, right under the statue of the Blessed Virgin Mary, first row."

After Mass my father always takes us girls for a ride to Borden's Bakery where we drive around the back and pick up fresh hot loaves of bread and chocolate covered donuts; then we drive home and have breakfast, pickled pig's feet, cinnamon buns, donuts, fresh bread. My father cooks bacon and eggs. After breakfast, which is really lunch, my parents go upstairs and change. Then they sit in the verandah except when it is cold in which case they sit in the living room. My sisters and I clean up from breakfast and get the chicken and potatoes ready for Sunday supper. After that my father always takes us for a Sunday ride except when we go out to a friend's house. I often go to my friend Mavis's house. I like her house. Her mother bakes cookies. The house is clean and she has a room of her own. Mavis and I go out across the fields over to the graveyard. We have a brown bag full of cookies from her mother. We go up and down the paths reading tombstones making up stories until it is almost dark. Then I go home.

When I get home the chicken is done. My sisters and I make gravy, mashed potatoes and vegetables. Then we have Sunday dinner in the dining room using the good dishes my mother loves. They are cream with big brown and green leaves and bushes. When dinner is over, my sisters and I do the dishes while my parents watch television or listen to the radio. After the dishes are done, we clean up and walk ourselves up over to the church for benediction. I always hate this except for the time Father Ryan's robes caught on fire and Mr. Reulinski had to jump over the front pew and roll Father Ryan down the altar steps.

After benediction we go home, and before we had television, we'd listen to the Leslie Bell Singers, Boston Blackie; after television arrived, we'd get home from benediction just in time to see Ed Sullivan. I see The Beatles, Elvis Presley, although I am not supposed to because the nuns say that Pat Boone is more Christian. Sometimes we play cards. My father packs up the car so he can leave in the morning with all of his sample cases full of unbroken biscuits and candies.

Every weekend is exactly the same, always the same; except for holidays like Christmas, Easter. Then we drive to Moose Jaw to be at my Grandma Katie's house. She makes a big dinner. All my aunts and uncles are there with their children. My mother always ends up having a fight with one of her sisters and won't speak to her until the next holiday. My father laughs and plays cards with the men. My uncle Bill always gets drunk but he gives us money. Then we drive home. My sisters and I are in the back seat of the car. My father gives us each our own window in the car so we won't fight. My sisters each get a side window and my father gives me the back window. Father says is better than the side window because it is bigger. I like watching the moon jump all over the sky and I can't figure out how it gets all over the place when the road is so straight. After we get home we always have some milk and a cinnamon bun, except when it is too late, in which case we all go to bed.

I don't know why my heart aches when I think of those days, or why when I shut my eyes sometimes I find myself standing in the back alley just behind our pink house. I think, well maybe I am like those brown wasps I read about; they go back to where they were born when they are dying. Well maybe I am dying and that is why I am wanting to go back. I actually do go back, two years ago, and go to see my best friend Mavis's mother, Mrs. Reulinski.

I love their house; it's always full of children. Mrs. Reulinski is always pregnant, except when she is nursing a baby. I like that because I can sneak a look at her breast. They are big and the nipple is almost the size of the baby's head. My mother does not allow us to see her breasts. Mrs. Reulinski's sister Bertha has a baby at the same time so Mavis and I go to see her too. It is a chance to see another breast. Only, on the right side of her nipple is an enormous abscess, draining away.

So while I am visiting Mrs. Reulinski her sister Bertha drops in. Mrs. Reulinski says, "You remember Clara don't you Bertha, Mavis's friend when she was little." I say, "Oh I remember you, you had an enormous abscess on your breast." Imagine that, not seeing someone for forty-five years and then saying that!

My mother's aunt had cancer of the breast. They cut her breasts off and lots of stuff under her arms. She goes back to the farm from the city hospital she is in. After she is home for a week she gets up one morning, cooks breakfast and when her husband and boys go out into the fields to work, she shoots herself. Her obituary says, "The entire community was shocked to hear of the passing of Mrs. Frank Haegel. She recently underwent surgery for cancer and had been sent home from the hospital and was thought to be having a good recovery. She is survived by her sisters: Mrs. William Dombroski, Mrs. Joseph Wilenski, Mrs. Anton Werner, Mrs. Jacob Siemens." You'd think when you lose a breast and half of your chest you would be entitled to a first name.

What if I can't find my breast after I die? Will I ever see it again? And will I recognize it? I've only looked at it from looking down and in the mirror; I've never actually stared at it directly. Maybe there is a big warehouse full of parts that have been removed, bins of breasts, uteri, ovaries, appendixes, and legs. People wandering around trying to get a match. It would be simpler for us all to mark them with an indelible marker like they do with televisions and computers. So you have a number. What if, what if I do recognize my breast and someone else is wearing it? How do I get it back? What do I say? I know, I know, I go up to her and just say, "I am sure you don't know this but that is my breast you are wearing." What if she says buzz off? Well I just chase her down and say, "You don't know what that means to me. It is part of my body and I miss it. Please give it back." Then the woman says "BUZZ OFF!" again, and I am desperate so I grab her by the back of her blouse and pull her to the ground and sit on her, "Look you, that's my breast, and I mean to have it back. You don't want it anyway, why, it's broken—that's it, *broken*. You don't want a broken breast do you?" She sees the light and returns my breast.

I listen as the clock chimes twelve. I clean all weekend. On Saturday I divide my apartment into three sections, wipe down the floors first, then mop and vacuum. In the kitchen I clean the oven, the fridge, the floor, then I bake a chocolate cake from the Watkins cook book and cinnamon buns. Saturday night I watch television and have popcorn. Sunday I find a church and go to High Mass and after I find a bakery where they sell chocolate covered donuts. I have breakfast of bacon and eggs, cinnamon buns, fresh bread and I find some pickled pig's feet at Safeway. Sunday afternoon I roast a chicken and go for a walk in a graveyard where I walk up and down the rows reading the names on the tombstones. Sunday night I have my chicken dinner with mashed potatoes and I use my good dishes, the ones with the pink flowers around the rim. I can't find a place that holds benediction anymore but I listen to the radio for a while. I watch a rerun of Ed Sullivan. I pack my bag and get ready to go into the hospital tomorrow for my surgery. I have a bath and I look in the mirror at my breast for a long time.

It's early Monday morning. Everything is nice this weekend, just like it used to be nice for Daddy. I don't want to be mad or angry or make a fuss, so I wait until now.

> **CLARA** *stands, exits behind the screen. She turns the screen around so the panels now show prairie blue sky, wheat fields. We hear a shot.*

[End]

Life of the Party

A MONOLOGUE BY

SARA O'LEARY

Life of the Party was produced for the Brave New Play Rites Festival in Vancouver in 1996 with the following cast and crew:

KAYLEE: Valeska Gonzalez

Directed by Conibear

SETTING: *Sparsely furnished apartment. Table and two chairs. Bed, dresser and standing mirror to left. Two doors off to right.*

SCENE ONE — KATIE'S APARTMENT

KATIE *is alone in her apartment. She has a tube of icing and is gluing together layers of miniature cakes from an Easy-Bake Oven. She is wearing a gaudy retro cocktail-style dress. There is a file folder of clippings sitting on the table.*

KATIE: If you are a guest at a social occasion it is always appropriate to take something along with you. That's why I made this cake. My mother taught me these little niceties. But I don't know what I should write on the top of the cake. The couple who are having the party are celebrating the fact that their building went condo and they bought their unit. So? "Happy Unit Warming?" But, I mean, the unit should already have been warmed—they've been living there seven years. Actually we're been invited to congratulate them on their rampant consumerism. It's like when people who have been living together half their adult life decide to get married. Either they want kids or some jazzy new appliances. I'm so tired of buying wedding presents. You end up buying something completely useless because you get to the point where you're in the store and you see something and you think, "Who would buy that?" And then you do. It must have been easier when bachelors lived with their parents until they married virgins and got a home of their own. Then they needed towels and pots and pans and glasses and tablecloths and sheets and toasters and blenders—wait, when were blenders invented? I definitely remember Mother having a blender when I was little because we used to make chocolate surprise milkshakes. The surprise was that she put spinach in them. I never knew until I had a milkshake made by somebody other than my mother and I was like, "Where's the green flecks?" I don't know if her blender was a wedding present. I'm certain, however, that life used to be simpler. In the good old days. Before I was born.

She scrawls something on the cake top with the icing tube.

Cheers! My name is Katie, but you can call me Ka-Ka-Ka-Katie. (*hums song and swirls about*) It sounds very romantic, doesn't it. Ka-ka-ka-katie, beautiful Katie. Actually, my father used to stutter. I never noticed though when he was saying anything else and I always thought that was my name. He could say Bob, I remember that much clearly. Bob, he'd say and it was a whole symphony of adulation. My son, my son. And then there was me. Going around telling people my name until the first grade teacher sent me to a speech pathologist.

> *She goes to look at herself in the mirror. Then walks away and*
> *quickly looks back—trying to catch herself offguard.*

Have you ever noticed how impossible it is to see yourself. I mean just the way you must look to other people when you don't know anybody is looking at you. I think my face kind of goes all slack—like this—and that I look like my tongue is too big for my mouth and I slept too many nights on my right side and my head got lopsided. It's just about impossible though to catch yourself not looking. Trust me. I know. Mirror, Mirror, on the wall. Who's the foolishest one of all?

> *She pulls out a box of paperback self-help books, piles them up*
> *into little pyramid and then knocks them down.*

I used to try and understand why I am the way I am in the larger context of my family. My father obviously never wanted a daughter and as for my mother I think she would have been happier with a mynah bird. It could just repeat everything she said back to her and they'd get along just fine. You've got to think for yourself, that's what my mother always says.

My brother, Bob. He's gay. Don't tell him I told you. Not so much that he'd mind you knowing—just that he doesn't know himself. No, that's not true. Forgive me, I lie. He just doesn't like to admit it. I remember standing there watching them put Daddy into the ground and thinking, "Well, at least Bob can relax now." Only he hasn't. If anything he's worse. I swear to weeping Jesus, he's gonna end up with a wife and kids one of these days. Does anybody have any idea what happened to Oscar

Wilde's sons? They probably ended up really twisted. Probably became lawyers or something.

She pulls her dress over her head and throws it in the corner.

My psychic told me that I might as well stop trying to understand my family because all my unresolved stuff was actually from a previous life-time. That was sort of a relief. Sort of. It turns out that many many life-times ago I was actually that guy in Arabian Nights. Sultan Schahriah. The one who had all the virgins killed until Scheherazade came along and tricked him by telling him stories for a thousand and one nights. Anyway this is the real reason why I've never been able to find true love through all my subsequent visitations to this planet. But tonight, tonight is the very first time in hundreds of years that the planetary alignment will coincide with my personal chart so that my transubstantiary bur-den may be lifted. Tonight is the night that all is made clear. And of course I have nothing to wear.

She twirls in her little slip and pulls a face at herself in the mirror.

I went through a phase of neurotic narcissism where I kept getting my hair dyed and cut and bought a succession of new frocks—they weren't just dresses, they were frocks!—each one a brighter colour than the last. And all because once, about a year ago, I dressed up as a bag lady and walked up and down all over downtown. All sorts of people passed by me but nobody I knew recognized me. Nobody saw me at all. It's like that fantasy you have when you're a kid where you take a magic potion that turns you invisible. I was never so frightened. I shouldn't have done it. I shouldn't have found out how easy it was to disappear. I didn't need to know that.

She pulls out a huge file of clippings from newspapers and maga-zines, then pulls out newspaper page.

I read this thing where it said that one of the greatest fears for women is becoming a bag lady. I thought that might make me feel better, but it didn't.

She searches through a file, then holds up a picture to the audience.

Look at this. Dum dum de dumb-dumb. Here come the brides. You can't beat those Moonies for throwing a wedding. What is it . . . thirty-five thousand couples? And more via satellite. Another 325,000 around the world via satellite. Satellite. Jesus-copulating-Christ. Look at all the teeny little brides. (*holds out to audience*) Here, try this. (*whips magnifier out of pocket and holds it up to picture*) Better? Look, I think this one here and this one in the twenty-seventh row are wearing the same dress. Imagine the mortification. Apparently the couples had all just met. Just met. What a flipped out first date. Arranged marriages. Closest I ever came was when our grade seven teacher picked pen pals for the whole class. Guess I don't need to tell you how that turned out. (*hums "Return to Sender"*) Kind of pathetic, isn't it. What if this was your wedding picture? I don't know . . . d'ya think the Reverend Sun Myung Moon could find me one of these itsy-bitsy little grooms?

She claps file shut.

When I first started calling the psychic hotline it was because I wanted to know if I'd ever get married. My best friend, Claudette, had just gotten married to this fellow that she'd met on the bus. She'd known him two weeks. And then they moved to Newcastle because that was where he was from. "Newcastle," she sighed. Doesn't it sound romantic?" He was only visiting here. The day we went to the registry office he joked and said he'd gone travelling to find himself and he'd found Claudette instead. She sorted of giggled and blushed in a way that made me wonder if I'd ever really known her at all. But I had known her. All our lives. She was the first one to learn to ride a bike and I was the first one to kiss a real live boy. And now she was gone and it might have been on a shuttle flight to Venus for all I was ever going to see her again. "We'll write," I said. "I'll call," she said. We both knew it was over. Only she was flying off into the sunset or sunrise or whatever it would be with this man and I was being left behind to wither on the vine. Or bus. Or whatever.

Claude wasn't just my best friend she was also my roomie. When she soared off into the happily ever after I was left with an apartment I couldn't afford. So I moved here. It's small, I know, but it suits me. I mean, Sarah Bernhardt made all kinds of money but she slept in a coffin, right?

She lies down on floor and then hops up again.

It's pretty hard to be a Sarah Bernhardt these days. I used to work in a corporation. I was a steno. Steno-pad, steno-chair, steno-gal. I was the only girl on the floor who could type and whistle at the same time. I think the other girls were jealous. I suspected several of practising at home. I tried teaching a few of my favourite co-workers, but it was like trying to teach a poodle to Watusi. I whistle really quietly, only slightly louder than breathing, but still sometimes the words to my songs showed up in other people's reports. Anyway, now I do box office for this theatre company and I'm really much happier. It's like I was getting allergic to beige pantyhose or something. I couldn't cope with all the normalcy. Everybody at the theatre is pretty weird and I get to meet all kinds of cool people. Not that I could ever be an actor. Way too scary for me. Standing up there, like in your underwear, in front of all those strangers . . . (*turns to audience*) I mean, wouldn't it freak you out?

She pulls on a black dress.

I don't have a date for the party. That's a little embarrassing but it's just too hard asking a guy out.

She picks up an imaginary phone.

Hello, is that you? I've been trying to get up my nerve to call you for weeks. My name? Well, actually that's confidential. (*turns away from phone and blanches*) I'm doing a survey. Would you mind answering a few questions. No, sir, it's nothing to do with the government. Oh, thank you very much. We do appreciate it so much. Did I mention there might be something by way of an honorarium in this for you, Mr. . . . (*consults imaginary list*) Wright, is it? Well, not an honorarium so much as a prize of sorts. Well, actually, that's confidential as well. Shall we begin? First question: How do you feel about marriage? (*pulls face and hangs up*)

Anyway, it doesn't matter. I mean if this is the night I'm to meet the love of my life—the sun in my sky, the dollop of Dream Whip on my bowl of Jello—if this is the night, then it's hardly necessary to bring a date.

> *She checks herself in mirror one last time, blows herself a kiss, picks up cake, and then shuts out light.*

SCENE TWO

> *Lights on.* **KATIE** *is sitting at one of her two chairs pulled slightly forward. The cake is sitting on the table. We are still in* **KATIE**'s *apartment as she is actually relating the events which transpired at the party. She is alone throughout.*
>
> **KATIE** *is sitting on a chair talking animatedly with somebody on her right, then being interrupted by somebody on her left who wants her attention—back and forth while she is drinking a cocktail, laughing and making extravagant gestures. Suddenly she looks out and begins to address the audience.*

KATIE: Life of the party. I just love parties. Party, party, party. The truth is I just barely even know the hosts. I mean I know them to know them but not to send them a card for Christmas or call them if it's their birthday. Birthdays. They probably have them separately. Although look at them. It's hard to believe either one of them could manage to go to the bathroom alone. I think it's kind of pathetic when grown-up adult people hold hands, don't you. I think public displays of affection belong in private. I'm really here because of that fellow over there. (*points*) No, not him. My god, what do you take me for? Desperate? That man, the one with one ear lobe a little longer than the other. (*stands on chair to point him out*) You didn't notice? Really? Anyway, he's crazy about me. Can't keep away. It's like he's a honey bee and I'm all piston and stamen and pollen and perfume. Well, I know he's way over there. Don't you think we're capable of any discretion at all?

She stands all alone and turns in circles, looking at those around her until the gesture becomes exaggerated into a strange little pirouette.

Look at me. I'm a bachelorette. I'm bachelorette #1. Ask me anything.

She looks at herself in the mirror, teases her hair, and then brushes it down flat, and then repeats.

The thing about going crazy in the privacy of your own home is that nobody cares. You can walk around naked, paint yourself blue, eat nothing but dog biscuits. Going crazy in your house is child's play. I like to throw away my marbles at parties. I started off small—going to parties at people's houses and having baths. Other people's bathrooms are so interesting, don't you think. The most unexpected people have secret sins. If I ever have a party I plan to plant all sorts of interesting things for people to discover. I bought this toy gun. I keep it in the cutlery drawer. I used to keep it in my bedside table but that was just so obvious.

Throughout this speech she is removing things from an imaginary bathroom cabinet.

Nearly all of my friends have been married at least once. Not that I think that's the be-all and end-all of a woman's existence. I mean do I look like I'm my mother. (*to audience*) Yeah, well, same to you, Mister. I have this one friend, Janibeth, (that's her name, she made it up) who's been married twice and to the same man. "Darling," her mother said at the rehearsal dinner, "this isn't a wedding, it's a relapse." I don't believe it—not a single band-aid. I mean it's not that I want to be married, or need to be married but just that's it's getting embarrassing. Like everybody had graduated and gone through some initiation ceremony that you know nothing about. All you know is what they tell you. Ha! wrinkle cream. But his or hers? It's like when you go for lunch with somebody and they say, "Oh I saw this great movie." And you say, "Oh, I hear the pasta salad is good" because you just know this is going to be unbearable. And they are just oblivious to you and your subtlety. Oh ick! Suppositories. They start off . . . "it had that guy in it. You know he was in the thing with the big party . . . where they all go to the house in the country . . . we saw it together, didn't we? At the place on Broadway? It was raining? Anyway, he's in it only he's skinnier now. And it's all set in the desert. Australia. No, Africa. Something that starts with an A. And at the end he tells her that he hadn't really slept with the other one. The one who kept all the dogs. This was after her brother burned down the garage. It was really funny. You should see it." That's what it's like when people try to tell you about how they feel being married. Only it's worse. Because they have to lie at least some of the time. The only thing worse is someone telling you about a dream they had.

> *Back to the party. She's standing and gazing at someone with a rapt expression.*

And then what did you say to him? You didn't. Not really. Omigod. I can't believe how brazen you are. You big brazen thing. You big bronze brazen boy. Where are you going?

> *She looks around, picks out a man and sidles over to talk to him.*

Hello. My name's Kay. (*she waits an incredibly long time for a response*) Well can't you take a pill for that these days? Shudders and walks away.

> *She is apparently listening to someone until she can't stand it and interrupts.*

Is that your real hair? No really, I like it. I do. It reminds me of a guy I used to sleep with. Maybe you know him? Raggedy Andy.

KATIE: (*sitting across from man/empty chair*) When I left home for the first time I was so lonely I thought all my hair would fall out from grief. I couldn't sleep, didn't sleep for weeks. I listened to shortwave radio broadcasts and thought about becoming a missionary. I told my mother about my insomnia and she said, "You probably miss your father's snoring." My father snores so loud that our next door neighbours moved away the year I was in grade seven. Do you really want to hear all this? Mother said it was because Mr. Jenkins was shell-shocked and what could you expect, but even Mrs. Jenkins said she was glad to be going. Mother made me a tape of father snoring and I play it every night, and pretend I'm back in my old room with the blue-flowered wallpaper that matches the bed spread, and that my parents are in their room down the hall, and that the world is a safe place and nothing will ever happen to me.

She looks at audience.

This can't be real. This guy's a fantasy. He hasn't interrupted me once. Are you real? Somebody call 911. I think this man is dead.

She's talking to someone.

So we say we're going for cappuccino and he says he doesn't do pasta.

She laughs uproariously then realizes she is alone. To audience.

I don't really do small talk. I mean I never seem to get the scale right. Either it's so small that it's like "Peep, peep, I'm just a little mouse under your chair." Or else it's like I've just revealed the most awful thing anybody could reveal at a party. Like I've eviscerated myself in public. Is it possible to eviscerate a person or is that only chickens? Does it have something to do with having feathers. Am I digressing?

She goes back to cruising for conversation.

What do you do for a living? (*pause*) Well, I guess it is a personal question. Only if you ask me, all questions are personal. (*pause*) I suppose it does depend on the kind of answer. (*pause*) Try me. (*pause*) Well, I took a cab actually, and that's because I've been phobic about driving ever since the night the family Dodge caught fire as we were driving home from my Grandfather's funeral after he dropped dead from a heart attack after he found out that my Grandmother who he married when they were both twenty hadn't really come from Scotland as she claimed, but from France, a country that my Grandfather refused to admit the existence of at all because of something that happened in his childhood, which we will never discover because he's dead. Also, she was actually

thirty years old and had been married before. (*pause*) A yellow cab.
  She wanders off, stares into space, then is approached.

Really, I don't think I've ever met a garbage man before. (*pause*) So who
takes out the garbage at your house. (*laughs until she realizes she's alone,
then hums "Alone Again, Naturally".*)

  Lights out.

SCENE THREE

  Lights on. **KATIE** *is sitting alone where she was at the end of the
  last scene. To audience.*

KATIE: Do you remember that ad that used to be on TV where there's
  this guy at a party and he's standing there and somebody says
  something only he doesn't answer and then, too late, he turns and
  points at his ears. And then there's this little kid watching her
  mother get smashed and she makes her dolly smoke cigarettes
  and drink whisky. No wait. It's just the deaf guy in this one ad.
  And then the writing comes on. Or maybe it's a voice. ALONE AT
  THE PARTY? What was that ad for anyway?

  KATIE *opens a drawer in table. She takes out a knife and cuts
  her cake.*

  Lights out.

  [End]

Day Shift

A MONOLOGUE BY

MEREDITH BAIN WOODWARD

Day Shift was produced for the Brave New Play Rites Festival in Vancouver in 1992 with the following cast and crew:

LOUISE: Annabel Kershaw★

Directed by Brenda Leadlay

(★Appeared courtesy of Canadian Actors' Equity Association.)

OTHER PRODUCTIONS/PUBLICATIONS OF *Day Shift*:

Theatre Barrie, Barrie, Ontario, June 1996

Day Shift was published in *Escape Acts*,
edited by Colleen Curran, Nuage Editions, 1992.

SETTING: *The kitchen of a trailer on a rural backroad. There's a chair, a lamp, a kitchen counter, and an old shoe box with papers in and around it. It's dusk.*

LOUISE, *in her thirties, has been looking through the box. She wears no-one-will-see-me-so-what-does-it-matter clothes: a housecoat, long underwear, a baggy* T-*shirt. She stares out the window. After a few moments she turns on the light, moves to the kitchen counter, and, picking up a box of macaroni and cheese dinner, tries to read the directions. She gives up, throwing the box on the counter. She stands for a moment, staring out the window again. Finally, she picks up the phone and dials a number.*

LOUISE: Shirley? Yeah, it's me. Louise. Listen, uh . . . Yeah . . . Listen, I'm quittin' at the cafe . . . Hold on! I'm givin' ya a month's notice, okay? . . . I'm not just walkin' out, I'm givin' ya notice . . . Well that's what I'm tellin' ya. Four weeks. Okay?

You can so get along. You can hire someone else . . . There's Linda. What about Bonnie? There's lots of them that'll—sure it's tourist season coming up, but there's always something, right? Thanksgiving, Christmas— and I gotta get outta here, Shirley. I just gotta leave.

No, I'm not upset about anything. Really . . . It's okay. Walter explained. Said he was sorry . . . No, I'm not mad, I've just . . . I dunno, Shirley, I'm just goin' that's all . . . Maybe Kelowna. I hear they got some good programs at the college there. Nicky's doin' that florist thing, right? Maybe I'll do that, or I got a cousin working in Cranbrook. Maybe I'll—no, no! I like workin' for ya, I really do. . . . Well, I'm not so crazy about the day shift, but I told you tha—Shirley! I told you when you switched me. I like workin' night shift much better . . . There's nothin' wrong with days, I just like night shift much bett—What? . . . Oh, now you're gonna give me night shift back . . . Yeah . . . Yeah? . . . Oh boy. I just can't Shirl . . . I've made up my mind. I mean I appreciate the offer and all, but I just can't stay here forever.

I dunno what brought it on. . . . It's just . . . (*laughs*) You wanna know what brought it on? What really brought it on? (*laughs*) I put seed in the bird feeder this morning. (*laughs.*) Yeah. (*laughs*) No, I just got lookin' at stuff . . . Those dead apple trees. The empty chicken house. Cripers! What an eyesore. . . . Yeah, exactly. And then that road outta my place. . . . I dunno, Shirl, I've been starin' at that road for what, thirteen years? It's all I see from the kitchen window. Makes me crazy. I don't even have to look anymore. I know it off by heart. All its twists and turns. Every pothole. Every tree. Every goddam stone.

Yeah, well, you wanna know something? Before I started workin' early shift? I'd walk out to the end of that road every morning and just wait for someone to drive by—anybody—so I could wave. . . . Yeah. Every day. . . . No, finally, the French couple started building their place and I figured, great! I'll practise my French. "Bon jour! Bon jour!" (*laughs*) . . . Yeah, it was fine till they answered back . . . Me? No. In high school I was lousy in French, but I always wanted to get good at it. It's on my list, right? . . . You know, the list that you have of things that you'll do someday when you get time or money or—everybody's got one. . . . Well I do. And speakin' French is on there. I just never got around to it. . . . Yeah, so then these people move in. And their darn dog speaks better French than I do. No kidding, they talk to the dog in French AND English and it understands. They've got a goddam bilingual dog! It makes you think. . . . Well, you make promises to yourself, you know? And then one day all they are is disappointments. Things you never did.

Yeah . . . (*laughs*) You did? You never told me that! No way! . . . . (*laughs*) Well, once upon a time, I was gonna be an actress . . . I always—Yeah, that's right. . . . Did you see that? At the high school? . . . *A Doll's House*. . . . That was years ago, I didn't think anyone remembered that . . . No, I wasn't the one that did the dance. I was the other one . . . That's okay. It was a while ago . . . Then they asked me in town, right, they wanted me to do something in that show they did—you know, the one they made up about the early days? . . . Yeah, well I sing a bit . . . No, I have an okay voice . . . Well they asked me to do it so I guess—nah, I didn't. . . . Well, I just didn't, I dunno. Too far to drive. Well you know, in the snow and that. But I've still got the program from *The Doll's House* . . .

The thing is, Shirl, I've got these old shoeboxes here and they're just filled with stuff like . . . Well, I dunno, newspaper articles, pictures, little . . . poems, sorta, on napkins and soup can labels and—yeah, well I write 'em when I'm workin' and that . . . I dunno. About people mostly. You know . . . just—people, for gosh sakes.

Okay. Like Morley. He'll come in and sit like he does for hours just starin' at his coffee, right? And it just makes me think . . . Well, I dunno, just what he's thinkin' about and that, or he'll say somethin' weird, or just how he looks I mean he scares me sometimes, but he's kinda. . . sad at the same— . . . Well, no, I don't LIKE him or anything, not like that, come on, Shirley, the guy's a fruitcake . . . It's just lonely for a guy like that. I dunno . . .

Or Ruthie. I mean there she is sniffin' and smokin' everything that comes her way. She looks dead half the time; I've never seen anything like it . . . No, I just talk to her sometimes when it's slow. She's had some pretty tough times, I kinda feel sorry for— . . . I dunno what I'm gonna tell her. Why should I tell her anything? I'm not her mother . . . She's kinda pissed off at me right now, if you wanna know . . . I dunno. We were just sittin' around after my shift one day. And all of a sudden she says, "What do you want from me, Louise?" . . . Yeah. (*laughs*) That's what I said: "What could I possibly want from you, Ruthie? What do you think you have that I could possibly want?" . . . I mean, here's this wasted out kid and she thinks—oh boy, who knows what she thinks—I mean, what does she see when she looks at me, for cripes sake . . .

Mike? Yeah . . . Well, when he, uh, when Mike got, uh, cancer and, uh, he had that voice box put in and that? He hated how it sounded, all raspy and that, right? . . . I know he was hard to understand, Shirley, that's not the point . . . Well, he'd never say anything to me, but—it was awful for him. People would act funny, you know, wouldn't talk to him any more . . . I dunno . . . so I wrote a little sort of thing about . . . and when he died? When he finally died? . . . Well . . . I . . .

Anyway maybe I'll put 'em all in a book, right? . . . Well Nora wrote that book about her childhood and got it all printed up herself and they were sellin' 'em at the Red and White. I could do something like that. . . . Well that's just it, Shirley. I've got this feeling that I could keep stuffin' things in that box for ever and nothin' would ever get done. Nothin' would ever change.

Oh come on, Shirl, a raise? Did you hear a word I said? . . . How much? . . . You serious? . . . Walter'll never go for it, I can tell you that right off. . . . Well, I dunno, Shirley, even if he does go for it . . . I know it's a lot of money. I'm not sayin' it's not a lot of money, I'm not sayin' that at all, it's a lot of money, I know that. I just don't think—I mean, I just gotta get out of here, Shirley. My gosh, every time you turn around the garden's overrun with weeds or the wood needs splitting or the waterline needs to be unplugged, and everybody's always askin' how your tomato plants are doin' or tellin' ya how big a zucchini they can grow, and I hate gardening, Shirl, I hate it, I'll be glad to walk away from that pile of rocks . . . Well Mike's not here, is he? So he doesn't get to say anything. If Mike cared so damn much about what happened to his land, maybe he shouldn't of smoked so damn many cigarettes or something. . . . Shirl, Mike's been dead almost four years. This is not sudden. I've had lots of time to think. Lots of time . . . Anyway, that's why I'm—

What? . . . What? . . . Get outta here! A trip to Reno? You never said anything about a trip to Reno. Get outta here! . . . I know we had a good time last time. You don't have to tell me. I know that. We had a terrific time, I never laughed so hard in all my life, I honestly don't think I ever did, it was great, you don't have to tell me . . . When are you going? When? . . . I won't be here then, Shirl, that's what I'm tellin' ya. I won't be here . . . But—no, listen. I just—no, I can't Shirl. I can't . . . SHIRLEY, I'M NOT STAYIN'.

What? . . . Listen, honestly, it has nothin' to do with Walter. I told you, he apolog— . . . Shirley . . . Well, I don't like it eith— . . . I do not ask for it. How can you say such a thing? . . . Shirley! . . . You know . . . Oh boy. I'm sorry, but he was drink—Shirley, he was drinkin'! . . . I don't care if he's going to AA, he's drunk when I come in to open up at seven o'clock in the morning, and he's all over me every chance he gets. And I'm not the only one . . . I'm sorry. That's just the way it is.

Shirley? Are you there? . . . Are you okay? Are you crying? . . . Oh gosh, I didn't mean to hurt your— . . . I'll miss you too . . . I will so miss—I do so care! What are you talkin' about? . . . Shirley! Don't get mad! I just gotta—SHIRL? SHIRLEY? GODDAM IT!

Shirley's hung up on her. **LOUISE** *puts the phone back in the receiver, composes herself, then redials.*

Shirley? Louise. Listen, I'm sorry if I pissed you off, but I— (*A beat. Sighs.*) Okay, listen. I'll stay another couple of months . . . yeah . . . just to get you through the tourist rush . . . Yeah. . . yeah, but then I'm outta here, Shirley. I mean it. Are you listening to me? Then I'm outta here.

[End]

I'd Like to Throw a Party

A MONOLOGUE BY

KATHY FRIEDMAN

I'd Like to Throw a Party was produced for the Brave New Play Rites Festival in Vancouver in 2005 with the following cast and crew:

BETTY: Helene Bolduc

Directed by Jenny Hereward
Costume Design: Karen Mirfield
Sound Design: Chris McLeod

CHARACTERS

BETTY: *an artist in her late twenties.*

SETTING

A live/work artist's studio. Present day.

SCENE

An easel stands downstage right. A small table with a sketchbook on it stands next to it. A stack of blank canvasses leans against a wall. BETTY *enters, carrying a specimen jar filled with a brown substance.*

BETTY: (*singing*) We are the champions, no time for losers, cause we are the champions—of the world!

She composes herself.

Hi there. My name is Betty and I'm chronically constipated. Or, was constipated. Look, just take a look at this. (*holds up the jar*) Today, the world rotates, like a pig on a spit. Today, everything changes. I just took a shit.

How exactly does one collect such a sample? Two words. Plastic wrap. The recommended method is to stretch some over the toilet bowl. What I prefer is a little outside of the mainstream, but I lay the plastic wrap out on the ground, and crouch.

As you can see, it finally worked. I felt something gather inside me. I'll skip over the details of the hour I spent in agony. I swear, they should give epidurals for these things. But finally, for the first time in eleven days, something fell out of me. She's a real beauty, too. Full of elegant folds and hidden mysteries.

(*talking to the jar*) Looks like I've finally accomplished something, eh Poo? She agrees with me.

BETTY *walks over to the table and sets down her jar. She selects*

> *a canvas and places it on the easel. She opens up some tubes of*
> *paint and begins squeezing them onto a palette.*

So I've finally got something for my doctor to analyze. If that isn't a good omen, I don't know what is. It's been four months since I painted anything. (*opens her sketchbook*) Already four months since you left. It's been peaceful, like my ears were full of water. I wanted to see how long I could stay under. How long I could hold my breath. But I'm ready to do this. You always thought of yourself as my muse, didn't you? Well, I'll be fine without you. I'm still the same person. I'm still an artist. And I'm going to paint your portrait.

> *She looks at the canvas, considering it carefully. She begins paint-*
> *ing tentatively.*

Of course my mother's overjoyed about all this. I remember how long I put off telling her in the first place about us. It was something I imagined in my head over and over again. In my superhero moments, when I disguised myself as a better person, I imagined being reassuring. (*earnestly*) "I'm still the same person I always was and no matter what, I'll always love you, Mom." At other times, particularly after actually speaking with my mother, I felt a bit more vindictive: (*Drill Sergeant*) "Mom. I like pussy. I like it a lot."

The strange thing is that I only fantasized about telling my mother. My father is so mild-mannered that I couldn't imagine him getting that upset over anything. The fact that her parents took her to her first Pride Parade when she was six didn't so much make me feel better.

I ended up going to their house for dinner one night, and I had this whole speech rehearsed. But at the time I couldn't remember it and I just kept hearing my heart beating in my ears like a drum roll.

It was almost the end of the meal when I started to panic. My mom was cutting fruit for dessert and she said, "Betty, can you pass me your plate." I went to hand it to her and said, "Mom, I'm gay."

Everything was silent and spinning. I looked down at my plate, hovering in my hand. It still had gravy and a few bits of rice on it and I thought about how it'd all be difficult to get off if this turned into a long discussion. So I put it back down and said, "I met a woman. I think you'd like her." At which point my mother left the room.

And then I started to cry. I still don't know why, I didn't even feel that upset. It had been a long time since I cried in front of my dad. But as I sat there, heaving and dripping, he reached out and took my hand. It got pretty sweaty but he didn't let it go.

Next time I saw him he was back at his newspaper and I was back to not revealing any of my feelings. Thank God.

(*sighs*) I guess it's understandable to hate your progeny for not living up to your expectations. I'd be devastated if Poo here got married and bought a minivan. Anyway, now that she's gone my mother thinks it's time I returned to the fold, lost lamb that I am. As if the fold would have me, as if it's down on its folded knees begging me to come back. We're going to have to have another little chat, but I'm putting that off as long as I can.

    BETTY *paints for a moment, then sets down the brush.*

I felt so free though, after I told them. I could talk to her about things I hadn't known I wanted to talk to anyone about. I was a truer version of myself with her, like a painting that's been refinished. She moved in, brought with her the most expensive collection of junk I've ever seen. She took me to openings, introduced me to artists. Paint started flying off my brushes with purpose. And she was there, at night, and our bodies slid like scarves.

But it ended. All things end. We started fighting. I started getting sick.
    Pause. **BETTY** *considers the canvas, then turns to the audience.*

It hit me at dinner one night and I couldn't walk. She had to carry me to bed. I almost passed out from the pain. She took me to the hospital and we sat in the waiting room. She held my hand, seemed so scared of what was happening to me.

I remember a few weeks later I couldn't sleep and I tried to go. I sat on the toilet for ages, watching grey bugs scuttle along our bathtub. But nothing came, so I went back to bed. She was awake and waiting for me, her mouth an envelope asking to be opened, the pain less as her tongue moved inside me.

What more could you have done? It was probably all my fault. I complained too much. Took too much for granted. You couldn't put up with me for very long.

(*defensive*) I had to stop waitressing. What else could I have done? The more I farted, the less tips I made. I'm sorry I got to devote myself full-time to painting and you didn't. Cold, frantic mornings, you pawing through drawers looking for pantyhose. Me lying in bed, completely useless. I hated seeing you like that, hated watching you resent me. I know it was hard on you, but if you love someone, you accept them. If you love someone.

Of course you couldn't lose it a little when you left. Too proud to let me see you fall apart, even then. It was so easy for you. Like you were just popping out for groceries. Fuck, darling, it's one thing to lie like a bag of frozen peas in my bed for six months, it's another to walk out on me the same way. Just pack a few things, crumple your face a bit, and tell me I can throw out or keep what I want. Leave just like that. Leave the computer, light bulbs, refrigerator, toilet, television. Everything empty and buzzing.

My health's gotten worse since. I've had so many tests. I'm scheduled for another colonoscopy, so they can shove a tube up my ass and look at my twisted, knotted insides. Whatever. I don't want to talk to doctors right now. I'd much rather paint, look at it and think: This has nothing to do with me.

It's great when you take a really good dump and that happens, right?

You look at it floating in the toilet afterwards, and it seems so unusual. And you can just flush it and walk away. But when there's something familiar in it there's a problem, a bit of carrot or corn or something recognizable. And it's this horrifying moment, 'cause our shit should have nothing at all to do with who we are.

    BETTY *looks at the canvas.*

What comes out of you, darling? What is it you would rather leave behind?

    Pause. **BETTY** *continues to scrutinize it.*

The perspective's not right. Everything's off. (*pause*) I can't do this. (*pause*) I just can't fucking do this. That's all that matters to me right now, you know. I'm alone, I'm constipated, I still miss you like hell, but if I could just be an artist—if I could be an artist, I'd have that one thing at least.

I don't know how much longer I can keep this up. All this silence. All this waiting.

    Beat.

Maybe I'll throw a party. She won't be invited. I'll call it a Turd Party. Everyone has to bring one of their turds, obviously, and we find shapes in each other's shit like, "Oh, yours looks like an ostrich" or even, "Yours looks like that time you walked in on your parents having sex."

    She lifts the jar and examines it, then, thoughtfully:

Or a face. Maybe my shit looks like a beautiful face. But it's so familiar that all I can see are the blackheads on the nose and bags under the eyes. The face of someone who moved inside me once.

It could be so simple, you know. My teeth would tear into you. I'd rip off a hunk of you with my incisors, grind you with my molars. Swallow you, feel you slither down my esophagus and splash into my stomach where you churn and dissolve into nothing. Then squeeze into my intestines, but you don't absorb into me. I twist inside out. I release you.

> *She considers the canvas for a moment. Then she picks up the jar and unscrews the lid. She grabs a piece of her feces between her fingers, feeling its texture, and begins to smear it on the canvas.*

What if . . . what if we put some here. Or maybe over here, on those big pouty lips of yours, and a little here to highlight your cheekbones. Can't forget about something for your eyes, I know how you loved to bat those lashes for the boys.

> *She steps backwards and begins breaking off pieces of feces and flinging it at the canvas.*

There. You. Go. And there. And there. That's for leaving me. And that's for being a selfish bitch. And that's for being able to go to the bathroom whenever you want. And that's for . . . for everything, for fucking every-thing.

> *She stops and surveys her work.*

Oh, you look stunning, Lianne. This is an absolutely gorgeous look for you.

> *[End]*

COMEDIES

Spanish Fly

BY

MAUREEN MEDVED

Spanish Fly was produced for the Brave New Play Rites Festival in Vancouver in 1994 with the following cast and crew:

PALMIRA: Tara Rosling
BRUNO: Dan Tinaburri

Directed by Paul Norman

OTHER PRODUCTIONS OF *Spanish Fly:*

Theatre Centre West, Toronto, Ontario, 1995

The Button Factory, Waterloo Fringe Festival,
Waterloo, Ontario, 1995

Beyond the Fringe, Vancouver East Cultural Centre,
Vancouver, B.C., 1994

Vancouver Fringe Festival, The Firehall Theatre,
Vancouver, B.C., 1994

Best of Brave New Play Rites, U.B.C.,
Vancouver, B.C., 1994

Steamy Spanish guitars collapse as fast as they rise.

SETTING: PALMIRA *lies across the table in a heap. She wears a red slip, her waist-length hair spreading around her like wild vines. Throughout the action, she clutches a stuffed dog—pummeled and flattened through years of tears and physical compression.* **BRUNO** *slumps in a corner, naked except for boxer shorts. The shadow of a beard decorates his bullish face.*

    Following the music, there is a ten second pause, then **PALMIRA** *bolts upright as if recovering from a dream. She screams. Another pause.* **BRUNO** *takes a swig from the bottle of hard liquor.* **PALMIRA** *scrambles anxiously.*

PALMIRA: Oh! Oh! Oh! (*looking down at stuffed dog in her hand*) Ma chien est triste. Ma chien est triste.

She moves dog about like a puppet.

PALMIRA: Ma chien est triste. Es tu triste? Oui. C'est triste. C'est . . .
BRUNO: If You're gonna talk like a fuck, at least do it in Spanish.
PALMIRA: . . . triste.
BRUNO: Stop talking to the fucking dog, Palmira. Are you psychotic? (*pause*) I asked you a question. I said are you psychotic?

PALMIRA *throws dog and hits* **BRUNO** *in the head.*

PALMIRA: I can't stand it, Bruno.
BRUNO: Take a shower if you're so buzzed out.
PALMIRA: I'm already drenched.
BRUNO: You're just making it harder on both of us.
PALMIRA: What's happening to us?
BRUNO: There was a time when people would call us civilized. But it's difficult. Experts say so.
PALMIRA: And to go through it together.
BRUNO: Heroic in the Homeric sense. Give us the key, Palmira. Give me the key. I need to go out.
PALMIRA: I don't have it.

BRUNO: Give me the key, Palmira.

PALMIRA: You know we can't leave. (*pause*) Until tomorrow.

BRUNO: I can't wait that long. Give me the fucking key.

PALMIRA: We can't leave until Pedro unlocks the door and the bulls have run.

BRUNO: The bulls.

PALMIRA: How long do we have?

BRUNO: One day.

PALMIRA: One day.

BRUNO: Eighteen hours.

PALMIRA: Then it's over.

BRUNO: Then we're free.

PALMIRA: Mmm. Inhale the air.

BRUNO: And you smell?

PALMIRA: The lemons hanging off the trees at Guell Parque.

BRUNO: We'll taste the tapas at the Ramblas. The one off the Barrio Chino.

PALMIRA: Those tiny pepper sausages. With beer. Can we still drink?

BRUNO: Of course. We're not alcoholics.

PALMIRA: Oh, goody. Give me some.

She grabs for bottle. **BRUNO** *draws it away.*

BRUNO: No.

PALMIRA: Why not?

BRUNO: It's all there is.

PALMIRA: Give me some, or I'll . . . I'll kill you.

BRUNO: If I gave this up it will kill me.

PALMIRA: Fucking, sissy. I'll give you something to fear. I'll cut you with my big knife.

BRUNO follows the trajectory of **PALMIRA***'s gaze. They bound to the floor and* **PALMIRA** *pulls out an enormous meat cleaver.*

BRUNO: You wouldn't. Not over this.

PALMIRA: I would, motherfucker. Then I'll just sit back and watch the waterworks.

BRUNO: You're only doing this out of some sense of lack. That's all this is, you know, some sense of lack.

PALMIRA: Don't feed me your Freudian bullshit.

BRUNO: It's not Freud. It's (*pause*) actually later than Freud.

PALMIRA: Lying weasel. I'll cut you.

BRUNO: Okay, okay. I think it's post-feminist. From one of those self-help books you're always reading.

PALMIRA: Bastard. Don't patronize me. Just because you have a PhD and I only have an MA.

PALMIRA *jabs him with the cleaver and cuts him.*

BRUNO: Cunt. You fucking cunt. You cut me.

PALMIRA: Don't call me a cunt.

BRUNO: You call yourself one all the time.

PALMIRA: I'm a woman. I'm allowed to say it. As a woman the word cunt is my domain.

BRUNO: Help me.

PALMIRA *stalks the stage with cleaver.*

PALMIRA: From the same root as county, kin, and kind. From the Latin cunnus, Middle English cunte and the Old Norse kunta. Cunabula, a cradle. Cunina, a Roman Goddess. Or, or . . . shit!

BRUNO: I'm dying.

PALMIRA: (*falters, then triumphs*) Cunctipotent, all powerful. The word is not slang, but a true language word and of the oldest stock.

There is angry yelling from street level. PALMIRA *spits out window.*

PALMIRA: Are we making too much noise for you, Senora Rivera? Why don't you go and clip a few of those coupons you love so much?

BRUNO: Help me, Palmira . . .

PALMIRA: It's just a dent.

BRUNO: . . . and I promise I won't call you a (*pause*) that thing anymore. You have my word.

PALMIRA *puts down the cleaver and moistens the corner of her slip with her spit and dabs* **BRUNO**'*s wound.*

PALMIRA: My love. My deepest love.

BRUNO: I can feel your spit entering me. Ah, I feel better.

PALMIRA: Better, better, better. How can anyone feel better?

BRUNO: My love, what is it?

PALMIRA: I can't possibly last.

BRUNO: But we only have seventeen hours and fifty minutes to go.

PALMIRA: Each minute is a screeching tire. It's intolerable.

BRUNO: Let me oil those tires.

BRUNO *grabs for her, she pushes him away.*

PALMIRA: How can you think about THAT now?

BRUNO: I'm sorry. It's been so long. *(looks about uneasily)* What is it? Christ.

PALMIRA: You should know, Bruno.

BRUNO: The bulls?

PALMIRA: What else?

BRUNO: They seem so close.

PALMIRA: My tiny baby. My bunny wunns.

BRUNO: Don't . . .

PALMIRA: You know they can't hurt us if we're inside. You're pathetic.

BRUNO: Inside we're safe. Inside we're safe. Inside we're safe.

PALMIRA: Shut up. Shut up. Shut up. I can't stand the pain.

BRUNO: What about me? I can't stand it.

PALMIRA: What about me? I can't stand it.

BRUNO: Let's try some visualization. You first, then me.

PALMIRA: Why should I go first? I won't be your little experimental rat!

BRUNO: Okay, then I shall go . . .

PALMIRA *shoves him out of the way.*

PALMIRA: Why should you go first? Get out of my way. What do I do?

BRUNO: Imagine something pleasant.

PALMIRA: The pain is overwhelming.

BRUNO: Just try.

PALMIRA: I can't.

BRUNO: Just close your eyes and try.

He passes his hand over her eyes to close them.

PALMIRA: Nothing.

BRUNO: Water. You love the water, Palmira.

PALMIRA: What colour is it?

BRUNO: Uh, blue.

PALMIRA: What kind of blue.

BRUNO: (*straining*) The blue of (*pause*) water.

PALMIRA: What kind of blue? Describe it.

BRUNO: (*straining big time*) The colour of the azure sky when the sun cuts through it like a knife. The colour of turquoise when it's fished from the bed of the sea. The colour of your eyes when, when (*pause*) you wear coloured contact lenses and a piece of dirt gets caught in them and they glisten with your tears.

PALMIRA: I can feel the water, my love.

BRUNO *puffs up like a matador.*

BRUNO: Are the waves shifting about you?

PALMIRA: Yes, yes. Oh, yes.

BRUNO: What are you wearing?

PALMIRA: Nothing. Let me wrap my hand around . . . no! Not like that. I take it like this.

BRUNO: (*sweating*) Like how? How do you take it?

PALMIRA: In the sea. In the Aegean sea. And you spring out of the water like a panther, sinews dripping with clear pearls, each pearl reflecting a tiny rainbow. Your tattoo hard against your hard chest.

BRUNO: Tattoo? (*checks his chest*) Whose tattoo?

PALMIRA: My nipples. Oh, harder. Rub them harder. I love the little particles of sand cutting me, I . . .

BRUNO: Who? Who's rubbing your nipples?

PALMIRA: (*passionately and totally oblivious to* **BRUNO**) Jesus.

> **BRUNO** *pulls away in horror.* **PALMIRA** *opens her eyes.*

BRUNO: Jesus who? Palmira, when were you ever in the Aegean?

PALMIRA: It was nothing, my love.

BRUNO: Think carefully before you answer.

PALMIRA: It was just a fantasy to get me over my cigarette withdrawal.

BRUNO: We promised. Total honesty.

PALMIRA: If I could only have a smoke.

BRUNO: Who was with you in the Aegean, Palmira?

PALMIRA: Nobody.

BRUNO: Is that the truth?

PALMIRA: Yes . . .

BRUNO: You lying bitch.

PALMIRA: It is the fucking truth.

BRUNO: When were you there?

PALMIRA: I wasn't. Just one, Bruno. If I have one smoke I'll be okay.

> *He throws her to the ground and falls on top of her.*

BRUNO: Tell me who you were with or you'll never smoke again.

PALMIRA: Get off me, asshole.

BRUNO: Not until you give me what I want.

PALMIRA: I hate you. I'll kill you.

BRUNO: Tell me who you were with and I'll get you a smoke.

PALMIRA: You're bluffing.

BRUNO: I hid one. Just in case.

PALMIRA: Liar. You would have caved by now.

BRUNO: It's a miracle. But I swear on the Blessed Virgin, it's the truth.

PALMIRA: Where is it?

BRUNO: Not so fast. Tell me who.

PALMIRA: Jesus Gabriel I Portas.

BRUNO: Under the mattress. (**PALMIRA** *rushes to feel under the mattress. There is nothing underneath it.*)

PALMIRA: Nothing. You bastard.

BRUNO: I don't believe it.

PALMIRA: You tricked me.

BRUNO: I can't believe you fucked him.

PALMIRA: You're right. He's not much.

BRUNO: My priest!

PALMIRA: It's not like I never told you. Remember the postcard I sent you?

BRUNO: (*recalling*) Dear Bruno: the sheet is clean and crisp. (*pause*) Wish you were here.

PALMIRA: It was just the once.

BRUNO: You tell me you've seen my priest's tattoo and you say just the once. I can't believe you'd do such a thing. You're sick.

PALMIRA: He's the one who broke the vow with God.

BRUNO: The whole thing is unbelievable. What, you couldn't shoot for my best friend, my father, or my psychiatrist?

PALMIRA: Don't be so melodramatic.

BRUNO: Women who fuck their priests and the men who love them.

PALMIRA: He wasn't MY priest.

BRUNO: That's right. He was only your priest once removed. How did it happen, Palmira? Did you go into the confessional and start this phone sex kind of thing?

PALMIRA: It was just a friendship that got a little carried away.

BRUNO: Eating meat on Fridays is getting a little carried away.

Pause.

PALMIRA: For God's sake, Bruno, I didn't even like Jesus. (*pause*) If you must know, it was something else.

BRUNO: Passion.

PALMIRA: Yes.

BRUNO: And we're . . .

PALMIRA: Passionless.

BRUNO: You don't love me.

PALMIRA: No.

BRUNO: You never loved me?

PALMIRA: Never. It was never love. If anything you make me (*pause*) sick.

BRUNO: Then why do you stay?

PALMIRA: You make me feel safe, warm, like . . .

BRUNO: Nestor.

PALMIRA: Only Nestor is small and you're more complex. Why do you stay?

BRUNO: I love you, you crazy bitch. I want to make love to you every second, every . . .

PALMIRA: When I straddle you and you grab my breasts I feel my stomach rise.

BRUNO: I deserve happiness. I deserve to be married. I deserve a baby with one of those little tapestry hats.

PALMIRA: I don't see you buying Nestor any hats.

BRUNO: You don't expect me to buy HIM a fucking hat.

PALMIRA: That's just like you, Bruno. You never appreciate what you've got.

BRUNO: For crying out loud.

PALMIRA: We can take the money we save on cigarettes and buy Nestor a white christening dress with pretty embroidery and a tiny gold locket. And we can buy him a cradle with brushed cotton blankets and a mobile that plays sweet nurseybyes.

BRUNO: He's got a place to sleep.

PALMIRA: With us.

BRUNO: That's right.

PALMIRA: You're the cheapest thing I know.

BRUNO: I'm not buying a cradle for HIM.

PALMIRA: I could roll over. We'd wake up and our son will be soundless. Dead.

BRUNO: I don't hear him chattering his head off now.

PALMIRA: That's because he only talks to me. He hates you.

BRUNO: I slept with my parents when I was a baby. Whenever they moved I moved with them. It's as natural as a wave. Shit. Shit. Shit. Those are my happiest moments.

PALMIRA: When I hear you talk like that I fantasize that one of us will die, so the other will be free. Bruno, I think you should leave me.

BRUNO: I will never leave you. Without you I'll end up like those old men in cafés with soup and tiny crusts of bread in my beard.

PALMIRA: Fine. Then you might as well know the truth. As long as I live, I will never leave you. (*pause*) But I will never love you.

BRUNO: It's because you do love me that you won't leave. You just don't know what love is.

PALMIRA: Motherfucker. I just said I don't love you. How could I know that if I don't know what love is?

BRUNO: You've got intimacy problems.

PALMIRA: I have WHAT?

BRUNO: What do you call it when you are out galavanting with strange men while I sit alone at home night after sweet loving night waiting for you with a zucchini loaf and a bottle of gin?

PALMIRA: That's it. You don't respect my reality. I want you to respect my reality, Bruno. I want you to respect my fucking reality.

PALMIRA *makes for the door.*

BRUNO: What are you doing?

PALMIRA: If I stay here I'll bite your cock off and spit it out the window.

BRUNO *moves aside.* PALMIRA *reaches for the door and recalls it's locked.*

PALMIRA: Don't laugh at me, motherfucker.

BRUNO: I'm sorry. I just can't believe we've been having this conversation for ten years. (*They laugh hysterically.*) Every year. On the Running of the Bulls. Our annual tradition. We quit smoking to change our lives, yet everything stays the same. (*He pounds the wall.* PALMIRA *backs away in terror.*) Fuck. Fuck. Fuck. I can't go on like this.

PALMIRA: Maybe I should leave you.

BRUNO: Maybe I will leave you.

PALMIRA: You'll never do it. Just like you'll never quit smoking.

BRUNO: You're evil. Because of you I'm stuck on this hideous carousel of sadism and cigarettes.

PALMIRA: You know, it's not too late to go back the way things were.

BRUNO: And smoke? Never Pedro will think we're nuts.

PALMIRA: He already does. Remember the other ten times we tried to quit? He's expecting to find us Saturday fucking in a mountain of DUCADOS.

BRUNO: But we've gone further this time. Last year we only lasted ten hours. Then we got Senora Rivera to pin a carton of DUCADOS to the bedsheets.

PALMIRA: Ah, cigarettes.

BRUNO: It's terrible to think that as long as we're alive we'll never taste another.

PALMIRA: Remember that day when we sat in Gaudi Park, dazzling our taste buds with a WINSTON?

BRUNO: Like that day at the Barrio Gracia sucking GITANES while pretending we were sailors.

PALMIRA: Or the Mexican restaurant, smoking IMPALAS while pretending we were hombres.

TOGETHER: Olay!

They dance a tango.

BRUNO: Melliferous yet specific. Dangerous yet familiar. An espionage of the heart. Each cigarette has its own unique personality, its own peculiar bouquet. From the sweet campiness of SOBRANIS to the dignified reticence of DUNHILLS to the down home Leave-it-to-Beaveracity of CHESTERFIELDS to the jazzy urbanacity of KOOLS to the bullfighterociousness of DUCADOS to the Jean-Paul Belmondaciousness of GALOISES. Oh! Your skin, your hair. You're an addiction. I can't stop touching you, I . . .

He tries to kiss her and she turns her head away.

PALMIRA: No, Bruno. I can't. I need a cigarette, Bruno. I must have one. I'm going out of my mind. Out of my fucking mind.

BRUNO: No, no—we CAN'T!

PALMIRA: We've lasted one day. Who cares?

BRUNO: We did have more pleasure before we quit. It's not like it's even expensive in Spain.

PALMIRA: Yeah, its' not like America or—

PALMIRA and **BRUNO** (*together*): Sweden.

PALMIRA: (*excitedly*) Let's do it, Bruno. Let's kill ourselves. If we were Swedes that would be the next logical step.

BRUNO: We'll go to hell. Suicide is a sin.

PALMIRA: We're already in hell. Suicide's a relief. Anyway, I'm not Catholic.

BRUNO: But some of your best friends are. (*pause*) Okay, so how do you propose we do it?

PALMIRA: Let's jump out the window.

BRUNO: Well, it's a vertical move, even if it's in the wrong direction. Sure, what the hell. Let's do it.

PALMIRA: We'll do it together.

BRUNO: We'll hold hands and jump to our deaths.

PALMIRA: Straight down.

BRUNO: At least we'll have spent our lives together.

PALMIRA: Until death do us part.

BRUNO: We'll land on Señora Rivera.

PALMIRA: Crazy old bitch.

PALMIRA *steps towards the window.*

BRUNO: You can't be serious.

PALMIRA: I'm completely serious.

BRUNO: It's five stories. Maybe we'll break our legs.

PALMIRA: Are you going to sissy out on me?

BRUNO: We never do this. This isn't the way it's supposed to go.

PALMIRA: Your way is useless. (*pause*) Of course, it is YOUR way. What do I expect from someone with too much speed and not enough size.

BRUNO: Fine. Let's just get this over with.

PALMIRA: Wait. Nestor.

She grabs the dog.

BRUNO: We're going to kill ourselves and you're worried about that stupid puppet?

PALMIRA: He's not a puppet. He's my son.

BRUNO: Our son. I'm the one who chose him. (*scrambles wildly*) What's that noise? Who's there? For Christ's sake. Don't let him in. Don't let him in. You hear that? His hoofed feet stroke the carpet out-

side. His horns gore straight through wood. Blood splashes against
the walls like a flapping red cloth.

BRUNO *cowers in the corner.*

PALMIRA: Pathetic.
BRUNO: No, Palmira.
PALMIRA: Pathetic, pathetic, pathetic.
BRUNO: Don't say another word.
PALMIRA: Afraid of a few little bulls. You're a baby.
BRUNO: Not a baby.
PALMIRA: A capon.
BRUNO: Don't.
PALMIRA: Weak.
BRUNO: Well at least I didn't . . .
PALMIRA: What?
BRUNO: Nothing.
PALMIRA: Say it, Bruno.
BRUNO: Nothing. I said nothing.
PALMIRA: What? At least I didn't what?
BRUNO: Over my dead body.
PALMIRA: Well somebody's gonna die here, that's for sure.

PALMIRA *runs towards* **BRUNO** *with the carving knife and stops
an inch away from him.*

BRUNO: Go ahead.

PALMIRA *flinches slightly.*

BRUNO: What's stopping you?

BRUNO *motions for her to cut him.*

BRUNO: Come on.

PALMIRA *falters.*

BRUNO: You can't do it, can you? Know why? It's because you love me. Sure you do. Remember the time we fucked behind the castle in Gaudi Park? There was a family picnicking a few meters away. You were excited. Wet. Bursting.

PALMIRA: It was good sex only because I imagined you were someone else. *(laughs)* That's right, Bruno. Your worst suspicions are true. There were hundreds. Every day. Hundreds upon hundreds. Your father, your brother, your priest, your psychiatrist, your best friend, your mail man, your delivery boy, your house painter—the boys on the Vespas who whip in and out of alleys in the night like fireflies—the machos, the fags, the old, the young, the withered, the smooth, the dwarfs, and the giants. I had them all. I had them all because—you know what?—you could never please me. Even in fantasy. *(pause)* Even in fantasy.

BRUNO: You fucking slut!

PALMIRA: That's sad. Can't you do better than that?

BRUNO: You know I can do better than that.

PALMIRA: I wouldn't ask if I did.

BRUNO: The weather's perfect, Palmira.

PALMIRA: What?

BRUNO: It's gaming weather.

PALMIRA: Don't.

BRUNO: When the day is this beautiful I feel like throwing a ball.

He pantomimes throwing a ball. PALMIRA *runs to grab his hand, but he pushes her aside.*

BRUNO: Like knocking down the plastic bull in the fairgrounds.

PALMIRA: Stop it.

BRUNO: You're exquisite in your little red dress. You tell me you want to leave. Pedro tries five times, but he can't knock down the plastic bull. You tell me you want to leave. Me and Pedro exchange a glance. I'm in excellent form. I'm athletic. Virile. You're a wild animal. You steam past men. This is my challenge. To tame the wild Palmira. You turn to leave. I grab your arm. Roughly. Every man watches. They all want you, but you belong to me. I jerk you back to the gaming table. Pedro was always more athletic, but not this time. You approach me at the gaming table and tell me you want to leave. You say it loudly, so I can hear you over the crowds. Just one shot at the plastic bull. That's all it takes. Ha, ha!

PALMIRA: The crowd watches as you lift your hand to strike me.

BRUNO: One shot. Just one perfect shot. Bull's Eye.

PALMIRA: Not actually touching my skin. Just a warning.

BRUNO: I choose Nestor from amongst the cluster of prizes. He's innocent and I think: this is the true Palmira. I turn and you are gone. The crowd's a blur. I focus on the red of your dress.

PALMIRA: I am running and running and the dust is rising and rising and I can't see anymore.

BRUNO: I place Nestor in your arms. I ask you to move in with me. You agree.

PALMIRA: I agree.

They stare at each other for a long while.

PALMIRA: Bruno. (*pause*) Bruno. (*He turns his back to her.*) Bruno. (*long pause*) Bruno. Why won't you look at me? Why won't you look at me, Bruno? Why won't you look at me? (*rushes to the window*) Somebody. Somebody. Help us. Fucking help us. He's fucking killing me. (*crawls over to him on her hands and knees*) Talk to me, Bruno. Just for a second. Just talk to me.

BRUNO: Please.

PALMIRA: What?

BRUNO: Leave me alone.

PALMIRA: I need you, Bruno.

BRUNO: I don't know what to do.

PALMIRA: I'm really small, Bruno. Hold me.

BRUNO: I don't know what to do.

PALMIRA: Just take your arms and hold me.

BRUNO: Do you love me, Palmira?

PALMIRA: Sometimes I'm not sure, but, see, remember the way it used to be. My flesh as smooth as paper. You loved to touch it. Remember that? You'd stroke my flesh. Do it, Bruno.

She takes his hand and puts it on her thigh.

BRUNO: You said you don't love me. Do you love me?

PALMIRA: Shh. Shh. I think I can try.

BRUNO: I need you to love me. Can you do that, Palmira? Can you love me?

PALMIRA: Yes.

BRUNO: Do you really think so?

PALMIRA: Forget all this. Focus on something else. A distant memory. Stroke my thigh. There, see. Close your eyes. The sun is high in the sky. The wood slats of the dock toast our feet. And here— remember the baby bull, Bruno? It's here, sitting on the dock all alone. There's no one to save it. Someone took it away from the loving arms of its mother. The bull is crying on the deck. But you can't see its tears. Know why? As soon as they fall, the sun dries them up.

[End]

An American Drama

BY

DAVID MACKAY

An American Drama was produced for the Brave New Play
Rites Festival in Vancouver in 1987 with
the following cast and crew:

WILHEMINA LOMAN: Christina Spencer
EUGENE LOMAN: Alan George
WOODY LOMAN: David Mackay

Directed by John Stevens

TIME: *November 1955*
PLACE: *Brooklyn, New York*

SETTING: *The scene takes place in an attractively decorated, but unkempt townhouse. The set is divided with a living room on Stage R. and a dining room set on Stage L. There is a kitchen entrance, a staircase going up to the bedrooms, a front door and a closet.* **WILHEMINA LOMAN**, *a 35-year-old southern beauty queen who abdicated her throne to become a fat alcoholic housewife, sits playing solitaire at the dining table. She stops playing, looks cautiously around the room, and then pulls out a bottle of Jack Daniel's from under the table. She takes an incredible swig, rehides the bottle and resumes her dainty self.* **EUGENE LOMAN**, *a 41-year-old washed up pro-bowler, enters from upstairs.* **WIL.** *makes sure her bottle is well hidden from her husband. A foghorn goes off in the distance for some kind of symbolic meaning.*

EUGENE: Is he home, yet?

WILHEMINA: Nope.

EUGENE: And he hasn't called? Where is he? Why ain't he home?

WIL: 'Cause he ain't. Do you see him here? Do you think I'm lying?

EUGENE: No ... I know he's not here. His hat ain't on the rack ... (*opens closet door*) There's an empty hanger where his coat oughta be, No ... he ain't here all right, but what I'm thinking ... what I'm wondering ... the thing that puzzles me ... what I'm contemplating on is ... the question that's got my gut wrenched and ready to explode inside me is—

WIL: All right, shut up! What the hell are you so worried about?

EUGENE: WHY ain't he home? Maybe he knows I'm waiting for him ... Yeah, that's it. He knows I'm pacing these floorboards, wearing out the carpet and my shoes. And all the while he's taking his time, taking each step like the slow methodical march of a pallbearer ... Boy, is he in shit when he gets home!

WIL: Home?! (*She let's out a pathetic laugh that is the summary of her life*) You call this a "home"? ... A home has love. A home has children, a home has a white picket fence. (*gasps for breath before she cries*) A home has a dog named "Fido."

EUGENE: Not tonight, Wilhemina. For God's sake, woman, just once will you leave your dreams in your head.

WIL: These aren't dreams, Eugene. These are promises you made to me, your wife, remember. (*takes a small swig of J.D. from a small bottle in her breast pocket*) And like a young, silly, southern, semi-virgin, I believed you.

EUGENE: You're drunk!

WIL: I drink to forget.

EUGENE: You drink to get drunk.

WIL: . . . Okay. I'll give you that one.

EUGENE: (*crossing to front door*) Maybe he's not coming home tonight . . . or tomorrow, or the next day after tomorrow, or the day after that, or next Sunday, or Thanksgiving, or Christmas, or January 18th, or March 10th, or my birthday . . . what does it matter if it's a holiday or an occasion, or any day of the year . . . maybe he's just never coming back . . . Hold me, Wilhemina. (*breaks down*)

WIL: Oh, darling. (*getting up from table, she knocks over many hidden bottles under the table*) What's the matter? (*hugging him*) You're shaking all over. What's wrong? What's Woody done that makes you say he won't be coming back?

EUGENE: (*pulling slightly back, and pulling a letter out from his bowling shirt*) This letter came today.

WIL: (*reading the letter*) Repossessed? Eugene, is this true? Woody's out of the business? (*looking at envelope*) This is addressed to Woody, how did you get it?

EUGENE: I was making some tea in the kitchen when the steam must have carried into the living room and opened the envelope. And then a gust of wind from an open window must have blown the letter open. It fell on the floor, and just as toast always lands butter side down, well, letters always land written side up. I couldn't help but read it.

WIL: But it's cold outside. I kept the windows closed all day.

EUGENE: Gee, then, how do you figure it? But don't you understand, Wilhemina, Woody's gonna lose Daddy's shoe store . . . no . . . my brother's gonna have to work harder. He's gotta save the shoe store. Goddamn, where is he! (*crosses to door*)

WIL: Eugene, maybe Woody doesn't know about the store, I mean he's only fifteen minutes late.

EUGENE: I guess I have been a little over-anxious.

WIL: A bit . . . and I'll tell you something else, Eugene. When Woody comes home I think we should act like we know nothing at all about this letter. Let's see if Woody brings it up first.

EUGENE: You're right. (*taking her into his arms*) Like so many times before, you're right. You know, Wilhemina, sometimes I can't help thinking back, to what it was like, you and me, the way we were . . . memories, like the four corners of my mind.

WIL: I remember as child I used to hear the wind talking to me. A Georgian wind, with a sweet, sweet blowing voice, saying, 'Hey Wilhemina, you're the prettiest of all the southern belles.' . . . and I remember you whispering in my ear, saying how you was going to be the best bowler in all the southern states. How we was going to live in one of those fine houses on Rodeo Drive. I'd tend to the children while you bowled . . . (*in a dream*) Our kids, we had their names, "Hey Strike, come give Momma a kiss. Tell Daddy to wash his hands, Pin."

EUGENE: I was gonna have a different bowling ball for each day of the week.

WIL: And on Sundays, you'd pull out a big black special one with a real gold monogram with fancy lettering . . . (*coming back to reality*) but there's no house, we live with your brother. There's no children, and you don't have any balls.

EUGENE: (*pulling his hand out of his pocket, displaying three gimped fingers*) Do you think I wanted this to happen? Do you think I wanted to break two vital finger bones and do nerve damage?! (*instant spotlight*) There I was in Lane 4, just like every other Wednesday night. I was putting my fingers into my three favourite holes. I looked down that automatic return, and I swear I saw no ball returning! I swear. Just then I turned to ask Fred what the score was . . . for a split second I turned away . . . for a miniscule of a moment I looked the other way . . . for one eency weency, teeny—

WIL: All right, one more description then get on with it.

EUGENE: Itsy bitsy, second I turned away . . . when out from hell, out from the very flames of hell came an eighteen-pound bowling ball. It barreled through and rammed my fingers into the ball. I heard them snap. I felt the pain. Fred hadn't seen what had happened, so he called out, "Hey Eugene, knock down three more and you win, ya ba da ba doo!" I couldn't move my fingers . . . never again. Goddamn it, woman, you know how much I miss my balls!

WIL: Oh, I'm so sorry, Eugene. It's just that sometimes I get all dreamy eyed now and then. I feel the whole world resting on our little shoulders. And the wind isn't kind to me anymore. I hear a Brooklyn wind now, saying, "Hey Wilhemina, you're a fat ass!"

There's a rattle at the door

EUGENE: That must be Woody now.

WIL: Remember, Eugene, we won't mention the letter, play it like any other day.

EUGENE: Right.

WOODY LOMAN, *a 46-year-old soon to be unemployed shoe salesman enters. He has a thick New York accent, and at the moment is wearing no shoes. He crosses to C. Stage and out-stretches his hands to point out his shoeless feet.*

EUGENE: Hello Woody, how are you doing? ·

WIL: Hello Woody, how was your day?

WOODY: You ask a man with no shoes on in the middle of November, "how was your day?" . . . You guys are worse than the screwballs I have to put up with in the city.

EUGENE: Where are your shoes, Woody?

WOODY: Well, thank you for asking, Eugene, how quick of you to notice. I DON'T KNOW WHERE THEY ARE! All I know is that I'm standing on 43rd Street, waiting for my bus, with my shoes on. And as the bus approaches, I see the driver change his sign to Hijacked—Cuba, and it's an express, so it doesn't stop. So I watch a busload of warm, dry, grenade-waving terrorists zoom off into the Hudson. So here I am surrounded by panhandlers, people with pornographic pamphlets, quasi-religious guys asking me to shave my head and drink tea all day long. It was my worst neurotic nightmare come true. My analyst is going to make a mint of my next session. But they didn't take my shoes. Finally, my bus arrives, and it wasn't until I realized I was standing in a puddle that I noticed my shoes were gone. I ask you? Who would take a man's shoes right from under his feet?

WIL: (*sympathetic*) You don't know who took them, do you Woody?

WOODY: Yes, I do. Right now, there's some wino wearing a potato sack for a suit, and my seventy-dollar Oxfords.

EUGENE: You really don't know then?

WOODY: That's the thing about thieves, Eugene. They take things without telling you. It's called stealing.

EUGENE: It's called 'repossession.' (*hands him the letter*) The people who took your shoes had every legal right to.

WOODY: (*inspecting the envelope*) Been reading my mail again, huh, Eugene.

EUGENE: Woody, they're going to take Daddy's shoe store away!

WOODY: Good. They can keep it. Now I don't have to put up with that city anymore.

EUGENE: Listen to me, Woody. Daddy gave you his business to look after. Not to let it go down the drain. He gave it to you on his deathbed.

WOODY: Oh, I remember it well. There he was, old and frail, looking like a prune. And he said to me in a voice all crackling and whistling, "Woody, I'm leaving the business to you." . . . and then he started laughing, and laughing. The man choked on a guffaw and died. They couldn't remove his smile off his face in the casket. I hate that business. Good riddance.

WIL: Is it really that bad, Woody? I mean, if you give up the store, they'll be coming for the house soon.

WOODY: Oh, don't lay the guilt trip on me Wilhemina . . . Oh, you don't understand. Day after day, dealing with smelly feet and mismatched socks. Let's face it. I don't like working. Just like everyone else in this house.

EUGENE: Do you think I wanted this to happen!?! (*showing his gimped hand*) Do you think I wanted to break—

WOODY: Oh, shut up! You and your repetitive sorrows. Pick up the needle and move to the next lament. Can't you see what I'm telling you? I'm a dreamer like you, and you. I don't like shoes . . . I like chicken! I want to open my own Chicken restaurant. (*using his hands to emphasize a neon sign*) "The Garden of Eatin', Eat-In or Chicken Out." Yeah, a real southern-style restaurant.

WIL: Southern? Chicken?

EUGENE: And where would you get the money for this venture?

WOODY: We don't need money... Inside, we wouldn't have normal tables, no we'd have picnic tables.

WIL: With red and white plastic tablecloths. So you can wipe them up with one swoop of the J-Cloth.

WOODY: (*mimes wiping*) Whoosh!

EUGENE: Wait a minute, wait a minute. This sounds like it needs money. It sounds expensive.

WOODY: If we had money, then we'd have to open a real restaurant. All that cooking and grease, plus dealing with the public, but if we dream about it . . . it's perfect.

WIL: Woody, as soon as the people sit down, bam! A pitcher of beer goes down on the table. With frosty glasses . . . I'd be the waitress, let me be the waitress, Woody?

WOODY: All right. As long as I get to serve the chicken. (*seeing what he says*) A big platter of golden French fries. Not frozen, mind you, but fresh, with the skins still on them. And ridges that make people say, "How do they cut 'em like that?" And sitting in the middle of this mound of fries is the biggest and tastiest southern-style chicken you've ever seen. People's eyes light up, because this is what they came for.

WIL: No napkins, Woody, we just plop down a roll of hand towel right along side the chicken. To keep that country look.

EUGENE: Stop it, Wilhemina, stop it.

EUGENE *slaps her.* **WILHEMINA** *slaps him back. He slaps her again. (beat) They embrace with a sob.*

WOODY: I hear fiddle music playing.

WIL: (*breaking away from the embrace*) I see license plates from all the states, covering the walls. Georgia, Virginia, Oregon, even one from a Canadian state.

EUGENE: No!

· WOODY: And one-dollar bills Scotch taped to the ceiling, with compliments to the chef. "Best chicken I've ever tasted," "Woody for president!"

EUGENE: Stop it! In God's name will you listen to yourselves? Chicken, license plates, funny cut French fries? I'm telling you there's no such restaurant. I know how easy it is to get caught up in your dreams. Sometimes, I wake up in the middle of the night and I can't remember falling asleep. Understand? Other times I find myself leaving the bathroom with my fly undone. 'Cause I was dreaming, lost in thought. And nobody looks that kind of dreamer in the eye.

WIL: What were you dreaming of Eugene?

EUGENE: Nothing special. (*looks longingly at his gimped hand*) Nothing that at one time couldn't have come true.

WOODY: Eugene . . . did I mention the bowling lanes in the back of the restaurant?

EUGENE, *with difficulty, shakes his head.*

WIL: Three lanes, Eugene. With automatic scoring and you in charge.

EUGENE: Me? Behind the counter? With all those wonderful red and green shoes?

WIL: And behind the counter, in fancy neon letters, is "Eugene's Lanes."

EUGENE: No. No . . . No! You can't bowl with greasy chicken fingers!

WOODY: You calling my chicken greasy?

WIL: We'll have hand towels.

WOODY: Premoistened.

WIL: Besides, at the end of the automatic return is a dryer, blowing a warm dry air.

WILHEMINA *kneels and blows on* EUGENE's *gimped hand.*
EUGENE *smiles and looks forward. There is the sound of a bowling ball rolling and cracking a strike.*

EUGENE: Yes, sir, Lane 2 is now ready for you. Ten-pound balls? Of course, I've got them.

WIL: Another chicken for table eight, Woody.

WOODY: Hah, a man has no time to rest in this place.

EUGENE:	WIL:	WOODY:
Yes, the league meets here every Wednesday night	Why, yes, I am from Georgia.	Sorry, I can't give the recipe to away. You all come back, now.

TWO MEN enter with ACME REPOSSESSION uniforms and proceed to remove furniture while EUGENE, WILHEMINA and WOODY continue to dream.

EUGENE:	WIL:	WOODY:
Yes, I am Eugene Loman, once the best bowler. I'm looking for a comeback.	Actually, I lost twenty pounds since working here. It's all the running around.	It takes good common business sense to make this restaurant run so well . . .

Lights out.

[End]

Chow Baby

BY

TIFFANY STONE

Chow Baby was produced for the Brave New Play Rites Festival in Vancouver in 1991 with the following cast and crew:

MOM: Jen Blair
SISTER: Erin Jeffrey
BROTHER: Chris Cound

Directed by Rhiannon Charles

MOM *and her two kids: older* SISTER *and younger* BROTHER.

From the black:

SISTER: *(voice only, simultaneously with* BROTHER) Mom, who's for
   dinner?
BROTHER: *(voice only, simultaneously with* SISTER) Mom, who's for
   supper?
SISTER: Dinner!
BROTHER: Supper!
SISTER: Dinner!

*The arguing continues as the lights come up on a large, long
table. Most of the places at it are unoccupied.* MOM *sits at one
end. The kids sit either side of centre with* BROTHER *favouring
Mom's end. The head of the table remains unoccupied.*

BROTHER: I'm hungry!
SISTER: When're we gonna eat?
BROTHER: I'm hungry!
SISTER: I'm starving!
BROTHER: Me, too.
SISTER: Shuddup.
BROTHER: Mom—
MOM: Come on, you two. You know we have to wait till your father
   gets home.

Pause.

SISTER: When's Dad gonna be here?
BROTHER: Yeah. I'm hungry!

SISTER *and* BROTHER *exchange looks.*

BROTHER: Ouch! She kicked me!
SISTER: Did not.
BROTHER: Did so.

SISTER: How could I kick you? I'm sitting way over here.

BROTHER: Mom, she kicked me.

MOM: Children, please. (*to daughter*) Don't kick your brother. You know better than that.

SISTER: But I—

MOM checks her watch, gets up and paces.

MOM: I wonder where he could be . . .

SISTER: Maybe he's bringing someone home.

BROTHER: Yeah. Bet he bagged some tourists 'n' he's gotta cut 'em: up 'n' stuff so's they fit in the car.

SISTER: Gross! I hate tourists.

She sticks her tongue out at her brother.

BROTHER: Mo-om!

SISTER: (*to* **BROTHER**) You're such a wimp.

BROTHER: Am not.

SISTER: Are so.

BROTHER: Am not.

SISTER: Are so.

BROTHER: Am—

MOM: Honestly, you two! Can't you sit together for two minutes without fighting?

There is a strained pause by the kids.

BROTHER: She started it.

SISTER: Did not.

BROTHER: Did so.

SISTER: Did no—

MOM: That settles it. I'm likely to kill both of you if this doesn't stop. We'll just have to go ahead without him. (*The kids are suddenly very well-behaved.*) Now, who to choose . . .

BROTHER: Pick her.

SISTER: Shaddup. Pick him. He's younger.

BROTHER: Yeah, but she's older. And she's a girl.

SISTER: So?

BROTHER: Girls taste better.

SISTER: Do no—

MOM: (*sitting down*) I have to agree with your brother on this one. I think we should eat you.

SISTER: (*gestures to empty spaces at the table*) But we had Patricia for dinner last night. And Allison the night before.

MOM: Yes, but don't forget, we had that taxi driver for breakfast and leftover social worker for lunch. Such a nice fellow. Pity he wasn't bigger. I could've made a lovely casserole. (*pause*) No, I definitely think it's time for a girl.

SISTER: Okay, okay, let's go for a girl. Don't we have someone in the freezer?

MOM: No, I'm afraid not. All that's left in there are some ears and noses from last Thanksgiving.

BROTHER: Gross!

MOM: (*ignoring him*) They're hardly worth defrosting.

BROTHER: (*to* SISTER) We're gonna eat you! We're gonna eat you! We're gonna—

MOM: (*to her son*) Dear, shut up.

He mopes.

SISTER: What about in the pantry? Don't we have a can of Chef Boyardee or somebody?

MOM: Not until I've been shopping. I promised your father we'd eat you kids up first.

BROTHER: Can we have steaks?

MOM: I thought I'd try something different. Maybe that new Cajun recipe I clipped from the paper . . .

SISTER: I still think we should eat HIM.

MOM: We've been over this already, lamb chop.

SISTER: But he's such a brat.

MOM: I know. But that's no reason to eat him.

BROTHER: Yeah, vegetarian lips! (*to* MOM) Can I have seconds if I clean my plate?

MOM: We'll see.

BROTHER: What's for dessert?

MOM: I don't know yet, darling.

BROTHER: Can we have ice cream? I'm gonna make a double-decker sundae—

SISTER: I still say we eat HIM.

MOM: Now, lamp chop, how many times do I have to—

SISTER: He deserves to be eaten!

BROTHER: No, I don't!

SISTER: Yes, you—

MOM: I think "deserves" is a bit extreme, don't you?

SISTER: Nope.

MOM: I'm surprised at you, lamb chop. I've never seen this side of you before.

Strategic pause.

SISTER: He only deserves it cuz of what he did.

MOM: What did he do?

SISTER: Something really bad.

BROTHER: Did not!

SISTER: Did so.

BROTHER: Did not.

SISTER: Did.

BROTHER: Didn't.

SISTER: Did.

MOM: That's enough, you two! What did he do? (*to son*) Have you been biting off people's fingers again?

She checks for evidence on his face.

BROTHER: No, honest. I didn't do anything.

SISTER: Yes, you did. And I'm gonna tell.

MOM: So . . . ?

SISTER: I know why Dad's not here.

MOM: Oh, did he call while I was out? You really must learn to write messages down . . .

SISTER: He didn't call. (*pause*) He couldn't.

MOM: Why ever not?

SISTER: Because—

BROTHER: No fair! You promised you wouldn't tell. I gave you my allowance and everything. I hate you!

SISTER: Dad couldn't call because HE ate him.

BROTHER: I did not!

MOM: Oh, darling, you ate your father?

BROTHER: I . . . I . . .

MOM: Did you?

SISTER: Yeah, with ketchup, too. I saw him.

MOM: I asked your brother. (*to son*) Did you eat your father?

BROTHER: Yes.

MOM: How could you? Brothers and sisters I can understand. Even the occasional finger. But you know better than to eat your parents. I'm very disappointed in you. Perhaps your sister was right. Yes, I think I've changed my mind. We'll have you for dinner instead.

BROTHER: But, Mom . . .

MOM: No buts about it, young man.

BROTHER: No fair!

Awkward pause.

SISTER: So, when do we eat?

BLACKOUT.

[End]

Courting

BY

DAN HERSHFIELD

Courting was produced for the Brave New Play Rites Festival in Vancouver in 2004 with the following cast and crew:

HILARY: Becky Ferreira
JACK: Kevin Lee
MAURICE: Mack McGuckin
MICHAEL: Ryan Smith
DAISY: Maria Todd

Directed by Duncan Mack
Costume Design: Alexia Chen
Production Dramaturgy: Sampson Hsieh
Set Construction: Kent Lipsett

OTHER PRODUCTIONS OF *Courting*:

Vancouver Fringe Festival, Vancouver, B.C., 2005

Hillfest, University Hill Secondary,
Vancouver, B.C., 2005

New Writing, New Worlds, Gilmorehill Theatre,
Glasgow, Scotland, 2005

CHARACTERS:

HILLARY: *a receptionist at an investment firm, early twenties*
MICHAEL: *an accountant who works at* **HILLARY**'s *office one afternoon a week, late twenties*
JACK: **HILLARY**'s *waiter*
DAISY: **MICHAEL**'s *waiter*
MAURICE: *chef, very French*

SETTING: *A posh French restaurant with two tables and a door to the kitchen. At one table sit* **HILLARY** *and* **MICHAEL**, *and the tension is palpable. There is a bread basket on their table, and they each have a glass of wine;* **HILLARY**'s *is white,* **MICHAEL**'s *is red.* **JACK** *and* **DAISY** *are setting the other table, even though it is already set; they do this by continually exchanging cutlery from one place setting to the other.*

MICHAEL: I like your sweater.
HILLARY: Thanks.
MICHAEL: Is it new?
HILLARY: Sorta. New to me. From a yard sale.
MICHAEL: Oh, neat. Neat. Neat. (*beat*) You know what I find weird? How when people want a drink with no ice, they order it "neat." It just sounds so, I don't know, keen or something. It's like a teenager ordering his first drink. "I'm going to be having a scotch. Neat!" (*putting on a Sean Connery accent*) "No martini for me today, Miss Moneypenny. Get me a whiskey, neat."
HILLARY: Probably meant more like tidy.
MICHAEL: Oh. Yeah. I guess that would make more sense. Uncluttered with ice, as it were. (*beat*) I'll bet Titanic survivors would agree! (*beat*) The boat, not the movie . . . although let's face it, surviving the movie was no walk in the park either!
HILLARY: I liked that movie.
MICHAEL: Oh . . . Neat . . . (*drinks*) So, anything interesting happen at work yesterday?
JACK: (*without looking up*) Don't answer that.
MICHAEL: (*frustrated by the interruption*) So, having a good time so far?
JACK: Objection!

DAISY: On what grounds?

> JACK *and* DAISY *move,* JACK *to stand behind* HILLARY, DAISY *to stand behind* MICHAEL.

JACK: He can't ask a question which obliges my client to feign having a good time or come off as a bitch.

DAISY: He is entitled to validation if she demonstrates willing and knowing disdain.

JACK: When did she do that?

DAISY: She's speaking in sentence fragments, and she said she liked Titanic, which no one would admit to in this sophisticated a restaurant unless they were trying to hurt someone.

> HILLARY *motions as if she's about to interject, but then changes her mind.*

JACK: You should have raised those objections then. You can't just store them up.

DAISY: I was allowing your client some leeway. I thought you'd return the courtesy.

JACK: You thought wrong. As far as I'm concerned, my client is the wronged party.

MICHAEL: Oh, c'mon!

JACK: Sir? If you have something to say, you should tell it to your waiter.

DAISY: It's alright, Michael . . . Fine. Let us ask the question again, and we'll allow your client to make a noncommittal but friendly response, one which acknowledges the awkwardness but doesn't lay blame. Let's say she'll reply "Meh," but then shrug and laugh?

JACK: I'm sorry, I'm not going to advise my client to violate standard dating protocol.

DAISY: It wouldn't!

JACK: It would!

DAISY: Wouldn't!

JACK: Would!

DAISY & **JACK**: Maurice!!

MAURICE *emerges from the kitchen.*

MAURICE: Oui?

JACK: Maurice, if a man asks a woman on a date if she's having a good time, and she answers "Meh," wouldn't that violate standard dating protocol?

MAURICE: (*philosophical*) It is like the integrity of a soufflé in a box marked "Fragile" sent overnight express; it will all depend upon the delivery.

DAISY: Thank you, Maurice. Michael, please ask your question again.

MICHAEL: Are you having a good time yet?

DAISY: So far. It was "Are you having a good time so far?" I know it seems nitpicky, but it affects the tone. Please ask again.

MICHAEL: Are you having a good time so far?

HILLARY *looks at* **JACK** *for approval.*

JACK: Go ahead.

HILLARY: Meh.

HILLARY *shrugs and laughs, not terribly convincingly.*

MAURICE: Good enough.

MAURICE *exits to the kitchen.* **JACK** *and* **DAISY** *return to their initial positions.* **MICHAEL** *and* **HILLARY** *take a moment to compose themselves.*

MICHAEL: (*to* **DAISY**) Can we, umm, proceed?

DAISY: Absolutely.

MICHAEL: Okay. (*to* **HILLARY**) Good. (*beat*) So something funny happened to me the other day—

JACK: You're under no obligation to laugh.

MICHAEL: She knows that, alright? Jesus . . . So anyway, okay, I'm on the bus and I want to sit down, only there are no empty seats. But then I notice that there's a teenager who's sitting straddled across two seats. So I ask him politely to move, so I can sit down, and he responds "I like to sit on the crack!" (*no big response from* **HILLARY**) Fine. Don't laugh.

HILLARY: What is that supposed to mean?

MICHAEL: I just don't see why you had to make this all so confrontational—

HILLARY: Just because I didn't laugh at your story doesn't mean—

MICHAEL: Not that! This!! (*indicating waiters*) Just tell me why.

HILLARY: I've told you why! You sent me flowers! At work! After our first date!

MICHAEL: Girls are supposed to like flowers.

HILLARY: What, did you read that in *Cosmo*?!? Next time, read the fine print, which says they don't like them at work!

MICHAEL: I know where you work. I don't know where you live.

HILLARY: Well, to me, that would be a pretty good sign you're not at the flower sending stage!

MICHAEL: I just thought it would be a nice thing to do.

HILLARY: I get that, and I believe that, but still . . . And more than even the flowers, what bothers me is that you don't get why I'm upset . . .

MICHAEL: Is it the money? Because they weren't that expensive and I was happy to—

HILLARY: God, no, it wasn't the money! God!

MICHAEL: Well, then, what? I mean, if they bothered you so much, why'd you take them?

HILLARY: What choice did I have?

DAISY: Objection!

HILLARY: What?

DAISY: Maurice!

MICHAEL: Look, forget it, she can talk.

DAISY: Michael, you have to let me do my job. Trust me.

MICHAEL: But I'd like to—

DAISY: Michael, the date will continue. Just as soon as we get our ruling.

MAURICE *emerges from the kitchen and arrives at the table.*

MAURICE: Oui?

DAISY: Maurice, I'm making a motion that she be prohibited from arguing that the flowers were "forced upon her." She signed for them. This is a textbook example of a property transfer agreement.

JACK: He bought her the flowers, making them her property prior to her knowledge or involvement. Signing for them only acknowledged receipt of what was already hers.

MAURICE: I take it you have a precedent?

JACK: In Marquez v. Sewall, this restaurant ruled that even though the jewelry the defendant bought for their anniversary wasn't received until the day after due to courier error, he was not at fault because the purchase had been made on time.

DAISY: Maurice, that case involved a present for which there was implied consent. They'd been going out for a year, she knew a present was coming. Here, there is no implied consent, ergo there was no tacit contract, ergo the flowers were still technically his until she waived her right of refusal, which she did by signing for them.

MAURICE: Jack. Daisy. You two become more brilliant every day. I am beaming with pride. But since you cannot both be right, I rule in Daisy's favour. The girl cannot argue she had no choice in accepting the flowers.

DAISY: In light of this ruling, she should also be prohibited from stating that she didn't want the flowers.

MAURICE: Why is that?

DAISY: If she willingly and knowingly took possession of the flowers, how can she argue she didn't want them?

JACK: Maurice, these flowers were delivered to her by an intermediary and were given to her in the presence of co-workers and employers. Surely the involvement of these third parties creates enough uncertainty as to her state of mind to preclude any declarative statements as to motive.

MAURICE: Ah, très bien. Now, it is fortune's turn to smile upon you, Jack. My ruling is that she took the flowers by choice, but the reason is still unknown. (*beat*) I may return to my truffles now?

DAISY: Yes, thank you.

JACK: Thank you, Maurice.

MAURICE: De rien.

MAURICE *exits to the kitchen.*

MICHAEL: So I guess that's the big question then. Why did you accept them?

HILLARY *looks to* **JACK**. *He nods his consent.*

HILLARY: Look, I'll tell you. But I want you to really, really listen, alright?

MICHAEL: Fine.

HILLARY: Michael, I didn't want the attention. And if I didn't want the attention from getting flowers, can you understand how much less I'd want the attention from refusing them, or throwing them out?

MICHAEL: I guess. But why wouldn't you want the attention? Guys sending you flowers, that's good attention.

HILLARY: Not at work! And guys don't send flowers, boyfriends send flowers! You get flowers from people you're dating, not from people you've been on dates with. Do you see the distinction?

MICHAEL: Not really. I mean, how am I supposed to know when that happens?

HILLARY: You just do! And this, this was just way too soon. I mean, now Barry thinks we're "dating" dating, and it's bad enough dealing with a boss who's always prying into my business without him thinking we're in a relationship. Especially since he knows you!

MICHAEL: What does it matter what he thinks?

HILLARY: Because! Because now I have to act by all these different rules! Now, it's like I can't just not go on a date with you, I'd have to break up with you, you know? And it's our second date!

MICHAEL: But that's ridiculous . . .

HILLARY: That's dating. Dating's ridiculous! (**JACK** *and* **DAISY** *clear their throats*) I'm sorry, but it is!

MICHAEL: Look, you shouldn't care about what other people think. Let them think we're dating, so what? It doesn't have to change things between us . . . I mean, the only thing it might . . . never mind . . .

HILLARY: No, what?

MICHAEL: ...Well, it occurs to me that maybe, you know, if one were so inclined to see it in a certain way, well, it might kind of maybe mean that you couldn't see anyone else...at least for a while ...

HILLARY & JACK: What?!?

DAISY: Alright, hold on a minute. Let's not overreact. It may be a slightly radical interpretation of convention, but it's not without precedent. There are well-established rules dictating the amount of time that should elapse between relationships.

JACK: First of all, what relationship? And second of all, those rules are designed to protect the new partners, not the old, and you know it!

HILLARY: So what, I'm your property now?!?

MICHAEL: No one's saying that!

DAISY: Michael, allow me. (*to* **HILLARY**) No one's saying that.

HILLARY: I think I should consult with my waiter. (**JACK** *moves over to her side.*) It's private.

JACK leans in over the table to allow **HILLARY** *to whisper. Instead, she kisses him full on the lips. He stands upright again, slightly dazed.*

HILLARY: (*to* **MICHAEL**) That a long enough break for you?

MICHAEL: Oh! Oh! Oh, that's real mature!

HILLARY: You're calling me immature?!?

MICHAEL: No, of course not! *Titanic* was absolutely a movie made for adults, and not TWELVE-YEAR-OLD GIRLS!

HILLARY: You know, it won a little award you might of heard of! The OSCAR! For BEST PICTURE!

From this point until **MAURICE**'*s intervention, the waiters attempt to calm down their customers. At some point,* **MAURICE** *enters unnoticed and cuts off their argument, possibly before the end of the text provided.*

MICHAEL: Right, that means a lot.

HILLARY: You know the real reason you didn't like that movie?

MICHAEL: Because it was crap?

HILLARY: Because you're Billy Zane!—You think a relationship is a contract, not a give-and-take. Your flowers are just a blue diamond! You don't get how Rose could choose Jack, because you don't see what he could offer her. See, that's what you don't get, and what everyone who didn't like that movie doesn't get. Love is about unspoken understanding. They're from different sides of the tracks, but they make it work because they're there for each other. No matter how much things go against them, no matter who tries to stand in their way, no matter how much the boat sinks and how grim things seem . . . it's sweet, and you cynics can't appreciate sweet . . .

MICHAEL: Oh please. Who could identify with any of those characters? They were so cartoonish and hackneyed! "I'm the good guy! Love is great! I'm going to get you naked after knowing you for five minutes, but it's an art thing." "I'm the bad guy! Crush! Kill! Destroy! Drown the children!! I have money instead of feelings!" "I'm the rich girl. I can't understand love until a poor boy comes along with his wonderful life experience and educates me, because my world is all about manners, people with money are incapable of real feelings, thank God for the little people, with their simple minds and their pure hearts—"

MAURICE: SHUT UP! (*they do*) I mean, SILENCE! I think maybe now you are ready to order, yes? (*to* **MICHAEL**) Perhaps Monsieur would care for a hot dog? It too is ninety per cent asshole. (**HILLARY** *laughs.* **MAURICE** *turns to her.*) For Madame, I would recommend a molehill of paté. To you, it will no doubt seem like a mountain.

MICHAEL: Hey now, c'mon, that's not . . . I mean, who are you to judge us?

MAURICE: I'm the judge.

MICHAEL: Yes, well, be that as it may . . . We didn't come here to be mocked, we just came to . . . you know . . .

MAURICE: No, I do not. Why did you come?

MICHAEL: Well, you know . . . see if there was a spark . . .

MAURICE: (*to* **HILLARY**) And you?

HILLARY: Ummm, well, I mean, for me, it was a little more because I thought I had to, but when I agreed to the date, and even a little now, umm, yeah, I guess, looking for a spark . . .

MAURICE: Both of you? A spark? A spark?!? A spark of what? Could not be lust, because that you would already know . . . So then, a spark of . . . the other! Is that what you're telling me? You are looking for a spark of the other?

MICHAEL: Uh, yeah, I guess.

MAURICE: For this, you take up our time? This you could not figure out on your own? For this, you take up a table, two tables in fact, that could have been used by those who had already found their spark?!? Mon dieu!! (*beat*) Wait here!

MAURICE exits to the kitchen.

JACK: (*to* **HILLARY** *and* **MICHAEL**) I'd finish that wine now if I were you.

They drain their glasses. **MAURICE** *returns from the kitchen bearing a fairly large piece of stereograph art. He places the bottom of the frame on the table, displaying it to them.*

MAURICE: Do you know what this is?

HILLARY: 3-D art?

MAURICE: Yes, but it is also something more. It is love. The way you look at 3-D art is the way you should look at the person you love. Your eyes should become wider. Your blinking should slow. You should stare deeply, afraid to look away, fearing that if you do, it will disappear, never to be seen again. You should feel that you can see dimensions that no one else can or will ever see. To everyone else, it is just surface, but to you, it is deep and it is beautiful. Look at the art. Look at it! (*They do.*) Now, look at each other. (*They do.*) Is there a spark?

HILLARY: I don't think so.

MICHAEL: Not really.

MAURICE: Might there ever be?

MICHAEL: Probably not . . .

HILLARY: I'm sorry.

MAURICE: Date dismissed. Without prejudice.

MICHAEL: (*after a pause, to* **HILLARY**) C'mon. I'll give you a ride home.

HILLARY: (*after a pause*) Alright. (*to others*) Thanks.

They exit. **MAURICE** *lays the stereograph art on the table and exits to the kitchen.*

JACK: (*shouting after* **HILLARY**) Call me!

JACK *and* **DAISY** *sit at the vacated table.* **MAURICE** *returns with wine for all. He stands where he stood with the stereograph art.*

JACK: (*toasting*) Good job as always, boss.

They drink.

MAURICE: Bah, it is nothing. It is just King Solomon's logic: you cut a baby in half in front of a couple, and neither of them puts up a fuss, chances are it was not their baby. You do it once, you've done it a million times.

JACK: I suppose.

DAISY: It was nice to hear the 3-D art speech again. Nights like this, it helps to know that someone's that passionate about anything . . .

MAURICE: Ha! I'll tell you a secret, chérie: in truth, I cannot even see it!

DAISY: Really?!?

MAURICE: Well, I can see it, in the sense that I don't run into it, but it doesn't, how you say, (*makes popping sound*) pop out at me. This one hangs over my stove. It drives me crazy. It plays with me as if I were a child's toy. It makes me so frustrated I just want to spit in the soup!

DAISY: (*incredulous*) Well then why would you use it as your metaphor for love?!?

MAURICE: Because it drives me crazy. Because it plays with me as if I were a child's toy. Because it makes me so frustrated I just want to spit in the soup! (*beat*) Yet I still look at it, for it, every day, knowing that if I manage to see it once, just once, then it will be mine forever.

DAISY: Oh.

They all look at the stereograph art for quite some time.

JACK: It's a duck.
MAURICE: I knew it!!

[End]

Iraqi Karaoke

SHERRY MACDONALD

Iraqi Karaoke was produced for the Brave New Play Rites Festival in Vancouver in 1999 with the following cast and crew:

CORK: Martin Blaiz
LYNNETTE: Emily Stone

Directed by Lu Nelson

SETTING: *The play takes place in the living room of* CORK *and*
LYNNETTE. *Tammy Wynette music plays "Stand By Your Man."*

    LYNNETTE *enters, carrying a laundry basket, wearing a sparkly
cowgirl outfit, complete with fringes, sequins, and boots. She sings
along to the words of the song as she picks up dirty laundry that
is scattered about the room. Hearing* CORK *arrive, she stands
poised for his arrival.*

    CORK *enters and takes off his jacket. He walks past* LYNNETTE,
*goes directly to the source of the music and turns it off. He goes
over to the television, turns it on and sits down to watch it.*

    Sounds of war: bombs, missiles etc. are heard. There is CNN
type music.

NEWSCASTER: The skies over Baghdad are illuminated tonight . . .
The security chief issuing a forwarning in elevating a post-event
premature ejection for desert hounds of the nearby checkmate
division . . .

    LYNNETTE *parades back and forth in front of* CORK *who ignores
her. Finally she turns off the television.*

CORK: Hey, that's the war you turned off there.
LYNNETTE: It's just a television show.
CORK: It's not just a television show, Lynnette. It's "War in the Gulf."
LYNNETTE: Yeah and it's in my living room.
CORK: Don't forget the bedroom.
LYNNETTE: That too.
CORK: I like "War in the Gulf."
LYNNETTE: I liked "Cold War" better.
CORK: Not me. Not enough action.
LYNNETTE: Don't blame the war, Cork. You were in a slump.
CORK: Can't help it. Stand-offs don't do anything for me.
LYNNETTE: At least the pace was good.
CORK: We can't do "Cold War" anymore, Lynnette. Doesn't make
    sense. The enemy's busted up into a million tiny little pieces
    now.

LYNNETTE: I can't discuss politics right now, Cork. I got a karaoke contest to get to.

CORK *pulls* **LYNNETTE** *to him and kisses her.*

CORK: Iraq—

He reaches under her skirt.

LYNNETTE: Not now, Cork.

CORK: Looks like we're going to need heavy duty immobilizing equipment.

LYNNETTE: Cork—

CORK: Alegiant Prowlers . . . F-16s . . . G-17s . . . patriots . . . scuds . . . wasp intruders . . . thrust action launchers . . . approaching strike zone—

His hand goes further up her skirt.

LYNNETTE: Cork!

LYNNETTE *jumps up.*

CORK: What?

LYNNETTE: These sequins are hand-sewn. The skirt alone took me three weeks. I gotta go. If you're late, they disqualify you.

CORK: You're going to leave me here all alone?

LYNNETTE: You're not alone, Cork. You got the war.

CORK: I want you to stay here and watch it with me.

LYNNETTE: There comes a time in every woman's life where she's gotta move on. I can't stay home and watch the war forever.

CORK *turns the television on.*

NEWSCASTER: . . . the strike zone is completely within reach. Thrust action launchers are on standby . . . here at Operation Desert Storm. And now back to Wolfe, at the Pentagon . . .

LYNNETTE *turns the television off.*

CORK: What?

LYNNETTE: You haven't told me how I look.

CORK: But they're going back to the Pentagon.

LYNNETTE: Forget the Pentagon, Cork. I worked my fingers to the bone on this outfit.

CORK: Alright, let's have a look.

LYNNETTE *models for* CORK.

LYNNETTE: Well?

CORK: What am I supposed to say?

LYNNETTE: Just say what you think.

CORK: You sure?

LYNNETTE: 'Course I'm sure.

CORK: The outfit's not bad, but the hair—

LYNNETTE: What about the hair?

CORK: It's a different red every time I see it.

LYNNETTE: I'm perfecting the look. And it's not red, it's strawberry blonde.

CORK: That's not strawberry blonde.

LYNNETTE: That's what it says on the package.

CORK: Well, whatever it is, it's fake.

LYNNETTE: So what?

CORK: So what? Everyone knows you really have black hair.

LYNNETTE: It's the effect that counts.

CORK: It don't match. Red hair, black pussy. It's unnatural.

LYNNETTE: Nobody's gonna see my pussy. It's karaoke, cork, not a striptease.

CORK: I see your pussy and it don't match.

LYNNETTE: Well, you don't have to see it if you don't want to. You can sleep on the couch until everything matches again.

CORK: Maybe I don't wanna wait.

CORK *pulls* LYNNETTE *to him. She sits on his lap.*

CORK: Hold on . . .

> CORK *turns on the television. He begins kissing her and touching her while watching the television.*

NEWSCASTER: . . . strategic paralysis of the entire strike zone with minimal collateral damage. That gives the checkmate division considerable advantage. Desert squirrel will not be able to elude forces for much longer . . .

> LYNNETTE *jumps off his lap and turns off the television.*

CORK: Hey!
LYNNETTE: I'm sorry, Cork. I have to go.
CORK: Don't leave me, Lynnette, not like this.
LYNNETTE: Sorry, Cork.

> *She walks away.*

CORK: You're not going out looking like that are you?

> *She stops.*

LYNNETTE: What do you mean?
CORK: You look like a spectacle.

> *Pause.*

LYNNETTE: You don't really think I look like a spectacle do you?
CORK: Well look at you. Those sequins.
LYNNETTE: It's a costume. It's supposed to make me look—
CORK: What?
LYNNETTE: Dazzling.
CORK: And that red hair.
LYNNETTE: It's strawberry blonde!
CORK: You'll be up there shaking your ass for everyone to—
LYNNETTE: It's karaoke, Cork. I don't shake anything. I sing.

CORK: How much do they pay you?

LYNNETTE: It's a contest, dumbbell. They don't pay you to be in a contest.

CORK: Well what do you get if you win?

LYNNETTE: You get to be in another contest. A bigger one. In the city.

CORK: In other words, nothing.

LYNNETTE: Brother that's just something you'd say, isn't it?

CORK: Sometimes I just don't understand you, Lynnette.

LYNNETTE: Sometimes I get the feeling you don't understand anything.

CORK: What do you mean?

Pause.

LYNNETTE: You're my husband.

CORK: So.

LYNNETTE: You're supposed to be—

CORK: What?

LYNNETTE: Supportive.

CORK: I am supportive.

LYNNETTE: You said I looked like a spectacle.

CORK: You told me to say what I thought.

LYNNETTE: Yeah, but not that.

CORK: Well what do you expect, Lynnette? You keep pushing at me to give you an answer. And when I give you one, you don't like it. That's why it's better if I just sit here and keep my big mouth shut.

LYNNETTE: I don't want your big mouth shut. I want it open. With compliments coming out of it.

CORK: I was just sitting here all peaceful watching the war.

LYNNETTE: Oh yeah, the war. You'd hardly believe it's a war. Press a little red button and boom whole cities are wiped off the map like you were brushing crumbs off a tablecloth. Can't hardly understand what they're talking about.

CORK: That's because it's a high tech war, Lynnette. You're not supposed to understand what they're talking about.

LYNNETTE: Sounds more like a board game to me. Never even hear the word blood.

CORK: It's globalized television coverage, Lynnette. No one wants to hear the word blood.

LYNNETTE: No, just words like strategic paralysis and collateral damage.

CORK: Ooh Lynnette, can you sit on my lap when you say that?

LYNNETTE: Oh, Cork.

CORK: Come on Lynnette.

LYNNETTE: No, I'm going to this contest. And I'm gonna win.

CORK: Jesus, Lynnette it's just a karaoke contest.

LYNNETTE: Never know who's gonna be in the audience. Someone important could be out there, someone looking for a singer.

CORK: No one important's gonna come here to listen to no karaoke country singing.

LYNNETTE: It's more than just that. It's doing something for myself.

CORK: Well then do it. And stop dragging me into it.

LYNNETTE: You're my husband stupid, I'm supposed to drag you into it.

CORK: Make up your mind, either you're doing something for yourself or you're not. Just leave me out of it.

LYNNETTE: Okay, if that's what you want. (*goes to door*) I'm going now. (*no response*) Cork? I said I'm going now. (*still nothing*) I'm taking my red hair and my black pussy . . . (**CORK** *jumps up and runs over to her.*) That's just like you: say the word "pussy" and you spring to attention.

CORK: I'm just looking out for you.

LYNNETTE: Yeah? Which part are you looking out for?

CORK: I want you to be realistic.

LYNNETTE: I don't want to be realistic, I want to be happy.

CORK: Why don't you get a job, make some money, that'll make you happy.

LYNNETTE: There are no jobs, dummy. Not in this town.

CORK: I don't know about that. I hear they're looking for chambermaids down at the Stowaway.

LYNNETTE: Good, Cork, why didn't I think of that? That'll make me happy. Why would I want to be a singer when I could scrub the shit out of toilets instead.

CORK: Well you go ahead then, go out, make your fame and fortune singing with a karaoke machine. But if you wanna know the truth, I think your chances of fame and fortune are better if you stick to toilets.

Pause.

LYNNETTE: It was just too good to be true. I kept telling myself, Lynnette, something's gonna happen to ruin it. Cork'll say something . . . You know I've been getting ready for weeks, working on my song. Why didn't you ruin it for me in the beginning, before I learned all those words, before I sewed on all those goddamn sequins?

CORK: But you know, Lynnette, you are cute.

LYNNETTE: Sometimes you make me so mad I could just . . .

CORK: What.

Pause.

CORK: I don't know why you get so worked up about nothing. It's karaoke. It's not even real.

LYNNETTE: Just takes one word. Sometimes it's not even that. Sometimes it's just the expression on your face. You're like a tiger waiting to pounce. All you have to do is raise an eyebrow and the life is ripped right outta me. It's effortless for you. How does it feel to have that kind of effect on a person?

CORK: What about the effect you have on me?

LYNNETTE: I don't know. What kind of effect do I have on you?

Pause.

CORK: You make me crazy. I can't get enough of you. Even with the red hair.

LYNNETTE: Strawberry blonde.

CORK: Strawberry blonde. (*pause*) I love you, Lynnette.

LYNNETTE: If you loved me, you would come to the contest.

CORK: I don't know, Lynnette. Karaoke?

LYNNETTE: Come on, Cork. It'll be fun. I might even shake something for you.

CORK: But . . . the war . . .

LYNNETTE: The war'll still be on when you get home. They have twenty-four hour coverage now.

CORK: I'll come with you. Watch your contest but then . . . the minute we get home . . . the TV is going on and that dress is coming off.
LYNNETTE: Alright.

Pause.

CORK: Iraq . . .

Pause. **LYNNETTE** *considers and then:*

LYNNETTE: Kuwait . . .
CORK: Coalition Forces . . .
LYNNETTE: Ground Force Detachment . . .
CORK: Desert Storm . . .
LYNNETTE: Desert Shield . . .

They move towards each other.

CORK: Checkmate Division . . .
LYNNETTE: Strategic strike zone . . .
CORK: Collateral damage . . .
LYNNETTE: Auxiliary disfigurement . . .
CORK: Stealth Champions . . .
LYNNETTE: Wasp Intruders . . .
CORK: Critical Rap Sector . . .
LYNNETTE: Deliniar bioptics . . .

They kiss. She breaks away and exits. He is about to follow her when he goes back for one more hit off the television.

NEWSCASTER: . . . Coalition Forces scored well today, another direct hit . . .

CORK *makes some sort of victory gesture, follows* **LYNNETTE** *out the door, leaving the television turned on.*

NEWSCASTER: Critical Rap sector and bilateral units maintained total control, while offshore collateral immobilizers secured secondary targets.

Music over "Stand by Your Man" as the **NEWSCASTER***'s voice continues and the lights begin to fade.*

NEWSCASTER: Cluster stallions are now on standby. Use of deliniar bioptics are expected to reduce radically the inferred expectations of target decentralization . . .

Sounds of bombings mix with the **NEWSCASTER***'s voice and the music as the lights fade to black. The* **NEWSCASTER***'s voice gradually fades out as well.*

NEWSCASTER: Clandestine retreat factions elevate the need for synthesis and subsequent reintegration of carbon infused elements in a one, one hundred and o six hundred eclipse of fuel injectors, allowing complete annihilation and bulk auxiliary disfigurement . . .

[End]

Fistfight with God

BY

KEVIN CHONG

Fistfight with God was produced for the Brave New Play Rites Festival in Vancouver in 1996 with the following cast and crew:

PONYBOY: Art Hand
AMELIA: Tracy Swaile
BRUCE: Chris Rowley

Directed by Meredith Vuchnich
Sound & Light Design: Jane Graham
& Meredith Vuchnich
Stage Manager: Jane Graham
Sound Engineer: Bruce Dierick

CHARACTERS

PONYBOY: *age 20-25*
AMELIA: *age 20-25*
BRUCE: *age 20-25*

SETTING: *An airplane. It may be best to portray the airplane as unrealistically and minimally as possible. Maybe only a couple of chairs and some sound effects are needed to give the impression of an airplane. The washroom is supposed to be to Stage Left, the pilot's cockpit to Stage Right. Seated together are* **PONYBOY** *and* **AMELIA** *facing Stage Right. They both appear to be nervous. Their heads tilt back against their chairs as the plane takes off.*

PONYBOY: Don't be afraid.

AMELIA: Thank you.

PONYBOY: I used to be afraid. Oh God, flying used to make me so nervous. But I learned to think about things which would make me feel better.

AMELIA: Oh, I see. What are you thinking about right now?

PONYBOY: French existentialist writer Albert Camus.

AMELIA: That's odd. Why Albert Camus?

PONYBOY: I don't know; I've never really thought about it. I've always liked his book *The Outsider*. It's one of my favourite books, you know. It's the story of a man named Meursault who kills someone and then feels no guilt about it. I read it in high school. One day, I skipped a P.E. class and I finished it in two hours. (*gets excited*) Wow, what a book, what angst. Right after finishing it, I killed a cat with a tire-iron.

AMELIA: That sounds horrible.

PONYBOY: I had a lot of (*accents this word*) angst.

AMELIA: That still sounds rather harsh.

PONYBOY: Well, I was angry at a lot of things. I was angry at my mother. Oh, what a woman. She always made me wear a scarf. She said that a scarf would protect me from the elements. And she said that she only felt it was safe for me to go out when I was wearing my scarf. But I didn't wear my scarf and one day I came home and she was murdered.

AMELIA: How tragic.

PONYBOY: Oh, isn't it? My male lover murdered my mother with a dildo. Then he cut her up and wrote my name in blood. I felt so horrible . . . I wasn't wearing my scarf. You know, Meursault, the hero in *The Outsider*, didn't give a rat's ass about his mother when she died. He was a horribly cold-blooded character. A man who refused to lie. I wanted to be like him after my mother's murder. I believed that would be the best way to escape the pain. Then I killed a cat.

AMELIA: You told me that.

PONYBOY: I'm sorry. I repeat myself often. When you repeat words meaninglessly it's called a tautology.

AMELIA: Thank you. I'll write that down.

PONYBOY: T–A–U–T–O–L–O–G–Y.

The airplane reaches its proper altitude. **PONYBOY** *and* **AMELIA** *take off their seat belts, though they're both a little tense.*

AMELIA: We're safe, I guess. Well, safer, at least.

PONYBOY: Do you know in real life Albert Camus was devoted to his mother?

AMELIA: No.

PONYBOY: It's true. When I found out how much Camus loved his mother, I began to feel guilty. If only I loved my mother more, maybe she wouldn't have died.

AMELIA: You're a sweet poor thing. . .

PONYBOY: Ponyboy.

AMELIA: Ponyboy.

She pats his hand.

PONYBOY: What's your name?

AMELIA: Amelia.

PONYBOY: Amelia.

AMELIA: Like Amelia Earhart. My mother's dream was for me to be a pilot when I was born. I don't think she would ever expect me to have such a fear of flying.

PONYBOY: It's an irony of life. My mother wanted me to be a pilot, too.

AMELIA: Well, that's ironic, too. Both our mothers wanted us to be pilots.

PONYBOY: I was thinking . . . Isn't it ironic how the hero in *The Outsider* didn't care at all about his mother while Albert Camus loved his?

AMELIA: I suppose that life is filled with ironies.

PONYBOY: You ever get that feeling, Amelia, that these coincidences that we find in our lives—

AMELIA: Aren't completely ruled by chance?

PONYBOY: That's what I was going to say.

AMELIA: Maybe we had the same thought at the same time for a reason.

PONYBOY: That's what I was going to say.

AMELIA: And maybe we're together, thinking the same thing, together, for a reason.

PONYBOY: It must be true. I don't know how many times I wished things would make sense.

AMELIA: Ponyboy, do you ever get the feeling that happiness is in front of your face? That you just have to grab it—

PONYBOY: That you have to make yourself vulnerable in order to get what you're looking for—

AMELIA: Be it happiness, or courage, or love.

PONYBOY: Amelia, I think I like you. I want to kiss you; I want to make popcorn with you and share it with you.

AMELIA: Oh, popcorn would be good right now. I'm very hungry and popcorn is a delicious yet nutritious snack.

PONYBOY: And you just can't have a little bit of popcorn either. Once you start eating it, you aren't happy until your fingers are buttery and salty and you're biting into unpopped kernels.

AMELIA: I like you very much too, Ponyboy. I like your eyes. I've always wanted to marry a man with the same colour eyes as yours. And your hands (*takes his hand in hers*): they're soft and damp . . . I suppose I like that too. It can't be a coincidence that we're sitting here together.

PONYBOY: Tell me something about you, Amelia.

AMELIA: I lost my virginity to a boy who really liked *Star Wars*. He would pretend that he was Luke Skywalker and I was the Death Star.

PONYBOY: Oh how delicious. Tell me more.

AMELIA: Well, right now I'm thinking to myself that I have to go pee, and that I'm hungry, (*pause, as she thinks*) and that I love you.

PONYBOY: I love you, too.

AMELIA: Now tell me something about you, my love.

PONYBOY: I'm going to flight school, you know. I thought it would make me less afraid of flying if I learned how to do it. Fly, that is.

AMELIA: Are you doing well?

PONYBOY: I'm tops in my class.

AMELIA: I've always had confidence in you.

PONYBOY: I couldn't have done it without you. You've given my life meaning and hope. I used to think my life was horrible. I used to think everything was gloom and despair. When I think about it, I realize how silly I was. I was so young. So obvious. Some people think that everything's existential angst short of a fistfight with God. Well, I laugh at them. Ha!

AMELIA: Ha!

PONYBOY: Amelia?

AMELIA: Yes?

PONYBOY: I don't ever want to live without you. Promise me that when we grow old and one of us has a terminal illness we'll kill each other.

AMELIA: We could drink liquid Drano out of shot glasses!

PONYBOY: Brilliant idea, darling. You're a real ideas person!

AMELIA: I am?

PONYBOY: You certainly are.

AMELIA: Oh, Ponyboy, you inspire me. From now on, all my brilliant ideas are dedicated to you, my darling.

PONYBOY: I can't believe how happy I am.

AMELIA: I feel like I'm drunk on champagne. I feel like I'm underneath an air vent during a hot summer day.

PONYBOY: Amelia, you are the best thing that has happened to me since that incident with my male lover and my mother.

They embrace and they kiss. **AMELIA** *pulls away.*

PONYBOY: What's the matter?

AMELIA: I'm sorry, I don't want to be nosy, but I think it's important I know. Are you still gay?

PONYBOY: Oh, no. You see, it was a bet.

AMELIA: A bet?

PONYBOY: I had a couple of friends who bet me that I couldn't live a homosexual lifestyle for three years. Do you believe me?

AMELIA: Yes, of course. There's no one else I trust more than you. They embrace. (**AMELIA** *pulls away again*) Did you win your bet?

PONYBOY: Oh yeah. My friends had to buy me two large pizzas.

AMELIA: Oh, I wish I had some pizza.

PONYBOY: I mean, do I act like I'm gay or anything?

AMELIA: Well, I don't think so. I mean, I wouldn't know.

PONYBOY: Be honest.

AMELIA: Oh, honey, you're all the man I would ever want. You're an extra serving of man.

PONYBOY: Thank you.

AMELIA: Do you think there'll be food soon?

PONYBOY: Probably.

AMELIA: Do me a favour?

PONYBOY: Anything.

AMELIA: I'm going to the washroom. All this excitement has excited my bladder. If they serve dinner, make sure you get something for me.

PONYBOY: Can do.

She gets out from her seat. They blow kisses at one another as she walks to the washroom. **PONYBOY** *looks reflectively out the window. Enter* **BRUCE** *pushing a dinner cart of some sort.*

BRUCE: Good afternoon, sir, for dinner tonight we'll be having—

PONYBOY: What the hell are you doing here?

BRUCE: You egotistical bastard? Do you think I was following you? It's been two years already. Did you think that we'd never bump into one another again, did you?

PONYBOY: No, I guess not. But it's been such a long time, I thought you had fallen of the face of the earth. What have you been doing, lately?

BRUCE: I'm an airline attendant.

PONYBOY: That seems like good, honest work.

BRUCE: You bet. I suppose you're on a vacation.

PONYBOY: Yes. With my new wife.

BRUCE: That's great. I always thought you were the type to settle down.

PONYBOY: Yeah.

BRUCE: I'm sure your mother loved the idea of her gay son getting married. How is she these days?

PONYBOY: She was murdered.

BRUCE: I'm sorry.

PONYBOY: An ex-girlfriend of mine did it. Strangled her with a pair of stockings. She got off by reason of insanity. It was a travesty of justice.

BRUCE: Well, that's terrible. (*uncomfortable silence*) I'm surprised that I would see you on a plane, you used to be so afraid to fly.

PONYBOY: I have it under control now. (*pause*) Bruce, do you ever think about us?

BRUCE: I used to.

PONYBOY: I see.

BRUCE: Well, what do you want for dinner tonight, pal? Beef or chicken?

PONYBOY: You know what I'd really like? I'd like a hot turkey neck sandwich.

BRUCE *takes out a turkey-neck sandwich from his cart and throws it at him.*

BRUCE: One turkey-neck sandwich.

PONYBOY: Oh, Bruce, you were always so literal. I was speaking euphemistically. What do you say about a stroll down memory lane?

BRUCE: You're kidding. What about your wife?

PONYBOY: She's in the john. How about it? When do you get off? Or should I say, how do you want to get off?

BRUCE: I'm a steward. I work the whole trip, smart guy.

PONYBOY: Let's trip the light fandango, Bruce . . .

BRUCE: (*sudden angry outburst*) You know I hate Procol Harum! Always pushing my buttons, aren't you?

PONYBOY: Please, Bruce.

BRUCE: I'm too smart for your crap now. Try if you like, but you're not going to get any action.

PONYBOY: Bruce, you're not the only who has changed . . .

BRUCE: God, not another one of your great big promises. Because they usually end up with me broken-hearted and another cat murdered.

PONYBOY: We had good times, didn't we?

PONYBOY *grabs* BRUCE.

BRUCE: Don't touch me.

PONYBOY: But we did.

BRUCE: It doesn't matter. Because it's over. (*pause*) You're a real party-pooper. Here I am on a nice plane flight, doing what I enjoy most, and then of all the people you could bump into, of all the lousy flukes . . .

PONYBOY: But, Bruce maybe it's not an accident we're here together. It's ironic, you see. I think there's a reason why we're thrown together, it's not chance . . .

BRUCE: Have a good dinner.

BRUCE *exits with his cart toward the pilot's cockpit side of the stage.*

PONYBOY: No, Bruce wait!

PONYBOY *sulks. Enter* AMELIA *from the washroom looking refreshed.*

AMELIA: Hi, honey, I'm back. Did you miss me?

PONYBOY: (*unconvincingly*) Yes. Yes I did.

AMELIA: Have they served dinner?

PONYBOY: I'm not sure.

AMELIA *looks around at the other imaginary passengers on the plane.*

AMELIA: It seems everyone else is having dinner.
PONYBOY: Oh really?
AMELIA: Yes. Did they skip us?
PONYBOY: I don't know.
AMELIA: Well, this isn't right. We're in economy class, we're not stow-aways. We deserve to eat. (*she waves her hand and yells*) Steward! Steward!
PONYBOY: Calm down, will you?
AMELIA: This isn't fair, you know. (*begins to yell again*) Steward!
PONYBOY: Listen.
AMELIA: I feel light-headed.
PONYBOY: Listen!
AMELIA: I feel young and obvious.

PONYBOY *slaps her. He starts shaking her.*

PONYBOY: Shut up! I told the steward that we weren't hungry.
AMELIA: Why the hell did you do that? (*pause*) Honey?
PONYBOY: Don't call me that.
AMELIA: Why did you do that?
PONYBOY: I just felt like it.
AMELIA: That's no excuse.
PONYBOY: I don't know you.
AMELIA: (*ignoring him*) I haven't eaten in fourteen hours. I was starving myself this whole week so I could fit into my bathing wear. This whole week, I've been living off carrots and gravy powder. . . . I feel malnourished.
PONYBOY: I don't want to talk to you.
AMELIA: Well, we're going to talk about it. We need to get things out into the open. I wanted to look good for you.
PONYBOY: Listen. If you're going to continue acting this way, I'm going to ask the steward for another seat.

AMELIA: God, why is this happening? Everything was going so perfectly, Ponyboy. It was like a fairy-tale—

PONYBOY: Steward!

AMELIA: You know, I couldn't even pee. There was an old man in there taking forever. I think he had Alzheimer's disease and was trying to committ suicide. Oh God, I know how he feels. I don't know what to do: cry or pee or both.

PONYBOY: Will you behave yourself, for Christ's sake?

AMELIA: I wanted to be thin and beautiful. I wanted things to be like they used to be—back when the plane was taking off. Tell me, Ponyboy have you found someone else? (*pause*) Oh God. What's she like? Is she prettier than me? Do . . . do you still find me attractive?

PONYBOY: I never have. I'm gay for Christ's sake.

AMELIA: You told me it was a bet.

PONYBOY: The only bet I made was the one I made to myself that I wouldn't puke when I looked at you, you smelly bag of pickles. I was doing fine as a heterosexual, until you sat next to me. Eww, just looking at you makes me want to screw men. You're about as desirable as a used kleenex.

AMELIA pulls out a kleenex and starts to blow in it.

AMELIA: I know you don't mean that.

PONYBOY: Well, honey, you're in denial. I'm tired of you people who don't understand my lifestyle. I'm sick of your hatred and your refusal to accept me for who I am. It's people like you—closed minded, dirty poo-poo pants—who killed my lesbian mother.

AMELIA: But I thought your mother—

PONYBOY: Listen. I'm going to repeat it until you get it: I'm gay, I'm gay . . . (*keeps repeating this*)

Each time he says "gay," PONYBOY pokes AMELIA with his finger. AMELIA vainly attempts to fight him off.

AMELIA: Please, Ponyboy, stop this . . . tautology.

Suddenly the plane starts shaking. Maybe the lights can turn on and off. **PONYBOY** *and* **AMELIA** *bounce around in their seats. Then the lights turn on and everything's normal for a brief while.*

PONYBOY: What was that?
AMELIA: I don't know.

The same thing happens again.

AMELIA: There it goes again.
PONYBOY: That was just once too many to be just an accident. *(starts yelling)* Steward! Steward!
AMELIA: *(with* **PONYBOY***)* Steward! Steward!

BRUCE *appears wearing a life preserver. He speaks to the entire plane.*

BRUCE: Hello, there. As you've probably noticed, we've had some problems keeping up in the air. This may seem like a strange question, and I don't want anyone taking this in the wrong way and panicking, but do we have any pilots whatsoever onboard?

A short pause. He exits.

AMELIA: Well, why wasn't your hand raised?
PONYBOY: I don't want to.
AMELIA: For Christ's sake, Ponyboy, you might not have your pilot's license yet, but you're our only hope.
PONYBOY: I can't.

The plane shakes around once more.

AMELIA: What did you mean by that?
PONYBOY: I mean, I'm not really a pilot. I don't go to flight school, either.
AMELIA: Are you saying you're lying?

PONYBOY: Yes.

AMELIA: I can't believe you did that. (*pause*) I suppose—did your mother want you to be a pilot, too?

PONYBOY: No, she didn't.

AMELIA: You're a bastard! I believed you.

She hits him (or pinches his arm). The plane dips down and begins descending. The actors on stage move accordingly.

PONYBOY: The plane's nose-diving.

AMELIA: Is that a technical term, fly-boy?

PONYBOY: How the hell would I know?

Pause.

AMELIA: Listen: I'm sorry I snapped at you.

PONYBOY: You had every right to. I didn't mean to lie. I should be sorry.

AMELIA: I'm afraid.

PONYBOY: Don't be. Think of Albert Camus.

AMELIA: Thank you. I will.

PONYBOY: Here, I have a hot turkey-neck sandwich for you.

AMELIA: Please, I thought you were gay.

PONYBOY: No, I didn't mean that . . .

He offers her the sandwich. She accepts. PONYBOY *takes a scarf from under his seat and wraps it around his neck.*

AMELIA: Thank you. You're very kind.

PONYBOY: It's the least I can do.

AMELIA: Oh God. I really need to pee.

Lights out.

[End]

The Reinvention of Minister Thorne

BY

TIM CARLSON

The Reinvention of Minister Thorne was produced for the Brave New Play Rites Festival in Vancouver in 1996 with the following cast and crew:

MINISTER THORNE: John Murphy★
THE TAILOR: Chris McGregor★

Directed by Richard Wolfe★

(★Appeared courtesy of Canadian Actors'
Equity Association.)

CHARACTERS:
MINISTER THORNE
THE TAILOR

SETTING: *A chair and a desk. Newspapers and magazines are strewn about. Clothes hang on a coat rack.*

SCENE ONE
*THORNE addresses the people. The **TAILOR** is standing in the shadows.*

THORNE: You are all aware, no doubt, of the trials and humiliations of Minister Thorne. I know suffering intimately. And you, the good people of West Recession know suffering as well. And although we may think we can bear little more suffering, we will perservere through our common resilience.

Suffering was suffocating West Recession before the good people voted the Common Sense Party into power. I doubt voters forget the Great Shortage of 1996 or the Unspeakable Downturn of '98. Again, delegates, we see dark clouds rising. I fear more suffering is at hand. We must band together in our common resilience. Let us align ourselves to lead West Recession into the renewal of 1999.

I am ready, good people. I am inspired. As an experienced sufferer, I am ready and willing to suffer more for the values and the way of life of West Recession. I humbly seek your support as the Common Sense Party candidate. Good night and God bless.

SCENE TWO
*Lights up. **TAILOR** is unpacking clothes. **THORNE** is undressing as the scene progresses.*

THORNE: He should be grateful.
TAILOR: Naturally, sir.

THORNE: I'm taken for granted—
TAILOR: Not at all—
THORNE: No—I am tolerated—
TAILOR: —sir.
THORNE: Barely tolerated.
TAILOR: I don't think—
THORNE: I can't think about that now.
TAILOR: Precisely.
THORNE: Turning my humiliation into advantageous position is a tricky bit of business.
TAILOR: Exactly.
THORNE: I've gained humility. But it was humiliation, nevertheless.
TAILOR: That was the past, not the future.
THORNE: I know I know. My humiliation—
TAILOR: Yes, sir—
THORNE: I've worn it like a cloak.
TAILOR: You're stamina and bearing have impressed, sir.
THORNE: Nonsense.
TAILOR: Absolutely.
THORNE: I'm sure my humiliation made for great comedy in the corridors, cellars, broomclosets and stairwells of power?
TAILOR: Certainly not, sir.
THORNE: You and the other party servants had a good laugh?
TAILOR: Never cracked a—
THORNE: Whispered amongst yourselves. Shouted anonymously in the press.
TAILOR: Not at all, sir.
THORNE: It's only natural—
TAILOR: Rest assured, sir, I go to great lengths to ignore the rampant lies, uninformed whispers, dehumanizing cartoons and mocking editorials that broadcast your humiliation globally—sir.

Beat.

THORNE: Things get blown out of proportion.
TAILOR: Most assuredly, sir.

THORNE: I should think Chief Minister would be grateful for my accomplishments.

TAILOR: Your humiliation alone, sir, will assure you a place in the history—

THORNE: Not only that! As constituents surely remember and the record clearly states, I voted for all progressive initiatives that facilitated the economic renewal we enjoy today.

TAILOR: Unforgettable.

THORNE: I was the leading light on a Common Sense subcommittee which created innovative brainstorming techniques to construct a great number of phrases in significant sentences in numerous subsections of various bills.

TAILOR: Ground-breaking.

THORNE: Trickle-up. That was mine!

TAILOR: Revolutionary.

THORNE: Unfortunately, my indiscretions were more fascinating than my legislations.

TAILOR: Unfortunately.

THORNE: One small misunderstanding lead to another and another lead to allegations of sexual impropriety, fraud, embezzlement, wiretapping and other charges the jury spent so little time in pondering.

TAILOR: Scant consideration.

THORNE: Thirty days in jail is not an easy thing to live down. But the good people of West Recession recognized my strength and resilience in the face of adversity—something the Chief Minister will never understand.

TAILOR: A sin, sir.

THORNE: My appearance should reflect this. Poise in the face of adversity.

TAILOR: (*opening the suit bag*) After consultation with party officials, I took the liberty of selecting this suit just for you, sir. I know you'll like it.

TAILOR drapes THORNE in a green suit jacket. **THORNE** *looks at himself in the mirror, slowly becoming angry.*

THORNE: Off!

TAILOR: You hit your zenith in the polls when I dressed you in green, sir.

THORNE: Off! Take it off!

TAILOR: A twenty-nine per cent approval rating, sir.

THORNE: Off!

TAILOR: Perhaps something in bold stripes, sir?

THORNE: Aaahhhhh!

TAILOR: Houndstooth?

THORNE: No! Gray! Solid gray!

TAILOR: Gray will not inspire voter confidence, sir.

THORNE: Surely my policy record and capacity for suffering—not to mention the promise of compassionately efficient common sense—is all the voter needs to feel confident.

TAILOR: The Chief Minister suggested—

THORNE: (*grabs the* **TAILOR**'s *lapels*) The Chief Minister? The Chief Minister suggested! I suggest you forget the Chief Minister's suggestions.

TAILOR: He is something of an expert in—

THORNE: —in nothing but playing Chief Minister Bond.

TAILOR: Does the Minister prefer deep, dark charcoal or a more cheery light gray?

THORNE: The middle gray is best.

TAILOR: Will the Minister please excuse me while I retrieve something in a pleasing hue of middle gray.

THORNE: Be quick about it.

TAILOR *exits.*

THORNE: He should be grateful. The Chief Minister wants to recreate me in his image does he? Image guru is he? Well, good for the Chief Minister. Prince among politicians. But a bastard among men.

What does he know that wasn't gained under my tutelage? He used to shake my hand and say as much. Introduced me as his mentor. Did all he could to help me. Hmm. Nice disappearing act during my humiliation—media smear, trial, conviction, incarceration. Not a word of encouragement or regret. Too tired from his late-night service in the Knife-in-the-Back. I went to jail and he woke up on top. Bastard of a man. But a prince among politicians. And a vulture among princes.

Thought he had me out of the way—stripped me of all he could, for all he needed, stripped me of all I had. Now he wants to swoop down from his vulture high and scavenge my carcass again. He is a vulture among carcasses. And a bastard among vultures.

Nevermind. The people of West Recession will support me. I will appeal to their goodness, their consciences, their suffering. I'll deliver the vote.

SCENE THREE

> **TAILOR** *enters carrying a makeup bag.* **THORNE** *is seated at the desk, still in his underwear.*

THORNE: He should be grateful.

TAILOR: Naturally sir.

THORNE: He'll owe me when I deliver West Recession.

TAILOR: I'm sure. (**TAILOR** *hands* **THORNE** *an envelope*) A dispatch from the Chief Minister. The latest poll.

THORNE: The question?

TAILOR: Can the humiliated Minister Thorne deliver West Recession unto the Common Sense Party?

THORNE: The numbers?

TAILOR: Thirty-nine percent. Down half a percentage point.

THORNE: Accuracy?

TAILOR: Plus or minus three per cent nineteen times in twenty.

THORNE: Our interpretion?

TAILOR: We feel insecure.

THORNE: The Chief Minister lends me no support.

TAILOR: His support is tied to the polls.

THORNE: Bastard!

TAILOR begins giving THORNE a massage, which becomes increasingly violent.

TAILOR: The Minister has a lot of knots.
THORNE: The tension of humilation.
TAILOR: Sags and bags.
THORNE: The deep, dark depths of my suffering.
TAILOR: Creaks and cracks.

TAILOR cracks THORNE'S neck. THORNE screams.

TAILOR: Why suffer needlessly?
THORNE: Leadership is suffering.
TAILOR: Theories are useless unless applied.
THORNE: I hadn't thought of that. It's just a theory.
TAILOR: You need a new path.
THORNE: Ethics. The high road will be my comeback trail.

TAILOR wrenches THORNE's arm behind his back.

TAILOR: The high road is the fast track to greater humiliation at the polls.
THORNE: Perhaps middle road is best.
TAILOR: It affords a wider view.
THORNE: There is no reason why the middle road cannot intersect with the high road at some point . . . in the distant future.
THORNE: Consider the low road.
TAILOR: Or . . . the back road?

TAILOR massages THORNE's back.

TAILOR: I think the tension has eased.

TAILOR throws THORNE into a chair.

TAILOR: The polls say you look rather haggard. (*applying whiteface*) A decrease in gravity to brighten the face. Your support is among the traditional Common Sense voter, but you must do more to court the youth vote sir.

He pierces **THORNE**'s *nipple.*

TAILOR: Fifty-one per cent of the good people of West Recession prefer plaid.

He holds up a plaid suit. **THORNE** *steps into decrepit pants.*

TAILOR: Pundits report the good people of West Recession want to hear no more about suffering.

TAILOR *helps* **THORNE** *into a ragged white shirt.*

TAILOR: Common sense dictates the improved Minister Thorne must wear his optimism as a second skin.

TAILOR *puts a mismatched tie around* **THORNE**'s *neck.*

TAILOR: Survey results suggest the new Minister Thorne must give the people a sense of security.

TAILOR *helps* **THORNE** *into his suit jacket.*

TAILOR: Confidence is the armor of today's Minister Thorne. Let's work on your speech.

He opens **THORNE**'s *mouth and brushes his teeth with an electric toothbrush.*

SCENE FOUR

THORNE, *wearing a red clown nose, steps into a spotlight.*

THORNE: People of West Recession, the long dark night of suffering has come to an end. Let's speak no more of suffering. (*beat*) Let's speak of optimism, confidence and security. (*beat*) Our great future inspires me. (*beat*) Optimism, confidence, security—a vote for Common Sense.

Confetti and streamers fall on **THORNE**. *The* **TAILOR** *hands him a phone.*

THORNE: . . . and congratulations to you on the humiliation of your unworthy opponents, sir. (*beat*) Let me just say, Chief Minister, that I am eternally grateful. And I'm prepared to serve and suffer in the most humiliating circumstances you can devise. (*beat*) Thank you, sir. Good night.

Curtain.

[End]

W. V.

BY

ANDREW WESTOLL

W. V. was produced for the Brave New Play Rites Festival in Vancouver in 2003 with the following cast and crew:

STIGS: Dom Fricot
MEL: Tammy Gillis
SAM: Erwin Rosales

Directed by Natalie Gemmell
Costume Design: Melissa Novecosky

CHARACTERS:

SAM: 27 years old, aspiring writer. He's wearing faded blue jeans and a smoking jacket with pens in the breast pocket.

MEL: 27 years old, **SAM**'s long-time girlfriend. She's wearing smart, business attire.

STIGS: 26 years old, generally annoying hang-around. He's wearing grubby clothes and a pair of diving goggles over his eyes. He carries a backpack everywhere he goes.

PROPS:

1 couch / 1 TV
1 desk / 1 cardboard box
1 office chair / 1 backpack
1 wristwatch / 3 pairs of diving goggles (different styles)
5 bags of groceries / 1 purse
1 laptop computer / many sheets of paper
2 manila envelopes / 1 waste paper basket
1 piece of rope / 1 book of stamps
1 video game controller

SETTING: Lights come up on a living room in a small apartment. There is a couch Stage Right with a TV mounted on a cardboard box in front of it. There is a desk with a chair Stage Left with a laptop computer and papers scattered everywhere, waste basket beneath. **SAM** is lying on his back on the ground between the couch and the desk, spread eagle, with a sheet of paper in his left hand. **STIGS** is sitting on the couch playing video games and wearing a pair of diving goggles. His backpack is beside him on the couch. **MEL** enters through the door, loaded down with bags of groceries and her purse. She looks down at **SAM**. She is unsympathetic.

MEL: What's wrong now? (*sets groceries and her purse down on the ground and shuts the door*)

SAM: I am a starfish.

MEL: Fine. You want some coffee? Stigs, you want coffee?

STIGS: No, I'm cool. Maybe some nachos, if you're making them.

SAM: A starfish, reaching out in all directions.

MEL: Some tea, then? Something with seaweed?

SAM: Not funny, Mel.

MEL: I can't stand it when you're like this.

SAM: So you go talk to the editor. (*holds a sheet of paper up in the air*)

STIGS: Another rejection letter.

MEL: Why do you get so upset over these things? (*grabs the rejection letter from* **SAM**) You've just got to forget about them.

SAM: Read it.

MEL: (*reads*) . . . failed to capture the essence . . . lacks compassion . . . not believable . . . it sounds like all the others, Sam.

SAM: Keep reading.

MEL: . . . and I wish you all the best in finding a new career. Jesus!

SAM: Yeah. Keep reading.

MEL: Sincerely, Michael Stark, Obituaries Editor. Obituaries editor? You wrote an obituary?

SAM: I can't even write a summary of someone's real life and make it believable. Do you know what that means?

MEL: Sam, someone's going to publish you.

SAM: I am at the bottom of an ocean of writers. I am a starfish.

STIGS: You know, actually, Sammy, starfish hang out in the tidal zones, man. Sometimes, like at low tide, they're completely out of the water.

SAM: So?

STIGS: So I'm just saying . . . if you were a starfish you'd at least be getting something published.

MEL: Stigs!

SAM: Fine. (*beat*) I'm a squid.

STIGS: Yeah. No. You can't be a squid either, Sammy. If you were a squid you'd have some ink, man.

SAM: That's it! (**SAM** *gets up and lunges at* **STIGS**. **MEL** *gets between them.*)

MEL: Guys! Not again! (**SAM** *and* **STIGS** *struggle to get at each other.*)

STIGS: No, you know what you are, Sammy? You're one of those faker fish.

SAM/MEL: (**SAM** *and* **MEL** *stop and turn around to face* **STIGS**.) Faker fish?

STIGS: Yeah. You know. Those fish with a part of their body that's evolved into something that looks real scary, but it's just a fake. For protection. To scare things off. Like big fake teeth. Or big fake spikes. You, Sammy, a part of you looks like a big important writer, with your pens and your jacket and these weekly mental breakdowns. Hell, you scream "writer," Sammy. But in reality, maybe you're not one. Maybe, in reality, you're just a fake.

MEL: Stigs—

STIGS: Trouble is, I think you might have faked yourself out.

MEL: Out, Stigs!

STIGS: I will now retire for the evening. (*His watch starts to beep.*) Oh, shit, hold on. (*takes off his goggles and replaces them with a new pair from his backpack*) You guys have a good night! (**STIGS** *exits.*)

MEL: What the hell was that?

SAM: I never know with that guy. (*beat*) But what if he's right, Mel? I've never even been published. Why do I think I'm a writer?

MEL: Shit, Sam. This is your problem. You listen to people too much.

SAM: Well, it's hard when they're all saying the same thing.

MEL: Sweetie, it'll come. You just gotta toughen up and keep focused on what you really want. Like W.V. (*makes a W and a V with her fingers against her chest and implores him to do the same*)

SAM: Yeah. W.V. (*makes the sign, without enthusiasm*)

MEL: Look, why don't you read it to me? Maybe you need a new perspective or something.

SAM: Alright. (*pulls his rejected obituary out of a manila envelope*) Here goes. (*reads*) Kitridge, Robert James, 83, liver failure. Robert James Kitridge, predeceased by his entire family's hopes and dreams, lived at 47 Blakestone Drive—

MEL: Sam?

SAM: What?

MEL: You can't start with that! Predeceased by his entire family's hopes and dreams? It's an obituary.

SAM: Trust me. It's the truth, ok. Just let me read.

MEL: Fine.

SAM: Robert James Kitridge, predeceased by his entire family's hopes and dreams, lived at 47 Blakestone Drive until two days ago, when he died. Now, his widow, Jane, lives there. Alone.

MEL: A little blunt, but go on.

SAM: When asked what she remembers about the first time she laid eyes on her husband of thirty-five years, Jane said, "Nothing. I rue the day."

MEL: Huh?

SAM: I know. Isn't it poetic? Rue the day. It's like I made it up.

MEL: Well, you can't write it.

SAM: Why not?

MEL: It's an obituary, Sam. For someone who died!

SAM: Look, you take what they give you. This ain't fiction, sweetie. Now, where was I? Alright . . . new paragraph. Robert Kitridge will always be remembered for his love of small animals, his lightning quick temper, and a tendency towards short spurts of unprovoked and seemingly self-indulgent violence.

MEL: What?

SAM: See, here I'm trying to allude to conflict and tension, the climaxes in the backstory. You know, to hook the reader?

MEL: But you're making him sound like a terrible person! Couldn't you just bend the truth a little, out of respect for the dead?

SAM: Look, there's only so much bending I can do before the truth just breaks in half and I'm left with The Death of Mr. Happy who refereed little league and raised $84,000 for organ donor research by selling small sections of his liver and the arteries in his upper thigh, ok? And I wasn't going there with this guy. I couldn't. Seriously, Mel. Stop interrupting. You're losing the flow.

MEL: Fine. Sorry.

SAM: Ok. (*beat*) Robert Kitridge's children, Bernice and Timothy, live in a bad area of town. When approached for comment they both claimed to be dead broke and, with a glint in their eyes, said, "Maybe Lucie left us something to make up for the horrible, horrible childhoods we both endured under his tyrannical hand." This reporter can only assume that "Lucie" is short for "The Dark Lord Lucifer," because both children enacted horns above their heads and narrowed their eyes when they said it. This is, however, just speculation, as this reporter was forced to cut the interview short when he noticed his wallet was gone and someone was stealing his car.

MEL: Sam?! Lucifer??

SAM: Yeah, I know. I mean, talk about realism! It really brings the characters to life, really rounds them out, don't ya think?

MEL: Are you done?

SAM: No, no. We've still got the third act. Robert James Kitridge had spent the last six weeks of his life confined to his bed, under the care of his immediate family, in a substantial and not-altogether-necessary amount of pain. His widow, Jane, said that watching her husband suffer was like "watching the first buds of spring nudge their way out into the light."

MEL: You can't be serious.

SAM: Yeah, they bragged about it.

MEL: Jesus!

SAM: And finally, the denouement! Funeral services will be held on Friday the 7th of December at Holly Home, and the party will continue well into the night and the following morning at various licensed venues around the city. Please call 1-800-DIE-LUCI or check the web at www.ourfathermyhusbandwasactuallyreally-lucifer.ca for more up-to-date info.

MEL: Sam? The man's dead!

SAM: And he was a bastard too! I'm not going to lie. What about journalistic integrity?

MEL: You need some practice. (*walks to the door, opens it, and yells into the hallway*) Stigs!

STIGS: (*from offstage, sounding sleepy*) What?

MEL: C'mere!

STIGS: I've retired for the evening! I can remember actually saying those words less than ten minutes—

MEL: (*very loud*) Stigs!!

STIGS: Ok, ok. I'm coming. Man! (*mumbling to himself*) People get involved with writers and they end up projecting all of this negative . . . (*out loud*) Ok, here I am. What?

STIGS enters wearing a robe and slippers. He is still wearing goggles, and he's got his backpack with him.

MEL: Ok. You sit right there. I'm going to ask you some questions, and Sam, you start writing. Pretend Stigs has just died.

SAM: Ha! Not a problem.

STIGS: What, did the faker fish evolve some talent? (*checks his watch*) How long have I been asleep?

MEL: Both of you, shut it! Stigs, just answer the questions. And Sam, just write, ok? Let's start with place of birth. Where were you born?

STIGS: Manitoba and Saskatchewan.

MEL: Stigs, you can't be born in two places at once.

STIGS: Yeah. Manitoba and Saskatchewan. What?

MEL: Those are two different provinces.

STIGS: No they're not. They're the flat one in the middle.

SAM: Oh my god, Stigs. Those are two separate and distinct provinces.

STIGS: What? Well, Christ, what's up with Newfoundland and Labrador, then?

MEL: It's an exception.

STIGS: Jesus! Well, then I have no idea where I was born. Man, it's like I got no roots . . .

MEL: Ok, let's move on. What did your parents do?

STIGS: Well, they worked for the province, but now I don't know which one!

MEL: Look, just forget about—

STIGS: We always just called it Maniskatchewan!! Oh, God! Mom and Dad! This is so cruel!

MEL: Stigs, it's ok. What did they do for the province?

STIGS: They were border police. (**SAM** *bangs his head against the desk.*)

MEL: Ok, forget about your parents. What kind of work do you do?

STIGS: I'm a marine biologist.

SAM: No you're not. You're the fucking paper boy!

MEL: Sam! No talking! Now Stigs, I'm pretty sure it's you that delivers our paper every morning, so—

STIGS: I just deliver papers on the side while I try to find work as . . .

MEL: . . . as a marine biologist.

STIGS: Yeah.

SAM: From the fucking Prairies?!

STIGS: Fine, a theoretical marine biologist. You know, someone's gotta do all the thinking and planning before people can just go out and chase whales and stuff, ok? Man, it ain't all Discovery Channel and wet suits.

MEL: Ok. Sorry.

STIGS: I mean, why do you think I wear these goggles all the time? Someone's gotta test this stuff before anyone actually uses it! Sure, it's just volunteer work, but whatever. Every little bit helps.

MEL: Ok, ok. Next question. Do you have any brothers or sisters?

STIGS: Yeah. Four of each.

MEL: And where do they live?

STIGS: Well, now I don't really know what to call it. Somewhere in the middle of the country, this side of Ontario, where it's flat and there're no oceans. God! My whole belief system's shot to hell now. Thanks a lot.

MEL: Ok, Stigs, just hold on a sec. Sam, what do you have so far? (*takes his paper and reads it*) Woah, this isn't bad.

SAM: Really?

STIGS: Really!?

MEL: Yeah. This reads like an actual obituary.

SAM: See, I really tried to capture the fiction of his life, the story, you know?

MEL: Sweetie, this is the best thing you've ever written. It's clear, concise, but it's also really moving. I mean, this part about him being completely dislocated, in every sense of the word . . .

STIGS: What?

MEL: . . . beautiful. I'm sure someone would publish this.

SAM: You think so?

STIGS: What the hell's that supposed to mean: dislocated, in every sense of the word?

MEL: Of course! Sam, this is amazing. Oh my God, this could be your start, your foot in the door. We could be on our way, Sam!

SAM: On our way to W.V.? (*makes the W.V. sign against his chest*)

MEL: That's right! On our way to West Vancouver. (*makes the W.V. sign*) Where the streets don't even have sidewalks.

SAM: Where no one's allowed to use power tools on Sundays.

MEL: Where the seawall is free of pesky baby strollers.

SAM: And hedges. We could have hedges, carve things into them!

MEL: Oh my God this is so exciting! All of our dreams are coming true! I love you so much Sam! (*They hug.*)

SAM: I love you too! (*still hugging*) So. I guess now there's only one problem.

*They both look at **STIGS**, who is sitting on the couch, oblivious.*

STIGS: What?

MEL: So. Stigs.

STIGS: So. What?

MEL: Why don't you tell me about those goggles again.

> **MEL** *goes to the table and starts putting pieces of paper into a manila envelope.* **SAM** *leaves the apartment.*

STIGS: Huh?

MEL: The goggles. You're testing them or something?

STIGS: Oh. Yeah, I've got a million pairs in my room. I have to wear a different one every fifteen minutes, to figure out which pair's the most comfortable. Like I said, it's just volunteer, but hey, it's a tough industry to crack.

MEL: Yeah, that's what I hear. Hey, would you mind licking this for me? I can't stand the taste. (*hands him the manila envelope*)

STIGS: Yeah, sure. Here ya go. (*licks it and hands it back*)

MEL: Thanks. So, what do you think of the pair you've got on now? (*starts writing something on the front of the envelope*)

STIGS: These? Well, I don't know. The strap's kinda nice. They seem a little loose around the nose, though, which I guess isn't all that good, 'cause I'm assuming that when you're diving you probably want a real tight seal.

MEL: Well, you'd think. Hey, you don't have any stamps on you, do you?

STIGS: Actually, I do. Here ya go. (*gets a book of stamps from his bag and hands them to her*) What're you mailing there?

MEL: Oh, nothing. So, those goggles . . .

> *As **MEL** puts stamps onto the envelope and **STIGS** talks, **SAM** comes back into the apartment. He slowly sneaks up behind **STIGS**.*

STIGS:Yeah. What I really like about this pair is the colours. I've read a
lot of books about it and I think that this blue with this green would
really go with a lot of stuff underwater, you know? This plays into
something I've been working on, my own personal theory about
marine biology. I think one of the most important things in underwater research is to feel sexy when you're diving. Like you're on a
confidence high, like nothing can stop you—the feeling you can
only get from being colour-coordinated, you know? Like when
you're in a bar and there's this girl you think is really hot and you
catch her eye and you're wearing your lucky shirt with your lucky
socks and the only thing between you and a little skinny-dipping-
for-two is some big dude with shoulders the size of—

SAM wraps a rope around STIGS' neck from behind, pulls it tight.

SAM: Who's the faker fish now, huh?!

*As he's being killed STIGS' watch starts to beep, and he struggles
to remove his goggles and replace them with a new pair from his
bag. He just manages to complete the change before he succumbs.
SAM lies STIGS' dead body down on the couch, STIGS' fingers
clutching at the rope around his neck.*

SAM: Now that's what I call journalistic integrity!
MEL: (*hands SAM the manila envelope*) You're gonna have to run if you
want to make the weekend paper.
SAM:Thanks, hon. Hey . . . W.V. baby. (*makes W.V. sign against his chest*)
MEL:Yeah. W.V. (*makes W.V. sign, too*) Ooooh. Just the thought of it
makes me tingle. (*They kiss.*)

*SAM walks out and closes the door. The lights drop, leaving a
spotlight on STIGS' upper body and face. His fingers are making
the W.V. sign against his chest. Spot stays for a few seconds, then
goes out.*

[End]

Wilson's Leg

BY

JASON PATRICK ROTHERY

Wilson's Leg was produced for the Brave New Play Rites
Festival in Vancouver in 2000 with the
following cast and crew:

BENTLEY: Sandy MacPherson
EVAN: Alex McMorran
WILSON: Steve Handelsman

Directed by Luke Beattie

CHARACTERS:

BENTLEY
EVAN
WILSON

SETTING: **WILSON**, **EVAN**, *and* **BENTLEY** *enter* **EVAN**'s *tree house. It is a pleasant summer afternoon The trees—agitated. The wind—bitter. The light—electrified.* **WILSON** *is speaking, but stops often to take breaths.*

WILSON: . . . and, like I said, just when the cops were running up to the house (*breath*) the house explodes, and there's all this fire everywhere (*breath*) and then all these guns start going off everywhere, just as this dog comes running up to the woman (*breath*) and the cops were running around the fence to check for his mother-in-law (*breath*) because she was in the cellar, and that was after he said he didn't have the phone (*breath*) and one cop said to the other that he was under the influence (*breath*) and that he said he never saw the sirens or the lights (*breath*) Anyways . . .

They have made their way to the centre of the tree house. **WILSON** *takes his backpack off of his back and pulls out a newspaper. He begins spreading pages of the paper onto the floor until the area in the middle is good and covered. When he is finished, he sits down on the covered area and extends one leg. All of this should look as though is has been planned and organized previously—should have the semblance of organization and delegation of duties.* **EVAN** *and* **BENTLEY** *could be doing things as well— such as covering the windows, or setting up candles or something—although they need not.)* **WILSON** *continues to ramble, but only when no one else is talking. He splices his sentences into the smallest silences.*

EVAN: Did you bring it?
WILSON: . . . the cop took him downtown. . .
BENTLEY: (*reaches into his backpack*) Yeah. It's right in here. Did you bring your stuff?

WILSON: . . . wanted to book him and pull prints. . .

EVAN: (*pulls a role of cellophane-wrap out of his backpack*) But I couldn't find any Happy-Wrap, so I had to get just the plain Super-Wrap.

BENTLEY: (*disdainfully*) Super-Wrap? Super-Wrap sucks.

WILSON: . . . they got into the station. . .

EVAN: Bentley, I couldn't find the other stuff. They didn't have anything else anyway. This stuff is fine. We don't need the other stuff.

BENTLEY: But, Evan, the other stuff is anti-bacterial.

EVAN: Super-Wrap?

BENTLEY: No. Happy-Wrap. Happy-Wrap is antibacterial. That's what we wanted: Antibacterial Happy-Wrap.

WILSON: . . . the guy was like "book this, ass-hole!". . .

EVAN: Why do we need antibacterial?

BENTLEY: (*pulls a large hacksaw out of his backpack*) If we're wrapping up his leg and the stump, don't you think it should be antibacterial to protect from infections?

EVAN: Who cares? As long as it's wrapped up then it'll be fine.

WILSON: . . . smacks the cop right in the face! It was so cool. . .

BENTLEY: We really should have Happy-Wrap.

EVAN: Whatever, who cares? Let's get going.

WILSON: Bam! Right in the face!

BENTLEY: Are you sure that it's okay that he's younger than us?

EVAN: He's in the same grade isn't he? That counts. That means he's in our age group.

WILSON: . . . and the cop starts bleeding, everywhere. . .

BENTLEY: Yeah. I guess you're right.

WILSON: . . . it was so amazing!

EVAN: Jesus, Wilson, wouldya knock it off! (**WILSON** *stops.*) Don't do that. It's really annoying.

BENTLEY: Are you okay, Wilson?

WILSON: Yeah.

BENTLEY: Do you feel all right?

WILSON: Fine, Bentley. I like hanging out. You guys are cool.

EVAN: You don't have to ask him how he's doing, Bentley. He's fine. We went over it with him already. He knows what he's doing.

WILSON: I know what I'm doing.

EVAN: It's Wilson's leg.

WILSON: It's my leg.

BENTLEY: I just wanted to know that he was having a good time, Ev. That's all.

WILSON: I'm having a really great time, Bentley. You guys are great. It's nice not having to go home and hang out with my parents again. But I was almost at the end of the story. So the guy runs outside to his Stingray, but his mother-in-law is outside. . . (*He is off again.*)

EVAN: Jesus, he started again.

BENTLEY: It's not that annoying.

WILSON: . . . and she's holding a baseball bat . . .

EVAN: Look, we have to decide who cuts first.

BENTLEY: It's a nice saw, hey?

WILSON: . . . and just as the cops are coming . . .

EVAN: Yeah. It's pretty shiny.

BENTLEY: Yeah, my dad just bought it.

WILSON: . . . she cracks him across the face with the bat . . .

EVAN: So you want to cut first since your dad just bought it and it's brand new?

BENTLEY: I dunno. Did you want to cut first?

EVAN: Well it is my tree house, but it's your dad's saw—

WILSON: CRACK!

BENTLEY: That's okay, you can go first. (*He passes* **EVAN** *the hacksaw.*)

WILSON: . . . but there's all these cows . . .

EVAN: Knock it off, Wilson! (**WILSON** *is silent.* **EVAN** *sets down his backpack and examines the blade.*) It's pretty sharp, huh?

BENTLEY: Yeah, it's brand new.

EVAN: They're so shiny when they're new.

BENTLEY: I know, hey?

EVAN: My dad just has rusty ones with webs and bugs everywhere. His shed is musty. Every time I go in there it messes up my clothes, and everything in there is so old and falling apart. I don't think he's gone into the shed for years, ever since he caught my mom screwing the gardening guy. He never builds anything or fixes anything anymore.

WILSON: I'm thirsty.

EVAN: Oh, except for last year, he was fixing the blade on the lawnmower—at least he was trying—and he was working in one of the springs, and it snapped, and he sliced off the tip of his middle finger—the whole tip! I was burning off my arm hair outside, and he screams: "Jesusmotherfuckingchristcocksuckingfuckshitty-brickfuck!"

BENTLEY: (*bursts into adolescent snickering*) That's so funny!

EVAN: (*yelling*) It was hilarious! Jesusmotherfuckingchristcock suck-ingfuckshittybrickfuck! He's such an asshole.

WILSON: Did either of you guys bring anything to drink?

EVAN: What? No. Don't be stupid.

WILSON: I'm kinda thirsty.

BENTLEY: I have a half a bottle of Happy Cola, but it's been in my bag for a week, almost, and it was my mom's, there's lipstick on the rim.

EVAN: Jesus, you buy Happy Cola?

WILSON: (*reaching*) Okay . . .

BENTLEY: My mom does.

EVAN: That stuff's crap. Super Cola has double the caffeine of Happy Cola.

BENTLEY: No it doesn't. Since when?

WILSON: . . . I don't mind. Can I have it?

EVAN: Since forever.

BENTLEY: But, Wilson, it's warm.

WILSON: I don't care.

EVAN: Really?

WILSON: Sure.

EVAN: That's fucking sick, dude.

BENTLEY: Okay. (*He fishes through his bag and fishes out the bottle, hand-ing it to* **WILSON***, who chugs half the contents.*)

EVAN *reaches into his backpack and pulls out two pairs of wood-working goggles. He hands one to* **BENTLEY** *and puts the other pair on himself.*

BENTLEY: What are these for?

EVAN: They're for the spray of blood.

WILSON: Do I get a pair?

BENTLEY: The blood's going to spray?

EVAN: Yeah, Bent. What did you think?

WILSON: Can I have a pair?

BENTLEY: I thought it would sort of just . . . gurgle out . . . I guess . . . I dunno.

EVAN: That's pretty stupid.

WILSON: Evan . . .

EVAN: I didn't get you a pair, Wilson. Jesus! I could only steal two. Just cover your eyes with your hands, we're the ones who have to concentrate.

BENTLEY: Here, Wilson, you can have mine. (*holds out his goggles to* **WILSON**)

EVAN: (*stopping* **BENTLEY**) Bentley, you have to use your pair. You have to be able to see when you do your cuts. Wilson's fine.

WILSON: I'm fine. (*puts his hands over his eyes and smiles*) See!

EVAN: Good for you, Wilson. (*rolls his eyes*)

WILSON: So after the commercials . . . oh, but wait, there's this one new commercial . . .

BENTLEY: Did you take the Tylenol we gave you, Wilson?

WILSON: . . . it has all these monkeys . . .

EVAN: (*to* **BENTLEY**) Are you ready? (*positions the saw over* **WILSON***'s leg*)

BENTLEY: Yeah. I guess.

EVAN: Okay, I'll make the first cut. (*puts the hacksaw over* **WILSON***'s leg and readies himself*) Prepare for lift-off! (*He is about to cut . . .*)

WILSON: Where's the cooler? (*takes his hands off his eyes*)

BENTLEY: (*hesitates with the hacksaw*) What do you mean?

WILSON: You need to put my leg on ice as soon as you cut it off. I told you yesterday.

EVAN: We do?

WILSON: (*confused*) Yes . . . I think so . . .

EVAN: Why?

WILSON: Because they always do it like that . . . don't they?

EVAN: They don't always, do they?

WILSON: I think so.

BENTLEY: I think he's right, Ev. I think they do put legs and stuff on ice after they cut them off.

EVAN: I guess we don't want it to rot right away. We want to study it.

WILSON: Cool.

EVAN: (*standing up*) I have a cooler in my garage. I'll be right back. (*goes towards the door*) Bentley, c'mere.

BENTLEY: (*goes to* **EVAN**) Yeah?

EVAN: (*quietly*) I'll be back in two minutes. If Wilson tries to leave, just stick him with this. (*hands* **BENTLEY** *a pocket knife*) Okay? (**BENTLEY** *is silent.*) Okay, Bentley?

BENTLEY: Sure.

> **EVAN** *exits.* **BENTLEY** *puts the pocket knife away and sits back down next to* **WILSON**. *Long pause.*

WILSON: That Tylenol's really kicking in.

BENTLEY: It is?

WILSON: Yeah. Whoa.

BENTLEY: Where did you move from, Wilson?

WILSON: Huh?

BENTLEY: Where did you move from? Where did you live before you moved here?

WILSON: I've always lived here.

BENTLEY: You have?

WILSON: Sure. My whole life.

Pause.

BENTLEY: I . . . I don't remember . . .

WILSON: It's weird, because sometimes people don't remember me, or who I am, or if they've met me before or not. My parents say it's because I'm a quiet person.

BENTLEY: You're not that quiet.

WILSON: I'm also predisposed to injury, so I have to stay home a lot and not go out.

BENTLEY: I broke my wrist once.

WILSON: Cool.

BENTLEY: I was on the roof of my house, with my brother. He's older than me, and he's really fat.

WILSON: Like, Fat Albert fat?

BENTLEY: Fatter. (**WILSON** *giggles.* **BENTLEY** *smiles.*) So we're up on the roof of my house, about two-and-a-half stories, and we had this trampoline in my back yard. So my brother tells me to jump. I'm like, "no way, dude." He tells me to jump again, and I tell him to fuck off. But he keeps telling me to jump, and he's telling me to jump, and he's telling me to jump. He wouldn't shut up. Jump, jump, jump, jump, jump, jump, jump. So finally I was like "Fine!" and I jumped off and missed the trampoline by ten feet and I broke my wrist. I had a cast up to my shoulder and I have a metal pin in my elbow.

WILSON: Wow.

BENTLEY: Yeah.

EVAN re-enters, cooler in tow, and plops it down in front of them.

EVAN: I found the cooler, but there's a problem.

BENTLEY: What?

EVAN: Watch out! (*opens the lid of the cooler and all three recoil from the horrible smell*) JESUS!

BENTLEY: Holy shit!

WILSON: Mama mia!

EVAN: You're such a dork, Wilson.

BENTLEY: What is that?

EVAN: There was this dead fish inside. I almost puked when I opened it in the shed. It was all rotting and sick and covered with puss and slime. I guess my dad caught it one day and just forgot to take it out of the cooler. It was so disgusting! I almost puked.

BENTLEY: We can't put his leg in there!

WILSON: (*snickering*) Evan puked . . .

EVAN: Why not? The way I figure, Wilson smells bad anyway...

WILSON: I smell . . .

BENTLEY: But . . .

EVAN: So his leg will probably smell, too. Right? Besides, it's gonna be all wrapped up, who cares if there's fish guts in there? (*takes the hacksaw and puts it over* **WILSON***'s leg*) Is everyone happy? Can I go?

BENTLEY: You didn't even rinse it out?

EVAN: (*putting his goggles back on*) We'll rinse it out later! Come on! I can't wait any longer. I've been waiting all day to do this. So let's go! Now! (*prepares to cut*)

BENTLEY: Wait!

EVAN: Jesus! What?

BENTLEY: I'll go first.

EVAN: You will?

BENTLEY: Yeah.

EVAN: Are you sure?

BENTLEY: Yeah. I will. It's my dad's saw.

EVAN: Fine. Christ. I don't care. It's your dad's saw. (*hands the hacksaw to* BENTLEY) There, just hurry up. This is gonna be so cool!

BENTLEY: Are you ready, Wilson?

WILSON: Yeah. Go for it.

EVAN: He's ready. Go.

WILSON: I'm ready.

BENTLEY: You're sure?

EVAN: Jesus!

BENTLEY: (*handing* EVAN *the Super-Wrap*) I'm sorry it's not antibacterial, Wilson.

EVAN: It doesn't matter!

BENTLEY: (*positions the hacksaw back over* WILSON*'s leg*) You have the wrap ready?

EVAN: Wrap's ready.

BENTLEY: How many cuts should I take before I give you the saw?

EVAN: I dunno. I'd say there's probably about forty cuts. But the bone is the hard part. Why don't you do up until the bone, and then I'll do the bone and the rest of his leg, okay?

WILSON: (*finishing off the rest of the Happy Cola*) You were right, warm Happy Cola does taste pretty bad. But actually with Super Cola . . .

BENTLEY: Okay.

WILSON: . . . you can win a free stereo . . .

EVAN: This is gonna be great!

WILSON: . . . and a TV, I think, but I'm not sure . . .

BENTLEY: Can you count me down?

EVAN: Yeah. Ready?

WILSON: . . . and with Diet Super-Cola . . .

BENTLEY: Ready.

EVAN: Three…

WILSON: . . . you can win . . .

EVAN: Two . . .

WILSON: . . . this car . . .

EVAN: One . . .

WILSON: . . . it's cool . . .

EVAN: GO!

> BENTLEY *is frozen.* WILSON *looks at him quizzically. There is a moment.*

EVAN: (*seething*) What are you waiting for?

BENTLEY: (*to* WILSON) What's cool?

EVAN: What are you talking about?

WILSON: Huh?

BENTLEY: I was just listening to what he was saying.

EVAN: Why?

BENTLEY: Because it was interesting, okay!

EVAN: Jesus, Bentley! It's only interesting because you only met him last week. If you had to listen to that shit for two months like I have then you'd think it was just as annoying as I do. Now stop fucking around and cut off his fucking leg. Stick with the plan!

BENTLEY: But—

EVAN: It's not like he's going to die! He'll be fine!

WILSON: I'll be fine.

EVAN: It's only his leg.

WILSON: It's no problem.

EVAN: He just fucking said it himself! What else do you need? We have the wrap, we have the goggles, there's the cooler. He even took the fucking Tylenol for Christ sakes! What more do you want? Come on! Hurry up! I have to go home soon and Wilson is going on vacation tomorrow so this is our last chance! We have to do it now!

BENTLEY: Wilson . . . ?

WILSON: Oh, this new sitcom has all of these guys from a cable company . . .

> **BENTLEY** *puts the blade back onto* **WILSON**'s *leg.*

EVAN: Don't be such a pussy.

WILSON: . . . and they all live in the same building . . .

EVAN: Just do it!

WILSON: . . . and the building is falling apart . . .

EVAN: CHRIST! COME ON!

BENTLEY: NO! (*stands up, drops the saw, and starts tugging at* **WILSON**) C'mon Wilson, get out of here! Come on! Go! Now! Go!

WILSON: (*solid*) Why? I don't want to go. Evan . . .

EVAN: (*recovering the saw*) I'll make the first cut.

BENTLEY: Leave! Leave ass-hole! LEAVE!

WILSON: What's your problem, Bentley?

EVAN: (*putting the hacksaw over* **WILSON**'s *leg*) I'll cut through the bone, then you can cut the rest,'kay?

BENTLEY: (*throws off all his gear, exasperated*) I'm leaving.

EVAN: Don't leave now! You'll miss the best part! Bentley . . . (**BENTLEY** *stops.*) Relax. Have a cigarette. (*pulls a pack of smokes out of his backpack and offers one to* **BENTLEY**)

WILSON: Can I have one?

EVAN: (*angry*) NO! (*tranquil*) Bent, you're my best friend. Stay. Stick with the plan. Think of how cool it's gonna be when we show up at school with a leg! A whole leg! If anyone tries to push us around, we'll just be like—WHACK!

BENTLEY: (*moves towards* **EVAN**, *takes a cigarette*) I guess—

EVAN: Stay, dude.

> *Moving slowly,* **BENTLEY** *sits, preparing to light a cigarette.*

WILSON: (*pulling a pair of garden shears out of his bag*) When do I get to cut off Bentley's finger?

BENTLEY: WHAT???

EVAN: Shit . . .

BENTLEY: FUCK!!!

EVAN: You're such a tool, Wilson.

WILSON: But you said—

BENTLEY: You told Wilson he could cut off my finger?!?

EVAN: What did I say, Wilson.

WILSON: The pinkie! He told me the pinkie!

BENTLEY: You told him he could cut off my pinkie!?

EVAN: WHAT DID I SAY!?!

WILSON: NOT TO SAY ANYTHING!!!

BENTLEY: YOU ASSHOLE!!!

EVAN moves for **WILSON** *as* **BENTLEY** *intercepts him. He punches him in the face and knocks him to the ground.* **WILSON**'s *mouth gapes open in disbelief as* **BENTLEY** *stands, hulking, over* **EVAN**. *Long pause.*

WILSON: (*smiling*) That was so cool!

EVAN: (*testing his lip for blood*) You suck, Wilson.

WILSON: That was amazing! You guys should have seen it! I wish someone was taping that! That was just like a real fight on TV!

EVAN: I wasn't really gonna let him cut off your finger, Bentley.

WILSON: That was like this movie I saw once, where there's this fighting competition . . .

EVAN: I just said that so he would think he was part of the club. That's all.

WILSON: . . . and it's the final battle . . .

EVAN: He wasn't gonna do shit!

WILSON: . . . except it turns out that one guy is actually the other guy's brother!

BENTLEY: Wilson, gimme a second. (**WILSON** *is silent.* **BENTLEY** *pulls the pocket knife out of his pocket, and opens the blade. He turns to* **EVAN**) I'm gonna stab you in the eye.

EVAN: What?

BENTLEY: If you're cutting off Wilson's leg, and Wilson is cutting off my finger, then I get to stab you in the eye.

WILSON: Cool.

EVAN: (*pause*) Which eye?

BENTLEY: Which one do you use more?

EVAN: (*contemplates*) My right one.

BENTLEY: Your left one, then.

EVAN: Who goes first?

BENTLEY: All of us at the same time.

> **EVAN** *thinks for a moment, picks up the hacksaw, and sits down.*
> *He takes off his goggles, and positions the saw over* **WILSON**'*s*
> *leg.* **BENTLEY** *moves over to* **WILSON**'*s other side, and sits down.*
> *He holds up his pinkie finger, and* **WILSON** *eagerly opens the*
> *shears, positioning the finger between the blades.* **BENTLEY** *brings*
> *the pocketknife up in front of* **EVAN**'*s left eye.* **WILSON** *giggles.*

EVAN: Who counts?

BENTLEY: We'll all count at the same time.

EVAN: Okay.

> *They look around at one another.*

ALL: Three . . . Two . . . One . . . GO!

> *Blackout.*

> *[End]*

DRAMAS

Aquarium

BY

STEPHANIE BOLSTER

Aquarium was produced for the Brave New Play Rites Festival in Vancouver in 1994 with the following cast and crew:

VERA: Kathie Laktin
RICHARD: Colin Kettenacker
WOMAN: Jean Paetkau

Directed by Sara Graefe

CHARACTERS:

VERA: *In her twenties.*
RICHARD: *In his thirties.* **VERA**'s *live-in boyfriend.*
WOMAN: *In her twenties.*

MUSIC—*ethereal, vaguely menacing. Music begins to fade as* **RICHARD** *enters.*

VERA: Do you know what today is?

RICHARD: (*distracted*) What?

VERA: I asked if you know what today is.

RICHARD: No . . . What?

VERA: You don't know. You really don't know. (*pause*)

RICHARD: Oh god, I'm sorry. I won't forget next year, I promise. I thought it wasn't for a while yet.

VERA: What wasn't?

RICHARD: Our . . . I don't . . . Christ, I don't know. Your birthday's in June. (*pause*) And our three-year's not until November. (*pause*) It was November, wasn't it?

VERA: The air smelled of rotting leaves . . .

RICHARD: Yes, yes, it was just after the Polynesian fish exhibit closed. (*pause*) Look, I really . . . Ted's gonna be waiting. He can't go without me, I've got all the gear. The fish are waiting, Vera. (*no response*) Okay, I admit it, I don't know. What am I forgetting?

VERA: It's six months since you told me you love me.

RICHARD: Oh come on.

VERA: Valentine's Day. On the beach. I remember the reflection of your face in the tide pool when you said it. It had been at least two months before that.

RICHARD: Okay, what's going on.

VERA: I'm leaving you. (*pause;* **RICHARD** *breathes*) Just think, if I'd let you go off fishing, you'd have been totally lost. You'd come back and I'd be gone and you'd call and look for me in the bedroom and finally . . .

RICHARD: Vere, are you all right?

VERA: You'd realize, finally . . .

RICHARD: Look, I love you, okay? Really. Come on, you don't like greeting cards, you hate cut flowers. (*pause, then seductive*) Wanna go look at the fish?

VERA: Christ.

RICHARD: We used to spend hours—

VERA: Past tense, Richard. (*He slumps on the loveseat, worn out.*)

RICHARD: So? So I used past tense. That doesn't mean it's etched in stone and buried, right? Okay: "We will spend hours looking at the fish."

VERA: We won't.

RICHARD: You can't say that.

VERA: I just did.

RICHARD: They're only words.

VERA: Painted glass, firemouth, blue gourami, damsel fish, pink kisser. Just words. I'd never heard them before. Remember how I closed my eyes? In the bedroom? The only light was the aquarium, blue-green, and there was that humming. And you said those words and I closed my eyes and put my fingers against your lips when you said them. My fingers inside your mouth when you said them. (*pause*) A deaf-mute learning to speak. (*pause*) You even made me believe this (*turns TV volume up and then down again*) was the sea. (*pause*) That was how I fell in love with you.

RICHARD: So you don't love me anymore.

VERA: Has there ever been a day since we met when I haven't said "I love you"?

RICHARD: I don't know.

VERA: I even used to send it to you. I'd stare into the swirling static until the flecks seemed to be coming toward me, falling, like water, and I'd think of you at work feeding the sharks or the cuttlefish. (*pause*) I'd feel the slow beat of their swimming, circles and circles, and I'd think, "I love you." (*pause*) Could you feel when I did that?

RICHARD: It used to be . . . oppressive. I never knew. I thought it was the heat. I'd want to take off my shirt. I'd put the fan on. Lately it hasn't been happening.

VERA: You've been happier.

RICHARD: Well, I wouldn't say that, exactly.

VERA: No, you wouldn't.

Pause.

RICHARD: So you really don't. You really don't love me anymore.
VERA: It's not me we're talking about.
RICHARD: Is that right.

VERA *gets up, starts walking around.*

VERA: I know who she is.
RICHARD: Who who is?
VERA: I don't blame you or anything, I just want you to know that I know.
RICHARD: What the—?
VERA: And I know why, too. It's because of the way she moves. So sure of herself, and slow. Fluid, like she has only the most delicate bones under her flesh.
RICHARD: Your bones . . .
VERA: (*simultaneous with* RICHARD*'s next line*) Your hands are so cold.
RICHARD: I am not having an affair. I am not having an affair.
VERA: Your hands feel like you've already killed a fish today. Cold-blooded. (*pause*) You know, sometimes I have to stick my feet out from under the sheets to cool them down. You've seen me do that? I get so hot sometimes. I need that slow cooling. Like wind near the sea . . . But your hands . . . That's a sudden cold. Like dry ice. I can see the fog rolling off you.
RICHARD: (*lightly*) I could wear gloves.
VERA: It's not about your hands, Richard. You always think it's about something other than what it's really about.
RICHARD: (*gets up, walks away*) Look, since I obviously don't understand what's going on with you, why don't I just go and meet Ted, who's probably pretty pissed off by now. And you can have one of your long baths with all the candles, and tonight I'll bring home the catch and we can clean it together and sort this stuff out. Okay?
VERA: I already called him. (*pause*) I said we had company coming so you couldn't make it.

RICHARD: (*stops in his tracks*) Christ. He didn't ask why I wasn't calling in person?

VERA: No.

RICHARD: (*pauses, walks again*) Well I'll just tell him we had a change of plans.

VERA: He said he'd ask Pete instead.

RICHARD: Nice of him.

VERA: Look, I just didn't want to pull a disappearing act. It seemed too easy. I wanted to say goodbye.

RICHARD: (*turning TV volume up*) To this? To all we have?

VERA: A TV, Richard? (*pause,* RICHARD *breathes;* VERA *turns volume down again*) I have this feeling. That she's coming today. (*his footsteps growing closer*) The air, it's . . . If I can just see you together, I think I'll feel—

RICHARD: Look, I've told you, there's nobody.

VERA: I can feel her. The air's . . . electric. (*pause*) You must feel it, I mean, I can feel it and I'm not the one—

RICHARD: I'm not sleeping with anybody. (*Pause. He comes towards her.*) If you'd just let me touch you.

VERA: (*pulls away*) I can't. Because I know you don't really want to. Your hands want someone, and I just happen to be here.

RICHARD: Who told you that?

VERA: I feel it.

RICHARD: So who is she? (*no response*) She's not somebody at work, is she? God, if you just nabbed some girl feeding the whales and invited her over . . .

VERA: It wasn't like that.

RICHARD: A guy should at least know who he's sleeping with, I mean—

VERA: You might not be sleeping with her.

RICHARD: What?! You just said—

VERA: I never said that. (*pause*) Maybe you only want her. Maybe you've never even touched her.

RICHARD: Christ.

VERA: Maybe no one's touched her.

RICHARD: Ah, that's what makes her alluring, huh? Or maybe she's not there to be touched.

VERA: She's as familiar as the patterns you see on your eyelids when you close your eyes.

RICHARD: I don't see anything.

VERA: You know she's more real than either of us. Can't you feel her? The way she moves, she's like those fancy goldfish with the huge fins. Orandas? So sleek, the water parts for them without a sound. They know they're beautiful, the knowing's inside their bodies. Sometimes they sway ever so slightly and they can feel you outside the glass, craving that movement. What's beautiful isn't the fish so much as the movement of the fish. And all you want is to be inside that movement. (*pause*) That's what you want, Richard. I know it is.

RICHARD: (*pause*) Is that what you want?

VERA: Yes. To be both woman and fish. I was for a while. But when you stopped loving me (*pause*) now I'm just a woman.

RICHARD: You're not. (*no response*) You know, I think . . . I think I can love you again. I think I'm starting to right now. (*pause*) I remember. The arch of your cheekbone, washed in that blue light—

VERA: It's too late.

RICHARD: Don't do this.

VERA snaps off the TV *set. There is a long pause.*

VERA: It's so silent.

RICHARD: You can't do this.

RICHARD gets up and heads for the TV, *but* VERA *stands in front of it.*

VERA: She knows the difference between static and the real sea, Richard. (*pause*) She's already yours. She's coming to see you.

RICHARD: Who is she?

VERA: All you've ever wanted. (*pause*) She's things you haven't even imagined you want.

RICHARD: And she's coming. To see me.

VERA: (*pause*) Close your eyes.

RICHARD: I won't see anything.

VERA: You will. (*pause*) Don't you want to see her?

RICHARD: Do you see her?

VERA: The edges of her. Wavering, growing clearer.

RICHARD: Right now?

VERA: Just close your eyes. (*pause*) Do you see her yet? The way she moves . . . I can see why you love her. (*pause*) Can you feel her getting closer? Circles of water widening out from her?

RICHARD: No.

VERA: Just keep your eyes closed. Just float there. (*pause*) Can you feel her now?

RICHARD: Something . . .

VERA: She sounds like h. Hush . . . Approach . . .

RICHARD: I think, maybe a little . . .

VERA: She's getting closer. You can feel the ripples lapping at your skin, the curve of her side growing nearer.

RICHARD: Yes . . .

VERA: Shimmering . . .

RICHARD: She's . . . perfect.

WOMAN: Hello.

VERA: We've been expecting you.

WOMAN *comes farther into the room.*

RICHARD: What? . . .

WOMAN: I know.

VERA: This is Richard.

RICHARD: A pleasure.

VERA: How does his hand feel to you?

WOMAN: Warm. Quite warm.

VERA: You can feel the blood under the skin?

WOMAN: Mmmm.

VERA: What colour is it?

RICHARD: (*to* **WOMAN**) What's your name?

WOMAN: (*to* **VERA**) His blood . . . it's terra cotta. The colour of rust. (*to* **RICHARD**) I don't have a name.

RICHARD: Come on. (*pause*) It's Rosalyn.

WOMAN: Perhaps . . .

RICHARD: You look like a Rosalyn.

VERA: More like an Amber, I'd think. The only stone that catches life inside it.

RICHARD: Ruby.

VERA: Veronica.

WOMAN: Veronica . . .

RICHARD: Rebecca.

WOMAN: I like the lilt of that. But perhaps Veronica . . . (*pause, to* **VERA**) Your name means true.

VERA: Yes.

WOMAN: Vera.

VERA: Yes.

RICHARD: (*pause*) Did you know that Richard means "wealthy and powerful"?

WOMAN: And are you?

RICHARD: (*seductive*) What do you think?

VERA: (*to* **WOMAN**) What colour is my blood?

WOMAN *crosses to* **VERA**.

RICHARD: (*abrupt*) Come on. It's turquoise. You can tell by her skin.

WOMAN: It's warm. Rose.

VERA: Try my cheek.

WOMAN: Warmer. Crimson.

VERA: My lips.

RICHARD: Rebecca . . .

WOMAN: Hot. Vermilion.

RICHARD: (*to* **WOMAN**) Let's try this again.

WOMAN : It's the same.

RICHARD: As hers?

WOMAN: As it was before. Terracotta. Rust.

VERA: (*to* **WOMAN**) You don't lie, do you? It's one of the things he loves about you.

RICHARD: (*to* **WOMAN**) I don't mind if you lie, Rebecca. Everyone lies.

WOMAN: I don't.

VERA: Richard lies. And he's not even aware he's doing it. He thought I made you up.

RICHARD: (*to* **WOMAN**) I didn't say that. I just didn't believe there could be someone . . . (*pause*) I've always seen you, every time I've closed my eyes. Rebecca. Would you like to look at the fish?

VERA: The aquarium's so big you could lie down in it. The fish against your skin. Painted glass, fire mouth—

VERA and **WOMAN**: (*together;* **RICHARD** *joins in at the end, drowning them out*) Blue gourami, damselfish, pink kisser.

RICHARD: (*to* **WOMAN**) You know about them? I can tell you—

VERA: About their intricate insides. The air bladders that keep them afloat. There are fish called mouthbreeders. And labyrinth fish. They hold air inside a cavity in the head, just above the gills. That's where the name comes from. Those narrow corridors of breath. (*pause*) He used to tell me those things. He used to teach me the fishes' names with the inside of his mouth.

RICHARD: (*stands*) I'll show you. Rebecca?

WOMAN: Later . . .

RICHARD: When it's dark. The fishes' shadows on the walls.

VERA: Two pink kissers. Or was it one? Kissing its reflection against the glass.

RICHARD: (*to* **WOMAN**) We'll move together, like we were made to do that.

VERA: I didn't love him, I loved the person I became when he moved with me. And I loved the names of the fish. Not his mouth, but the way it held those names and then let them go.

RICHARD *turns on the* TV.

RICHARD: (*to* **WOMAN**) Isn't it like a whirlpool? (*no response*) Like the sea. Swirling . . . The salt . . . Doesn't it make you want to close your eyes?

WOMAN: No.

VERA: My eyes are open.

VERA *turns off the* TV.

RICHARD: (*to* **WOMAN**) Did I dream you?

WOMAN: No.

RICHARD: Then you're real?

VERA: My eyes are open. I'm wide awake.

WOMAN: Yes. My eyes—

RICHARD: You're beautiful.

WOMAN: (*to* RICHARD) Are you real?

RICHARD: I think I'm just becoming—

VERA: You're going to be a fish now.

RICHARD: I can't swim.

WOMAN: Take off your shirt. Yes. The gills are here. They're for breathing underwater. (*He gasps.*) Good.

VERA: Your blood's growing colder. Blue. Very blue.

RICHARD: Blue gourami, damselfish, pink kisser, painted glass, firemouth. (*pause*) Now do you love me?

WOMAN: Do you love me?

RICHARD: Yes. (*pause*) I love you.

WOMAN: I love the woman whose name means "true."

RICHARD: (*He turns* TV *on*) Look. It's the ocean. Isn't it beautiful? (*pause*) I could change my name.

WOMAN: It's not about your name, Richard. It's the difference between outside and inside, above and below . . .

RICHARD: Which am I? (WOMAN *and* VERA *laugh.*) I don't mind if you lie. (*pause*) I'll try to go deeper.

VERA: We're going now.

RICHARD: In the bedroom. Where the aquarium is. The fishes' shadows. In the bedroom you'll love me. (*He turns the* TV *volume up slightly.*) Hear it? Destiny? Like hush. Approach. Can't you see the glow?

WOMAN and VERA: Yes.

RICHARD: In the aquarium you'll love me.

[End]

Passing

BY

ANNE FLEMING

Passing was produced for the Brave New Play Rites Festival in Vancouver in 1993 with the following cast and crew:

DAN: Erin Graham
GAIL: Kirstie Grant

Directed by Francine A'ness

(for DK, who had the courage to live it)

MUSIC: *"Walk on the Wild Side" by Lou Reed.*

SETTING: *DAN sits on one side of an institutional interviewing table, an empty chair across from her, reading a book, and listening to a walkman. DAN is seventeen. Deciding her sex might give you a moment's pause, but only until you realized she was, she must be, a teenage boy. She wears loose jeans low on her hips, a baggy t-shirt under another shirt and a leather biker jacket. She looks tough. GAIL, 28, professionally dressed, enters from behind her, walks briskly to the table, pulling out papers and pencils, not looking at DAN, who ignores her anyway.*

GAIL: Danielle Stewart? I'm Gail Henshaw, your . . .

She notices DAN's not listening, keeps talking.

GAIL: . . . court-appointed psychologist, here to take your young and no doubt tragic life into my hands and toss it to the lions of justice to mawl and toy with it as they will until they finally decide to rip you to shreds.

There is still no response.

GAIL: (*shouting*) Danielle!

DAN looks up angrily, looks back down.

GAIL: YOU'RE NOT MAKING THIS ANY EASIER! (*beat*) God, what a stupid mom thing to say. HEY! HEY! (*starts ripping up bits of paper and throwing them at DAN*) DANNY-BOY! HEY!

DAN takes off her headphones. Music goes tinny.

DAN: Noisy bitch, aren't ya?
GAIL: I have a good feeling about this interview already, don't you?

DAN gives her a steady stare.

DAN: Dominant mother, weak father.

She puts the headphones back on. **GAIL** *reaches across the table to pull them off.* **DAN** *takes them off before* **GAIL** *can. She turns off the sound. End music.*

DAN: Okay, the other way around. Dominant father, weak mother, no real female role model, therefore subject has taken on only positive identity, i.e. the male. Good enough?

GAIL: Well, no, not really. Ever see *Miracle on 34th Street*?

DAN: Anything like *Nightmare on Elm Street*?

GAIL: I don't know. Maybe. Anyway, there's this man who thinks he's Santa Claus—well, he is Santa Claus—and this unqualified, self-important psychologist tests his general mental state. Same general idea as this. Okay?

DAN: Whatever.

GAIL: Okay. Name, date, year, city.

DAN: Dan Stewart, October I don't know, 5th, 1982, Toronto.

GAIL: Any history of mental illness in your family?

DAN: Ha!

GAIL: Yes or no.

DAN: No. Not official anyway.

GAIL: How many times have you cried in the last week?

DAN: What kind of a question is that?

GAIL: Just a question.

DAN: None.

GAIL: Men cry too, you know, they even admit it sometimes.

DAN: None.

GAIL: The last month? (**DAN** *shakes her head.*) The last year? (**DAN** *shakes her head again.*) All right. When was the last time you cried? You must've have cried once in your life.

DAN: I bust my arm a couple of years ago. Falling down those stairs by Castle Frank. Compound fuckin' fracture, this little tip of bone sticking out. Yeugh, Jesus it was gross. Cried then.

GAIL: Ever cry for, say, emotional reasons?

DAN: Sure, when I was a kid. Didn't get me anything, though, did it?

GAIL: No emotional release? No feeling of relief?

DAN: Well, maybe that, yeah. I meant, like, no sympathy.

GAIL: You wanted sympathy?

DAN: Sure, don't all kids?

GAIL: And what did you get instead?

DAN: "Shut up, Dan. I don't have time for this. Look, I'm late already. You're driving me crazy, Danielle, Danielle, I said, shut the fuck up."

GAIL: This was your mom or your dad?

DAN: Oh, Jesus, here we go.

GAIL: Here we go where?

DAN: Didn't I tell you already? Dominant father weak mother vice versa broken home abandoned child understimulated overwhelmed take your fuckin' pick. Don't you have this all on file?

GAIL: Why don't you use your name?

DAN: I do.

GAIL: Actually, you don't. In fact, as I'm sure you're aware, Using an Alias is one of the charges against you. On four documented occasions you've used not Dan, but Daniel Stewart. Why not Danielle?

DAN: "Danielle, what a pretty name for such a pretty little girl! Why don't you grow her hair, Louise, such beautiful curls, just like a little doll. You must be so proud of her. Yes, your mommy must be so proud of you." Barf. People should get to choose their own names.

GAIL: So you didn't like being a girl.

DAN: Look, do we have to do this? You can make the answers up, I don't care, just, just, leave me alone.

GAIL *seems to take her at her word, starts writing. There is a longish pause.*

GAIL: (*as if reading what she's writing*) "Daily bouts of copious weeping . . . Mild, timid persona . . . Loved her little girl's curls, played with dolls . . . "

DAN: Stop it.

GAIL: "Wishes her name had more flourish . . . Daniella, perhaps, or Danielletta . . . "

DAN: Come on, stop it.

GAIL: Want to hear the rest of the questions I can make up the answers to? (*turns page of interview questions and reads them out mechanically*) If you didn't like being a girl, did you want to be a boy? Do you feel like a man in a woman's body? Have you ever thought of having a sex change operation?

She closes the file, and notebook, puts down her pen.

DAN: Could we just talk? You know, like normal human beings? Is that possible?

GAIL: Okay. What do you want to talk about?

DAN: When was the last time you cried?

GAIL *balks.*

DAN: Last week? Last month? Last year?

GAIL: Does it really matter? We're here to talk about you.

DAN: Fine. Go ahead. Talk about me.

She pulls out her book again.

GAIL: (*sighs*) You're seventeen, on parole for let's see, disturbing the peace, drunk and disorderly, underage drinking, vagrancy, and possession of narcotics, and now, now you've broken parole, you're up on another possession charge, plus corrupting a minor and using an alias.

She reaches over the desk, pulls **DAN***'s book down with her hand speaks to* **DAN***'s face.* **DAN** *pulls her book away and keeps reading.*

GAIL: You're in deep shit, Dan, and if you don't talk to me, you could be in even deeper.

DAN *doesn't move until she's decided* **GAIL***'s finished her little speech.* **DAN** *puts her book down on the table, crosses her arms,* *and looks at* GAIL. *They stare at each other, maintaining a silence long enough to be uncomfortable.* GAIL *is the first to look away.*

GAIL: This morning. I cried this morning.

DAN: About what?

GAIL: The sour milk on my Frosted Flakes.

DAN: That can really tear you up sometimes. Come on, what else?

GAIL: Oh, you know, nothing much—the extra toothbrush in the bathroom that's not mine that I can't seem to throw out yet. Stuff like that.

DAN: He dumped you, eh?

GAIL *looks sharply at* DAN.

GAIL: Basically. Sort of, yeah.

DAN: Drag.

GAIL: Yeah, well. How about you and Angela? Have you seen her?

DAN: You kidding? They got her under lock and key, her parents. Won't let her out of the house, won't let her answer the phone. They're fuckin' brainwashing her, man. It's sick.

GAIL: What do you mean, brainwashing her?

DAN Sending her to the Clarke fuckin' Institute. Making her into a nice little straight girl.

GAIL: So she knew you weren't a guy?

DAN: Not at first, but it didn't faze her when she did find out. I'm not the first girl she fell in love with, and unless they totally fuck her over, I won't be the last. That's what I'm worried about, that they'll grind who she is right out of her like a, like a—grapefruit on a juicer, until there's nothing left but a hollow shell. In a way, Ange has it worse than me. Nobody can do that to me, not anymore. Nobody has power over me—

GAIL: Except the law.

DAN: The law. Fuck. (*pause*) Six months she'll be sixteen, she can do what she wants, and me—well, who knows, eh?

GAIL: Think you'll try to see her after she turns sixteen? I mean, if you can?

DAN: There you go again. Questions. That's not normal talk.

GAIL: Sorry. Habit. Gets to be all you know how to do. "How does that make you feel?" "What do the snakes in your dreams mean to you?" "What can you do to make yourself feel less trapped?" You stop knowing what you think about anything. All you know is the right question to ask at the right time.

DAN: What happened with you and whats-his-name? Your boyfriend?

GAIL: My—oh. Jules. Jules fell in love with someone else—our therapist, as it turns out, which I think is pretty lousy, but—it happens, I guess. God, you're going to make me cry again. (*pause*) I wish there were windows in these rooms. What does the world even look like? I forget. Every day I forget. Blank, blank, blank, and then boom, it smacks you in the face.

DAN: It's a mystery, isn't it? Love. (*pause*) What a fuckin' ordinary thing to say. I hate being ordinary, but, hey—what I was going to say was, I care about Ange. I really care about her, but you know?—I've never told anyone this—I don't know if I love her. And now—I only think about her every day because, well, I kind of have to, don't I? I worry about her—I want to know she's holding out, she's keeping strong. I worry, but—that's all.

GAIL: It's a mystery all right.

DAN: Probably isn't good for me telling you this. I 'corrupt a minor' and I can't even say she's the love of my life, I can't say, what's that line? "It is the east and Angela is the sun." If I could, they'd have some explanation for it, right? True love. Thing is, she was the one who came on to me. We're at this party, right? It's like a month after we met. She keeps sliding her hand up my thigh and I keep pushing it away, shifting around, crossing my legs. She says she can't stop thinking about me, she thinks she's in love with me. I'm like, Oh fuck, what am I going to do? So I tell her. I figure it's only fair. I'm all ready for her to get up and storm out, but she doesn't. She thinks about it for a minute, then she kisses me, and whispers my name, my whole name—Danielle—and she slides her hand up my thigh again, and I don't push it away.

GAIL: (*genuinely*) Why are you telling me?

DAN: (*shrugs*) Don't you want to know?

GAIL: When I walked in that door—no. I thought I did, but—I wanted to come in, ask my questions, and get out. Way, way the hell out. But now—yes, I do want to know.

DAN: Do you have a marker? A pen'll do, but a thick magic marker would be better.

GAIL *finds a pack of Crayola markers in her bag, gives them to* DAN.

GAIL: Sometimes use these with kids...

DAN: Bonus. Colours.

DAN *starts drawing on the wall.*

GAIL: What are you doing? You want to be charged with vandalism, too? Dan!

GAIL *gets up. It's clear she wants to stop* DAN, *but she doesn't want to physically intervene.* DAN *keeps drawing—it becomes apparent she's drawing a window.*

DAN: You want curtains? Birds? Trees? (*draws*) I'm not very good, but—you get the idea.

GAIL: A window! (*smiles despite herself, relaxes and watches without speaking for a while as* DAN *draws*) Could you—could you do big puffy clouds?

DAN: Like this?

GAIL: Like that. Just like that.

GAIL *goes to the "window" and looks out as* DAN *finishes drawing.*

DAN: You always have great intentions, you know? And something always happens to fuck them up. The day I turned sixteen, bam, I left home. Outta there. I'm gonna get a job, anything, construction, dishwashing, doesn't matter. I'll get my own place, make a little money, go back to school. I thought once I was out of there I could get my life together. Didn't work that way.

DAN *sits down.*

GAIL: When I started this job? I actually thought I was going to help people, do you believe it? Who could be so naive? Twenty-two years old, clutching a psych. degree, thinking, all you have to do is understand a person, and everything follows from there. If you understand them, you can help them understand themselves, and if they understand themselves, they'll change their behaviour. But people don't want to change. They may want out of the situation they're in, but if they're gonna change, they'll do it in their own sweet time. So I gave up. Kept the job, though. Needed to pay off the loans. (*takes a marker and draws seagulls made of two upside down arcs out the "window"*) Those questions I asked you earlier? About whether you felt like a man in a woman's body? I'm sorry. There's more, too, that I didn't ask. I am, I'm sorry.

DAN: All my life, people have thought I was a boy, except when I was really little and my mother stuck me in dresses. Didn't matter what I did. I had long hair, and they'd say, "Wow, you've got really long hair for a guy." I'd wear earrings in both my ears and they'd say, "I've never seen a guy with both ears pierced before." I wore makeup once, just a little eyeliner, and this guy in the subway grabs my crotch—you should've seen the surprise on his face when he didn't find what he expected. Fuckin' should've kneed him in the balls but he moved off too quick. Pig. Or people would say, "Danielle—in English that's a girl's name." Public washrooms were the worst. I was always getting kicked out. Literally. A woman actually kicked me once. I learned to hold my bladder.

GAIL *comes close to* DAN *as if to touch her in compassion, then sits at the table instead.*

DAN: Sometimes I liked it, sometimes it made me uncomfortable— like what if I let them think I'm a boy and then they figure it out? But they never figured it out. And I discovered it was a hell of a lot easier letting them think I was a guy than trying to explain to them why a girl would look and act the way I did. A guy is just a guy, but a girl who looks like a guy—well, there's something wrong with her, you know? (**DAN***'s face screws up as if to cry.*) God, I hope Ange is all right. She shouldn't have to pay like this. Neither of us should have to pay.

*DAN cries silently. **GAIL** puts her hand on her arm. **DAN** recovers quickly, pulling away, wiping her eyes. She goes to the "window."*

GAIL: You know what I think? I think if my little report said you felt like a man in a woman's body, the judge'd be easier on you. It'd be like, Oh, okay, you're just confused. You think you're a man, and you're acting like one. We can fix that. Seriously. How often do they charge seventeen-year-old boys with statutory rape for sleeping with fifteen-year-old girls? Doesn't matter if she gets pregnant and has to have an abortion, or keeps it and ends up on welfare. Oh, they'd think that was unfortunate, maybe, but natural, the way of the world. But if I tell him you know you're a woman and you're just using your ability to pass as a man because it's easier and safer and people treat you better, well, that's just not allowed, that's wilful, deliberate fraud, and you're going to have to pay. And to consort with a fifteen-year-old girl at the same time, well—that's unspeakable. I don't know. I could be wrong.

GAIL goes to DAN at the window.

GAIL: So what do you want me to say?
DAN: Say what you want. Doesn't matter.
GAIL: But it does, I think it does.
DAN: (*pause*) Say, I don't know . . . (*confidently*) Say I'm a woman named Dan.

*They look each other in the eyes. **GAIL** nods, then leans forward, and kisses **DAN** lightly, non-sexually, on the lips, much to **DAN***'s surprise. **DAN** stares at **GAIL** as she gathers up her things and goes to the door.*

GAIL: How do you know the person who dumped me was a man?

She exits.

DAN *looks out the "window." She puts on the Walkman (up music, as before), puts her book in her pocket, and leaves.*

Fade to black. Fade out music.

[End]

Ice

BY

RUDY THAUBERGER

Ice was produced for the Brave New Play Rites Festival in Vancouver in 1989 with the following cast and crew:

KEITH: Simon McGlynn
MARK: Anirudh Chawla
DAVID: Daniel Davidson

Directed by Deb Pickman

CHARACTERS:

   KEITH: *mid-twenties, well-dressed*
   MIKE: *mid-teens, dressed in jeans and T-shirt*
   DAVID: *mid-teens, jeans and T-shirt*

   SETTING: *The play is set in a video arcade. Two machines should
be represented (by tables, desks or lecterns), one Centre Stage
with the player facing the audience, the other off to the side with
the player facing away from the audience. No other props are
necessary. Sounds of video games can be heard: popping, zapping,
beeping, music.*

      *The stage is dark. Sounds of video games can be heard.
Lights come up on* **KEITH**, *Centre Stage, playing a game of Time
Pilot. He plays with his arms crossed, left hand on the joystick,
right hand on the firing button. He plays with intensity and
exuberance, neither the stereotypical video geek staring vacuously
into the screen, nor the goon exulting in the violence and carnage.*

KEITH: I have a method. Left hand on the joystick. Right hand crosses, hits the firing button. (*plays*) I focus on the centre of the screen
where the spaceship is, but not on the ship itself. Do you understand? Not on the ship. If I focus on the ship, I'm too slow. I can't
see things coming. I get confused. No. I focus on the area around
the ship. It's like a force field. I don't let anything touch it. I
destroy anything that tries. (*plays*) You don't play these games with
your mind. Your mind is useless. You play with your eyes and your
hands. That's what I do. I detach my mind from my hands and
from my eyes. I attach my eyeballs right to my hands. My eyes see,
my hands destroy.

   KEITH *continues playing.* **DAVID** *and* **MIKE** *enter from Stage
Right.* **MIKE** *immediately looks disappointed.*

MIKE: Oh, man.
DAVID: What?
MIKE: There's a guy on my game.

DAVID: Yeah, I see.

MIKE: There's always a guy on my game. I mean, don't they understand? My name is up there, up top, number one, all-time.

DAVID: I know, I know.

MIKE: What's your problem?

DAVID: I'm getting a good look at the guy, okay?

MIKE: He's just a guy, wasting my time.

DAVID: No, that's not it. I know that guy.

MIKE: You know him?

DAVID: That's the Iceman.

MIKE: What?

DAVID: The Iceman. That's him!

MIKE: Bullshit. That's ICE? He's too old.

DAVID: I saw him in here a couple of weeks ago. I'm telling you, that is the Iceman. Jesus, look at him go.

KEITH: People complain about the violence, the destruction. Look at this, they say, knives, guns, bullets, missiles, lasers. Death surrounds you when you play. Death and carnage. They don't understand.

DAVID: He's hot, look. 200,000 already. He hasn't lost a man. What's your record?

MIKE: You know what my record is.

DAVID: Look at him. Look. God damn.

MIKE: I didn't know he played Time Pilot. I've never seen his name on the machine.

KEITH: The game doesn't live in the pictures. I could be a vaccine eliminating viruses or a baker wrapping loaves of bread or an old woman watering house plants. The game lives in my nerve endings. Lights pulse in my eyes. My hands move.

DAVID: God DAMN! Look at that!

MIKE: Let's go. I don't need to watch this.

DAVID: Your record's 600,000, right?

MIKE: 650,890. Let's go.

DAVID: I want to watch.

MIKE: Why does he have to play my game? Why does he have to be the best at every game? I hate that. His name is all over the place, on every machine. ICE. ICE. ICE. ICE. ICE.

DAVID: This is great!

MIKE: I'm leaving. I want to leave.

KEITH: Lights and sounds. My nervous system bonding to the machine. That's the joy of it. Joining with the game. Being the game. Everything else falling away.

MIKE: Oh God, the guy's inhuman. He's supernatural. Look at him. Hands crossed over. He looks half asleep. He doesn't move his eyes. Is he breathing? I can't tell.

DAVID: Look at his hands, the way his hands move.

MIKE: I hate this guy. I hate this son-of-a-bitch. That's my game.

DAVID: He's at 300,000.

MIKE: I can see that.

DAVID: He lost a man, look.

MIKE: Oh, thank God.

    KEITH *stops playing for a moment, massaging the fingers on his left hand.*

KEITH: When I lose a man, I can feel it in my hands. My fingers hurt, like I've twisted them, like I've moved them in some unnatural way.

He resumes playing.

DAVID: He's almost halfway and he's only down one man.

MIKE: Let's play something. I don't want to just stand around.

DAVID: I want to watch.

MIKE: Okay, screw you.

    MIKE *takes a coin and puts it in a game. He tries to play, but he can't keep his eyes off of* **KEITH**.

KEITH: The score's not important to me. The score is abstract, arbitrary. Sometimes, I'll just walk away from a game, leave it going. Why not? The game is the reality, not the score.

    MIKE *loses a man.*

MIKE: Shit!

He plays, loses another one.

MIKE:Shit!
DAVID: 350,000. Over halfway.
MIKE: Shit!

MIKE *beats on the machine, shakes it.*

KEITH: To complete a game, I have to lose. Those are the rules. I refuse to accept those rules.

He loses a man, waits, then resumes playing.

KEITH: Sometimes I just walk away.
MIKE: I should unplug the damn machine on him, make him start all over.
DAVID: 400,000.
MIKE:I could make it look like an accident.
DAVID: He's at 400,000. Look.
MIKE: I believe you. I don't have to look.
DAVID: He's only lost two men.
MIKE:This isn't such a big deal, if you think about it. It's only a game.
DAVID: It's your game, the only game without his name on it. Your game.
MIKE: I hate this son-of-a-bitch.
DAVID: 450,000.
KEITH: Every game has its own rhythms and its own melody. That's the secret. Understanding the game as a piece of music, filled with different nuances every time it's played. Some games are harsh, with staccato rhythms that vibrate in your bones. Others are softer, smoother. You listen to the game, let it play its song. That's the secret. If you know that, then every game is the same. You can do anything.
MIKE: Dave, Dave, let's go. We can come back later and see what he got. We'll see his name on the machine.
DAVID: No.

MIKE: I can't stand to watch. It's giving me a stomach ache.

DAVID: I don't care. I want to see.

MIKE: How does he do it? It took me a year to get good at this game. What right does he have to just come in here and take it away from me?

DAVID: Watch. Maybe you'll learn something.

MIKE: Bullshit! Look at this guy.

He approaches KEITH.

MIKE: You're not human, you know that?

KEITH: Leave me alone.

MIKE: This is my game.

KEITH: Get lost. (*loses a man*) Damn.

MIKE: Oh yes! Yes!

DAVID: Three men down. Two left.

MIKE: You are going down, buddy. Mr. ICE. Mr. Iceman. Going down in flames.

KEITH: Fuck you.

MIKE *makes sounds of explosions as* DAVID *pulls him back.*

MIKE: Two more, buddy.

DAVID: Mike, Jesus.

KEITH: The game has been corrupted. Something has touched it. Negative energy. Dark distractions. I hear the voices around me. I can see my hands moving. How can they move that way? How is that possible?

MIKE: Soon, buddy, soon.

DAVID: Don't be a jerk, Mike.

MIKE: I can't help it. It'd be so sweet to see this guy crash. I'm sick of seeing his name everywhere. ICE. ICE.

DAVID: He's up to 500,000.

MIKE: Two men. Just two men.

KEITH: I see shapes and colours. So many spaceships. So many enemies. How do I keep track of them? My hands feel like stone. My eyes are broken glass.

MIKE: He's losing it. Look.

DAVID: No.

MIKE: Look at him. He's going down.

DAVID: Shut up. If you weren't such a jerk.

MIKE: Boom! There goes one.

    KEITH *kicks the machine.*

KEITH: I'm being destroyed. My enemies are everywhere.

MIKE: One more, baby. One more.

KEITH: (*to* **MIKE**) I'm trying to play here, okay?

DAVID: (*pulling* **MIKE** *back*) Sorry. We're sorry. Let's go, Mike.

MIKE: Not now, not yet. I want to see.

DAVID: Later. We'll come back.

MIKE: I want to see it. I want to see it with my own eyes.

DAVID: Mike—

KEITH: Damn!

MIKE: Oh baby! Sweetness! Yes! Yes!

    KEITH *enters his initials into the game, then turns to* **MIKE**.

KEITH: I ought to kick your head in.

    He exits. **DAVID** *and* **MIKE** *stand for a moment, then go to the game.* **DAVID** *reads the score, while* **MIKE** *jumps around, ecstatically.*

DAVID: 534, 110.

MIKE: Safe. Safe. Yes. Safe!

DAVID: Jesus!

MIKE: What is it?

DAVID: Look. On the screen. The name. It's CAP. C-A-P.

MIKE: You said he was ICE. You told me he was the Iceman.

DAVID: I thought he was.

MIKE: CAP? CAP? Who the hell is CAP?

DAVID: I saw him play. I went to the machine afterwards. It said ICE, ICE, ICE all the way down. He played so awesome. I thought he had to be—

MIKE: I don't believe this. I do not believe this. If he's not the Iceman. Oh God. If he's not the Iceman—

*MIKE and *DAVID* stand still, staring at the video screen. Lights dim. The sound of video games is heard, fading.*

[End]

Love Child

BY

AARON BUSHKOWSKY

Love Child was produced for the Brave New Play Rites Festival in Vancouver in 2001 with the following cast and crew:

RACHAEL: Jacqueline Leung
LYNDA: Yvette Lu

Directed by Anita Majumdar

Lights up to reveal **RACHAEL**, *thirties, sitting in a coffee shop.*
LYNDA, *twenty-one, defiantly sits away from her at another table.*
They sip coffees.

RACHAEL: Come on, Lynda . . . please.

LYNDA: You can't make me.

RACHAEL: I know—

LYNDA: I'll spit at you.

RACHAEL: I'm just saying that sitting way over there looks even
worse . . . I mean—

LYNDA: I need my space, alright?

RACHAEL: It's . . . embarrassing.

LYNDA: Oh you think this is embarrassing.

RACHAEL: (*beat*) So, Lynda . . . where do we go from here?

LYNDA: Don't talk so loud.

RACHAEL: Well, I'm over here and, and—

LYNDA: Oh stop whining. God . . .

RACHAEL: (*beat*) I think about you all the time.

LYNDA: You do not.

RACHAEL: (*sighing*) I knew this wasn't going to work.

LYNDA: Where are you going? What's wrong?

RACHAEL: Look, Lynda . . . I decided to meet you because I thought
this was the right thing . . . I've felt horrible over the years . . . I
mean we've had so little contact. Until now.

LYNDA: And why's that I wonder?

RACHAEL: Because.

LYNDA: Because . . . ?

RACHAEL: Well . . . it's awkward.

LYNDA: Oh great, not only am I a mistake but I'm awkward too.

RACHAEL: Can we be serious? You aren't awkward. In fact, you're very
attractive. Anyway, this isn't just about you. I'm getting older now.
I'm coming to a crossroad in my life. I want to get things in order.

LYNDA: You're not dying, are you?

RACHAEL: No I'm not.

LYNDA: What's that, a bribe or something?

RACHAEL: What?

LYNDA: Ha. You like my sense of humour?

RACHAEL: I don't get it.

LYNDA: Well, maybe you don't get me.

RACHAEL: I think that's obvious.

LYNDA: Guess what: I'm a ho and I like it.

RACHAEL: What?

LYNDA: Ho, ho, ho.

RACHAEL: (*beat*) I'm sorry. Ho? What's a ho?

LYNDA: You're embarrassing, you know that. God . . .

RACHAEL: Could you be a little nicer to me? I mean, could you give it a try?

LYNDA: OK, I'll try.

RACHAEL: I mean I called you, didn't I? I know it's been a couple of years but . . . Look I'm sorry I don't, you know, include you more, honey, but—

LYNDA: Don't say "honey" to me, alright?

RACHAEL: Fine.

A moment.

RACHAEL: What have you done to your hair? It looks—

LYNDA *gives* **RACHAEL** *a look.* **RACHAEL** *stops talking.*

RACHAEL: Are you eating?

LYNDA *just gives her another look.*

RACHAEL: You look thinner.

LYNDA: Good. Great.

Another moment. **LYNDA** *lights a cigarette.*

RACHAEL: And you're smoking.

LYNDA: Can't fool you.

RACHAEL: You can't smoke in here.

LYNDA *butts out the cigarette.*

LYNDA: Happy?

Another moment. Finally **RACHAEL** *moves closer.*

RACHAEL: Do you realize that you, me and your father are the only three people in the world that know about . . . about what happened with you?

LYNDA: Yeah, us and about one hundred of my closest friends. Oh yeah, I forgot . . . don't tell anybody that your father won custody because your mom was too strung out to be a proper mom. I'm not keeping your shitty little secrets, it's not my job.

RACHAEL: I was 16 years old, alright! Your father . . . well . . . I was young and stupid. I got caught up. I almost drowned in the deep end. But now I'm over it. I'm better. I'm old and wise and I have a very nice, very ordinary life. I'm a soccer mom. I'm bored senseless and I love it. It makes me happy. Really (*pause*) really happy.

LYNDA: Goodie for you.

RACHAEL: Oh come on. Please allow me this. Can you do that?

LYNDA: (*sarcastically*) Yeah right. (*beat*) Have you told your—

RACHAEL: My husband is a busy man. He's a judge now.

LYNDA: Big deal. Have you told him?

RACHAEL: Now . . . look, let's be reasonable.

LYNDA: You haven't, have you?

RACHAEL: You are in your twenties, Lynda, the prime of your life, you have a life with your father—

LYNDA: Life?! Jerry is almost 60! He just got his second pace-maker. He drinks beer and steam-cleans drapes and watches curling on TSN. It's pretty exciting on Sundays at our place particularly in the winter. And oh, guess what . . . Jerry still doesn't have any friends, he never married, he never finished university and we collect food stamps. How's things going for you?

RACHAEL: Don't compare, please—

LYNDA: Why not? You have a nice split level four-car garage type house with what . . . four and a half bathrooms and a solarium? You have nice normal kids who take French immersion and play badminton—

RACHAEL: Tennis. They play tennis—

LYNDA: You know what I did this weekend? I took all our bottles into the recycling place and made eighteen bucks which I spent on socks and underwear at Wal-Mart. And I hate Wal-Mart. It's full of loser mothers just like you.

RACHAEL: Don't. Please.

LYNDA: It's no fun being a secret, mom. I want a new life. A new start.

RACHAEL: You are twenty years old now . . .

LYNDA: Twenty-one—

RACHAEL: It's too late for a new life.

LYNDA: I NEED a new family, new friends—

RACHAEL: At your age you should be dumping friends not trying to make new ones.

LYNDA: I can't make it, mother. I can't. I'm trying but I can't do it.

RACHAEL: Well, maybe you're not trying hard enough.

LYNDA: Fuck, you're hopeless. God!

RACHAEL: Lynda, I'm your mother. Treat me with respect! Can you do that?

LYNDA: Why don't you earn it first, mom.

RACHAEL: (*beat*) I'm leaving.

LYNDA: Leave away.

RACHAEL: I find you . . . really, really impertinent.

LYNDA: Oh that hurts.

RACHAEL: Alright, now I'm really going.

LYNDA: Fine. Auf Wiedersehen.

RACHAEL: Good.

LYNDA: Very good. I took German in high school. But then you wouldn't know that, would you? And oh yeah . . . I went to college for two years trying to get into university but I had to work driving Jerry's van delivering clean drapes to rich people just to get by and . . . well, it just didn't work out. Then I got a job checking gas meters, which was nice except for the dogs. But then I had to quit.

RACHAEL: (*beat*) Look, do you need some cash?

LYNDA: No, no. We seem to have an endless supply of bottles around our place. I have this theory about recycling, which some day I will explain to you. I have other needs.

RACHAEL: Fine. I'll see you around.

RACHAEL *goes to leave.*

LYNDA: No goodbye kiss? Come on, a little kiss . . .

RACHAEL: What?

LYNDA: Oh come on. What are you afraid of? I mean, what could possibly go wrong with a little kiss between consenting . . . mothers.

RACHAEL: What did you just say?

LYNDA: Surprise.

RACHAEL: Are you kidding me?

LYNDA: Not really.

RACHAEL: What happened Lynda?

LYNDA: I think you know what happened. You've had three of your own, right? No, four. My mistake. But thanks for asking. It's a little girl.

RACHAEL: What's its name?

LYNDA: Angela. Because she's an angel.

RACHAEL: Where is she?

LYNDA: Now . . . that is an interesting question.

RACHAEL: What are you talking about?

LYNDA: Let's see...where do angels go?

RACHAEL: What did you do, Lynda?

LYNDA: She's around.

RACHAEL: Being a mother is a very serious offence . . . I mean, responsibility.

LYNDA: Very funny.

RACHAEL: Where is she, Lynda?

LYNDA: She's in your car.

RACHAEL: What? (*looking out at her car*) Where? I can't see her.

LYNDA: She's lying in the back seat.

RACHAEL: WHAT?!

LYNDA: She's fine. She's sleeping. Time to go. (*gets her coat*) I want you to drive us home.

RACHAEL: (*beat*) What?

LYNDA: To your house. Me and her and you. The three of us. In your nice mint julep Jeep. To your house. Hippity-hop, like little bunnies. Uh . . . We should go pretty soon. She's been in there for a while. It's fairly warm out.

RACHAEL: I will NOT take her—

LYNDA: She just wants to . . . belong.

RACHAEL: Look, I refuse to be blackmailed.

LYNDA: You really should take us there. Honestly.

RACHAEL: Never!

LYNDA: (*sadly*) Well, you see . . . the father is going to be here soon and he's not a very nice man. He has a real mean streak to him. Prone to violent fits. He drinks, you see. A lot. But a real charmer. He could sell ice to polar bears. And he has a unusual way with the women. He charms and tricks you. He turns on you. And you think . . . this is all my fault, isn't it? It's all you can do to stop screaming inside your head. And you want to hurt yourself. You want to burn holes in your arms with cigarettes. You want to hit yourself with somebody else's fists. You want to drink until you drown. You want to float in a big blue sea of I forget. You want to disappear. But you can't because He's got a way of getting under your skin . . .

RACHAEL: Who is the father?

LYNDA: Does it really matter?

RACHAEL: Yes it matters.

LYNDA: Some guy . . . a friend of Jerry's.

RACHAEL: He has no friends . . . just drinking buddies.

LYNDA: That's right.

RACHAEL: Why?

LYNDA: I was scared, that's why.

RACHAEL: Why didn't you . . . ?

LYNDA: Why didn't you?

RACHAEL: This isn't real. None of this is.

LYNDA: I'm sorry . . . it happened . . . it happened. Oh God . . . god . . . it was horrible . . . horrible . . .

RACHAEL: (*beat*) Lynda? (*There is no answer.*) Lynda?

LYNDA: What?

RACHAEL: Tell me none of this is true. Come on, please, none of this is true, right?

LYNDA, *sobbing, tries to put her head on* **RACHAEL**'*s shoulder.*

LYNDA: I can't . . . I can't . . .

RACHAEL *pushes her away.*

RACHAEL: Stop that. Stop it right now! Tell me the truth. What's going on?

LYNDA: I told you, I did!

RACHAEL: What?! What?!

LYNDA: Help me, mother, please . . . I'm . . . I'm in a swirling, crazy river and you're on the shore. I can't hold my breath very long. I can't. I tried but I'm a lousy swimmer. I want to quit. I have to quit. Please help me. Throw me a line . . . do something, please . . .

LYNDA *grabs onto her mother for dear life.*

LYNDA: You have to. You have to. You have to. We're the same. Don't you see? We are exactly the same.

Lights fade.

[End]

Urban Shipwreck

BY

JAAN KOLK

Urban Shipwreck was produced for the Brave New Play
Rites Festival in Vancouver in 1991 with the
following cast and crew:

MARY: Laura Julia Gavini
PARKER: Chris Cound
EDDIE: Chris Ferguson

Directed by Terry Dawes

CHARACTERS:

MARY: *early thirties, wearing jeans and a loose print top in the hippie/earth mother style.*

PARKER: **MARY**'s *husband, slightly older, a mechanic; has a cautious mixture of disdain, admiration and fear of some of his wife's beliefs and attitudes.*

EDDIE: **PARKER**'s *friend from work, about* **PARKER**'s *age; quite vain about his dress and appearance.*

SETTING: **MARY** *sits on a sofa at a coffee table writing on a piece of paper. On the table there's an empty, amber wine bottle. She finishes her writing and picks up the bottle. She takes it over to a floor lamp and holds the bottle up to the light. She seems satisfied. She goes back to the coffee table, picks up a roll of masking tape, tears off a piece, tapes it halfway around the bottle and writes on it with a felt pen. Then she takes the page from the coffee table, rolls it up, paper clips it on top to make it retain its shape, and pushes it into the bottle. She takes the bottle over to the floor lamp again, holds it up to the light, then brings it back to the coffee table. She sits on the sofa and stares at the bottle on the table. There is the* SOUND *of a* DOOR OPENING *offstage.* **MARY** *takes the bottle off the table and puts it beside the sofa. Before anyone enters the room she speaks towards the sound.*

MARY: So what does a monarch butterfly know that we don't know?

> **PARKER** *and* **EDDIE** *come into the living room. They're a little loose, but not drunk.*

PARKER: A whole load a shit, I'll bet, from the way you asked that.

MARY: Yes, it does. Amongst other things, it knows how to find its way home on time. Even after travelling thousands of miles.

PARKER: Then that butterfly don't drink.

EDDIE: Not beer anyhow.

PARKER: So it's got an advantage over the rest of us.

EDDIE: And it flies—

PARKER: —so it doesn't have to put up with traffic jams. And I'll bet when it gets home it doesn't have to answer stupid fucking questions either. Or it wouldn't be in such a goddamned hurry to get there.

EDDIE: Those butterflies have crystals strapped to their backs so they can find their way, don't they? Strap Parker up with a crystal and he'll be home on time.

MARY: Aren't you amusing?

EDDIE: How you doin', Mary?

MARY: Just wonderful, I suppose. I thought I felt your vibrations in the vicinity.

EDDIE: Had the dee-lux model out today, did you?

MARY: Why did I know you'd say something like that?

EDDIE: 'cause you visualized me in your mind?

PARKER: My wife, Eddie, my wife. This isn't Louise at the shop, you know.

EDDIE: Just playin' around, man. No harm. Louise is somebody's wife, too, by the way. No harm, Mary.

MARY: You make me . . . Jesus, I don't know . . . You give me a chill. Like a horror movie. I get goose bumps like when some terror is hiding in the basement and you know it's coming up. You see the stairs. You see the door open. You see the back of the woman's head.

PARKER: What she's tryin' to say is your aura looks like shit. Beer, Eddie?

EDDIE: You got any tequila?

PARKER: You think shooters?

EDDIE: Some beer on the side.

PARKER: You wanna serve that up, Mary.

MARY: Serve yourself.

PARKER: Mary gets her hemorrhoids lined up just right, then she don't wanna move.

MARY: (*mimicking*) Mary don't wanna move because Mary ain't the one who wants a drink.

PARKER: See what I missed getting home late, Eddie?

EDDIE: Why the fuck am I still single, eh? Why?!

PARKER: Lemme get those drinks.

PARKER *leaves.*

EDDIE: You can't forgive me, can you, darling?

MARY: For what?

EDDIE: For makin' you all hot and bothered.

MARY: You think people don't know your filthy thoughts?

EDDIE: Cat can't talk to a dog?

MARY: What does that mean?

EDDIE: Somehow, you and me must be thinking the same thing. Otherwise you wouldn't be so upset.

MARY: I'm not thinking what you're thinking at all. But I can feel it. Every time you come in here. You don't have to say a thing. The atmosphere just gets . . . polluted . . . with your thoughts.

EDDIE: Well, shit. I should start bending spoons and stopping clocks.

MARY: You burn those thoughts into people's minds.

EDDIE: Let's not get too carried away there, Mary. I have a fantasy now and again. Far as I've heard, fantasies are still legal. Rumour has it, women have 'em too.

MARY: I'm not talking about fantasies. I'm talking about evil thoughts . . . that travel across the room. Into a school yard. In a restaurant. They've figured out how to measure those gamma rays and microwaves and infrareds and the other things we can't see. They'll be tracking your dirty thoughts soon, too.

EDDIE: My thoughts, Christ . . . You're leavin me in the dust there, darling. Let me just tell you what I think about you and me—

MARY: I don't want to know.

EDDIE: I thought you already knew. I thought you could read my mind.

They stare each other down. **PARKER** *comes back with a bottle of tequila, two shot glasses and a couple of beer. He puts everything on the coffee table and doesn't notice the tension.*

PARKER: Hey Eduardo. You hungry?

EDDIE: Not starved, but if you got something to nibble on.

MARY: Oh, Parker, you're not going to do that.

PARKER: Do what? My pickled worms?

MARY: That's what I thought.

PARKER: They're made to go with tequila.

EDDIE: I'm not into pickled stuff.

PARKER: Listen, you don't just eat these off a plate like spaghetti. You know the worm at the bottom of a mescal bottle?

EDDIE: That's a fuckin' hairless caterpillar, not a worm.

PARKER: It's a grub, same thing as a worm.

EDDIE: Mr. Expert.

PARKER: This is not bullshit.

MARY: Did you bring me a beer?

PARKER: You never said you wanted one.

MARY *gives him a look.*

PARKER: Have mine. I'll get another one.

MARY: I'll get it.

MARY *goes to the kitchen.*

PARKER: This isn't bullshit. These are like mescal worms. Or grubs or whatever. You get these nice ropey rain worms and you give 'em a bath and you put 'em into a little jar of tequila where they drink and shit and drown and pickle. Then you move 'em to the real bottle.

MARY *comes back with her beer.*

EDDIE: Oh yeah, sounds fantastic.

PARKER: I got the idea from Mary . . . and mescal. She tried cooking with worms. Tried making a worm and tofu burger or something.

MARY: Even I couldn't eat it.

PARKER: Tasted like shit on a bun.

EDDIE: Keep your worms, Parker.

PARKER: This is different. They're full of tequila.

EDDIE: Just gimme the tequila.

PARKER *pours the tequila and gives one to* **EDDIE**.

EDDIE: Hey, Parker. What am I thinking?

PARKER: Whadya mean? About the worms?

EDDIE: Nono. Your wife says she can read my thoughts.

PARKER: Yeah, well, Mary's got some cute tricks. What's he thinking, sweetheart?

MARY: You mean you can't feel it?

PARKER: Guess not?

MARY: Of course you can't feel it. You have no idea what I'm feeling . . . let alone thinking.

PARKER: I know what you're feeling.

MARY: What am I feeling?

PARKER: I don't know . . . frustrated or something . . . right? Drink up, Eddie.

They knock back the shooters and have some beer.

MARY: Even when I tell you, you don't believe I'm feeling what I told you.

PARKER: Sweetheart, Eddie's here. We're having a drink. We can talk about all that personal stuff later.

MARY: Eddie wants to have an affair with me.

PARKER: Eddie wants to have an affair with anything he can push his dick into.

EDDIE: That's such an unfair exaggeration, man.

MARY: (*to* PARKER) Is that all you can say?

PARKER: Don't fuck my wife, Eddie. Or I'll cut off your nuts and make 'em into earmuffs.

EDDIE: Come on, man, you're my friend. I'm not gonna fuck with my friend's wife.

MARY: (*to* PARKER) He knows how weak you are. He knows he can play with you and taunt you and taunt your wife.

EDDIE: I'll finish my beer and I'll be gone.

PARKER: Wait a minute, wait a minute. Wait a minute. Where's all this shit coming from, eh? What's Eddie done?

EDDIE: Yeah.

PARKER: Forget all this feelings stuff for a moment. Just tell me what he's done. Has he actually done anything? To you? Or to me—

EDDIE: Fucked if I know what I've done.

PARKER: Or to anyone else that we know?

MARY: There's radiation coming at us all the time. We don't know what half of it is and what we do know we've barely discovered. Gamma rays and microwaves and infrareds.

PARKER: What the hell has this got to do with Eddie?

MARY: Eddie's dangerous with his thoughts—dirty and evil. All these thoughts and feelings that ooze out of people. We're all affected by them. Good or bad. And if there's too much evil around we become evil. The evil works its way right into our cells, into our DNA. Babies know it most. They're little feelings meters. They can tell right away if something's wrong.

PARKER: Sweetheart, you can't really say about babies, can you?

MARY: I can say about babies. That's one thing I can say about for sure. When I had my baby—

PARKER: (*very gently*) You never had a baby, sweetheart.

MARY: I carried a baby inside me. And that baby felt everything in this house. That baby felt all the bad and evil between us then. That baby felt you out with another woman while I was pregnant with him. That baby knew you didn't want him to be born.

PARKER: Bullshit. That's enough!

MARY: That baby felt so scared and unwanted and unloved, it just shrivelled up and died before it had to be born.

PARKER: Eddie doesn't want to hear about this.

MARY: Eddie has to hear about this. Eddie has to hear what happens when there's too much evil.

EDDIE: If she wants to talk it out—

PARKER: We been over this and over it like a dog licking his balls. It's a bunch of bullshit. I don't want to hear anymore about it.

MARY: Come over to my side, Parker. You don't believe me about the baby, you don't believe me about Eddie. Come over here and look at it from over here. Try and look at it my way.

PARKER: It's not that I don't believe you. But what good does it do? What can we do about it? The baby dies. You talk to a psychic who says he sees some evil shit somewhere.

MARY: He said there was an evil aura around a person very close to me that the baby would have felt.

PARKER: (*to* EDDIE) You know Mary's a bitchin' fine woman in an awful lot of ways. But she gets her ideas, and she gets her mind set, and she can't see nothing but what she's put in her own mind.

MARY: The only thing any of us sees is what's in our own mind.

EDDIE: Ain't it so.

PARKER: Now I got this bottle of tequila that's just got this bit of a heel left in it, and she don't want me to drink it. (*pause,* PARKER *goes and starts addressing* MARY) But on the other hand she wants me to finish off this bottle. You know why? (*pause*) Mary wants this empty bottle. She keeps track of her life with empty liquor bottles. She'll take this bottle and write a note—a letter—and stick it in the bottle and put it in the garage. And that's how Mary keeps her diary.

MARY: I don't need that bottle yet.

She reaches around the sofa for the bottle she has put away.

MARY: I finished one tonight while I was waiting for you.

PARKER *takes the bottle from Mary.*

PARKER: Every one of 'em has a date on it, and a piece of paper stuck inside it, just like that one, like we're gonna float 'em out to sea any day.

He takes the bottle over to the floor lamp and holds it up like MARY *did.*

PARKER: Remember that car—I told you about it, Eddie—the one I wanna restore. It's been sitting under a tarp in my brother's yard for two years, 'cause I don't have room for it in the garage. There's bottles in our garage.

MARY: When the sun shines through that garage window on those bottles it's like I'm in a cathedral. All the colours. The light sparkling amber and brown and green. Yellow and red. Streaks of light reflecting and bouncing . . . scattering. When I go into the garage to put a bottle away or to arrange them differently, a hum starts in my head. I can't hear anything outside the garage, Parker. And the garage gets silent as the hum dies down, and there's only the sound of glass clinking as I move the bottles. It gets so very quiet. I swear I've heard a spider spinning her web. I could hear the silk threads brushing together and web twanging as she moved.

No one speaks.

PARKER: Mary took me into the garage to listen to a spider spin her web. And I heard it. (*pause*) It's not always easy to believe all Mary's words. But she knows about feelings.

EDDIE: (*quietly*) Listen, man. I'm gonna call it a night.

PARKER: No! (*pause*) And if Mary thinks she can feel some evil shit coming out of your mind—then I believe her.

MARY: Any bottle, I can look at the date taped to it, and let the sun shine through it and memories will play in my mind. Not all good ones or exciting. But parts of my life. Even when it's raining, and the bottles in the garage look like a dirty, angry glass ocean . . .

PARKER: Sweetheart, why don't we take this bottle out to garage. C'mon, Eddie, take a look at the bottles.

EDDIE: No . . . it sounds pretty personal.

PARKER: You been getting pretty personal with Mary.

EDDIE: No harm intended, man.

PARKER: Come take a look in the garage. Mary's got this cute set-up of bottles she's been collecting since we met.

EDDIE: Parker, this doesn't sound like just a cute set-up of bottles . . .

PARKER: (*viciously*) I know it's not just a fucking cute set-up of bottles. (*relaxes a bit*) Come look at it. Mary's put a lot of time into it.

MARY: It's not his place to come.

PARKER: I know. (*pause*) I was just seeing if he thought it was.

PARKER *hands the bottle to* MARY *as if it was a newborn baby. The LIGHTS FADE. They leave the stage.* EDDIE *is left drinking his beer.*

Blackout.

[End]

The Last Prayer

BY

KUEI-MING LIN

The Last Prayer was produced for the Brave New Play
Rites Festival in Vancouver in 2002 with the
following cast and crew:

TREE: Alexia Hagen
NIXIE: Orsolya Szabo
GUARD: Kwesi Ameyaw

Directed by Hayden Thomas
Costumes by Nicole Bach

(in memory of Peter Loeffler, with love and gratitude)

TREE: *innocent and dreamy old plant, no movement below knee, holding one flower.*
NIXIE: *the prisoner to be executed, exhausted*
GUARD: *in uniform*

SETTING: TREE *is on stage before scene begins, symbol of a clock. Could be done bare.* TREE *stands inside a fenced-in area, in a cage that is a temporary holding area for prisoners.*

GUARD *enters, taking* NIXIE *into the cage.* TREE *watches without much interest.*

NIXIE: Okay, already, quit dragging. I say, *quit dragging, will you?*
GUARD: Here it is, lady. (*locks fence*)
NIXIE: How long will it be?
GUARD: Your last day.
NIXIE: I say how long will it be?!
GUARD: Not to worry. Won't be long. In a blink of an eye . . . (*gestures execution*)
NIXIE: That's comforting . . . (GUARD *starts to leave.*) Hey, hey! Where're you going?
GUARD: To wait.
NIXIE: For what?
GUARD: For time.
NIXIE: Time?
GUARD: Come on! Of your execution! You know it. I know it.
NIXIE: I'm innocent! You saw that! I have been wronged! You let me go! (*rattles fence*) Let me out!
GUARD: Don't make it more difficult than it already is, lady. I don't want anything to do with you.
NIXIE: You just have—
GUARD: Save it. Rules are rules.
NIXIE: Injustice!
GUARD: Orders are orders. (*sighs*) Look, why don't you spend your last minutes in quiet prayer.

GUARD *exits.*

NIXIE: Come back! Come back here . . . (*kicks* TREE) you bastard! (*kicks again*)

TREE: ow!

NIXIE: (*surprised*) What was that? (*silence; punches* TREE)

TREE: Hey! Stop that!

NIXIE: (*rubs her eyes*) What . . . you . . . you . . .

TREE: (*yawns*) What?

NIXIE: You're a tree. (*circles around* TREE, *poking and observing*)

TREE: (*giggling*) That tickles!

NIXIE: (*laughing nervously*) Death is sure giving me a hard time leaving. (*pauses*) My name is Nixie.

TREE: (*shrugs*) What is a name?

NIXIE: Well . . . a word, perhaps, that people call you.

TREE: Hmm . . . a label, a sign?

NIXIE: Something like that.

TREE: What about boards that are hung or nailed on me?

NIXIE: No, that has nothing (*yawns*) to do with you. (*sits down*) So, tell me. What are you doing here?

TREE: Standing. (*pauses*) Ever since I can remember . . .

NIXIE: Oh.

TREE: I grew from this soil. (*pauses*) From a little seed. Did you grow from a seed?

NIXIE: No.

TREE: I didn't know that when I was still a seed. Perhaps you need water and sunlight.

NIXIE: I wish I can get out of here.

TREE: You can.

NIXIE: But . . .

TREE: You have legs. You can move around. You can squeeze right out that fence.

NIXIE: (*shaking her head*) Where would I go? (*she yawns*)

TREE: Anywhere! (*pauses*) Me? I'm stuck here. Still here. After five hundred years. (*pauses*) I wonder what it is like to have legs or wings. One can—

NIXIE: (*looks away*) There is no mercy out there. Not for me.

TREE: Hmmm . . . if I have legs, I would like to learn how to tap dance! Left shuffle step stamp, right shuffle step kick. (*giggles*)

NIXIE: I've worked hard all my life, honest and loyal.

TREE: Now, how does it feel to have wings? To be lifted off ground, flying across the world's highest mountain (*imitating a bird, whistling*) to be free from the burden of—

NIXIE: What have I done to deserve all this?

TREE: Well? Are you going?

NIXIE: Where is there to go?

TREE: Perhaps you like to climb on my branches. I have apples.

NIXIE: (*standing up*) Where?

TREE: What?

NIXIE: Apples.

TREE: Hmm . . . (*searches through branches*)

NIXIE: I haven't eaten for three days . . . (*yawning*) I'm so hungry I want to faint.

TREE: (*discovering one flower*) Oh! One flower! I guess they will be late this year. You can wait.

NIXIE: (*walks away*) No . . . (*starts crying*)

TREE: You must have hope in this flower. It will turn into an apple. It will. There is all the hope in the world in this one flower!

NIXIE: But there is no time . . .

TREE: Sap is leaking.

NIXIE: These are tears!

TREE: (*nods*) I've seen those—

NIXIE: What do you know? You're a wood.

TREE: (*sighs*) I'm here for a long long time. I see many things. I saw a tower built, dwelt, cheered, nested, fought in, crumbled, forgotten and rebuilt again . . . I saw the sun, star, moon, snow, rain, lightning, and the clouds of hundred colours . . . I have no feet but I see more things than a thousand explorers.

NIXIE: Today . . . (*starts shaking*)

TREE: Hmm . . . there is no trace of wind north, south, east or west . . .

NIXIE: I am afraid to go . . . (*pauses.*) very soon . . . (*silence*)

TREE: What is "afraid?"

NIXIE: It's when something horrible is going to happen and you don't know what to do . . . and nothing can be done.

TREE: What is that "something"?

NIXIE: The judge is cutting off my head.

TREE: Is that all?

NIXIE: I only have one head.

TREE: Perhaps it can grow back. When a wicked monkey breaks one of my branches, it always grows back sooner or later.

NIXIE: No, it can never grow back. Never, never!

TREE: Then why is the judge cutting your head? Your only one head?

NIXIE: It is a sentence.

TREE: Sentence?

NIXIE: Sentence to death.

TREE: Death?

NIXIE: Yes.

TREE: What is it? Is it something to eat? Something to wear? Oooo.

NIXIE: Like when a tree that is cut down, laying as lifeless as a stool.

TREE: Oh my . . . what bore it must be.

NIXIE: Yup. (*smiles mischievously*) Timber!

TREE: Ahh!

> **TREE** *shakes in fright, tries to move but is stuck to the ground.*
> **TREE** *struggles hopelessly.* **NIXIE** *laughs.*

TREE: It's not funny. (*gives up struggling*) I used to be blossomed with flowers and everyone loved me. (*pauses*) Mules sleep in my shades. Birds lay their eggs. Bees, butterflies, hummingbirds danced around. Couples drew hearts on my bark and come here as their "secret place" and I hear their wonderful tales. Children climbed on my branches and make necklaces out of my flowers. I perfumed and fed the whole village. (*pauses*) But each year, I seem to make less and less flowers, less and less apples. (*pauses*) Termites gnawed in and built their kingdoms. Dogs peed on me. And people are always complaining how I get in their ways and how ugly I look, all cracking and mossed. (*pauses*) I heard from one man that he will chop me down when I have no more flower left. (*pauses, then proudly*) I have one left. Hohoho!

NIXIE: Are you afraid?

TREE: Of what?

NIXIE: Death.

TREE: I don't even know what it is.

NIXIE: Then you should be afraid.

TREE: Nonsense. I wouldn't know it if I approach it. (*pauses*) But I would like to live on if I may.

NIXIE: And what will you be doing if you never be cut?

TREE: (*pauses*) Stand here, like I always have and always will, watching these wonderful little lives shuffling about, giggling . . . and giving them a soothing shade and a branch for perching and a flower for smiling and being here. Just being here . . .

NIXIE: Sometimes it's not fair . . . (*looks in distance, then to* TREE) You feel like a million termites growing inside. You can't do anything . . . you can't . . . there is no way. No one knows. No one understands. And you plod along like ripples in the stream . . . You reach the end; there is no where to go but to return . . . (*pauses*) I wish things can be different.

TREE: Everything that happens has a reason to.

NIXIE: Many reasons are unreasonable!

TREE: (*confused*) This is so odd . . . why are you (*pauses*) like this? This . . .

TREE *and* NIXIE *look at each other in silence.* SOUND *of a gong or some instrument.* GUARD *enters, unlocks fence.*

GUARD: Number one hundred and two. You're next! Time is up. (*notices* NIXIE*'s moment*) Oh! Finish your prayer. I will wait. (*stands still outside fence*)

NIXIE. Time . . . yes. Well! I must go.

TREE: Nixie—

NIXIE: But, thank you. (*leaving*)

TREE: Wait.

TREE *drops flower onto ground, smiles.*

NIXIE: What?

NIXIE *picks up flower.*

TREE: Now they will not chop you down.

NIXIE: But—

TREE: You have a flower!

NIXIE: You—

TREE: It's okay. I had a long life. It's for a charm.

NIXIE: One day, I don't know . . . a new young branch will sprout and ten million flowers will bloom from it. Then that person will never chop you down.

TREE: (*shrugs*) Well, nothing cannot be done.

NIXIE: (*kisses* TREE, *whispering*) Bless your soul.

Long pause.

GUARD: Let's go now, missy.

NIXIE: I am ready.

NIXIE *walks out of cage. She looks back at* TREE, *smiling. She turns and exits with* GUARD. *Silence.* TREE *looks down, then looks up, confused.*

TREE: Bless your soul . . .

[End]

Wagen

BY

DENNIS E. BOLEN

Wagen was produced for the Brave New Play Rites
Festival in Vancouver in 1987 with the
following cast and crew:

THE MAN: Keith Provost
GERMAN MECHANIC: Gavin Rhodes

Directed by David Wilson

An adaptation of this work appears in Dennis E. Bolen's
novel *Stand In Hell* (Random House, 1995).

CHARACTERS:

MAN: *A middle class, urban man, age thirty-five.*
GM: *A German mechanic, mid-fifties.*

SETTING: *The set is bare except for three objects: a workbench with tools, a tall stool and a Volkswagen Beetle (any vintage, pre-1990) with its rear end jacked up.*

The GERMAN MECHANIC, *wearing coveralls, is under the car working. The* MAN *sits on the high stool. There is an open case of beer on the workbench.*

MAN: . . . Yeah, but . . . There's this small matter of a couple of zillion people who got killed . . .

GM: *(heavy accent)* We were all working. *("Vee ver all verkink")* *(slides out from under car)* Do you know what that means?

MAN: Well, yeah . . . sure. I mean, I know you guys were pretty hard up there for a while—

GM: *(walking to bench)* Do you know what it's like to have no food. *(gets two bottles of beer)* Do you know what it's like having no pride?

MAN: Uh . . . well . . .

GM: *(poking* MAN'*s chest with bottle)* Just be glad you don't. Have a beer. *(gives him a bottle)*

MAN: Thanks.

They twist caps and drink in unison.

MAN: But . . . Jeez, right wing politics. Reactionary fanaticism . . .

GM: What do you want to do? Change the world or get your car fixed?

MAN: Well . . .

GM: I will give you a clue. Your seals are completely shot.

MAN: No kidding. Jeez, I didn't notice anything . . .

GM: *(sets the bottle by car, slides under)* No you did not and for a very good reason. The car was made strong. The car was made so you do not have to do anything with it right away. It was made to drive through deserts and forest and ice caps and keep on going no matter what. To run on whatever and go to wherever. Even if the driver is a fool. Even if he has something else on his mind. Even if he is drunk or ignorant or even dead . . .

MAN: (*drinks*) Gee, I find the steering's a bit funny . . . And there's a squeak in the rear end . . .

GM: I check it for you.

MAN: Thanks.

GM: Don't mention it.

The **GM** *is working with a wrench. He grunts, mumbles, makes car-working noises. The* **MAN** *drinks his beer, contemplates.*

MAN: You work a lot on the weekends like this?

GM: What I can.

MAN: (*off the stool, looking at tools on bench*) Nice stuff you got here.

GM: (*working*) What?

MAN: I said nice setup you got here. Just like the shop.

GM: Humph . . . Not quite like the shop. No compressor.

MAN: What? For air?

GM: Pneumatic wrench.

MAN: Oh.

GM: Very expensive.

MAN: I can imagine.

GM: Some day.

MAN: Sure. Just keep working. You can't be doing bad . . .

GM: Not bad.

MAN: . . . Regular day job and freelancing on the weekends like this.

GM: Not bad.

MAN: No income tax.

GM: (*slides out*) What do you mean?

MAN: Well, you don't report this weekend stuff do you?

GM: Report? (*picks up beer bottle*) What is this "report?"

MAN: I mean you don't claim the money you make off jobs like this one. No one would expect you to.

GM: (*gulps deeply from the beer, almost finishes bottle*) This is a good car. How long you had it? (*slides back under*)

MAN: Oh, hell. Long time. Had a van before that. And I had another Beetle too, that was a long time ago. High school.

GM: I was twenty-five years old before I had a car.

MAN: Hmm . . .

GM: Good car, eh?

MAN: Good car? (*drinks, walks around*) I don't know if you could exactly use a term like "good." These things were a phenomenon, really. Beyond good . . .

GM: What?

MAN: (*slaps fender affectionately*) These babies were all we used to drive. I mean, none of us were rich. But almost every other cat I knew could afford a used Bug. In those days a tank of gas for one of these things was, hell . . . buck seventy-five maybe. And repairs, heck, we did 'em ourselves. Everybody knew something about how to do one thing or another on 'em. My van, hell, I just used to keep oil and gas in the thing and it went and went and went. Bunch of us drove it clear across the continent one time. Just kept going. Picked up and dropped off people along the way. Drove when we wanted. Stopped anywhere. Didn't even have a map most of the time. God, what a time. Sometimes you'd wake up in the morning and there'd be people sleeping around that you couldn't remember seeing before. Course, we were all pretty heavy into smoke at the time. We made it to the coast and hung out all summer, headed back for school. What a time. Thing had a pretty wild paint job in those days. Had to repaint to sell it. Big peace sign on the front . . .

During the last few lines of the **MAN**'s *monologue, the* **GM** *has risen from under the car, finished his beer, thrown the bottle back in the case and opened another.*

GM: (*sternly*) Almost done. This is going to cost you, eh?

MAN: Say what? Thought we agreed on forty bucks . . .

GM: That was before . . .

MAN: Well, what all's the matter with it?

GM: Seals.

MAN: You said that.

GM: Very expensive job. (*grabbing a bottle*) Have another beer.

MAN: Thanks, but I'm still working on this one. What else is there?

GM: Adjustments . . .

MAN: Adjustments.

GM: Yes. Sorry to give you the bad news.

The **GM** *returns to work under the car, beer bottle and additional tools close by. The* **MAN** *paces.*

MAN: Sure not like the old days. No time to fix things anymore.

GM: (*working*) Do not worry. (*sarcastic*) Your "Peace Machine" will be running again in no time.

At this the **MAN** *turns his head sharply to look at the half-visible mechanic. A look of anger crosses his face. He chugs the remainder of his beer, wipes his mouth and goes to the workbench.*

MAN: Take you up on another one of these. (*gets a beer, twists cap*)

GM: What?

MAN: Never mind.

While the **GM** *slides under the car, the* **MAN** *looks over the tools on the bench and eventually settles, leaning casually on the bench. The* **GM** *slides back out, sits up and takes a drink.*

GM: Almost finished.

The **GM** *goes to the rear of the car and releases the jack. The car lowers. He pulls the jack away and wipes his hands on a rag.*

GM: You got cash on you?

MAN: Uh huh.

GM: No cheque?

MAN: Nope.

GM: Good. Just a few more adjustments.

The **GM** *raises the engine hatch and begins tinkering with a screwdriver. The* **MAN** *watches, drinks his beer, then shakes his head, smiling, remembering.*

MAN: God, that van, the more I think of it, wow, it got us through some adventures. It wasn't all good times, don't worry. I mean, those were strange days. We didn't mean any harm, but people thought we did. Kindly old grandfathers, guys who'd bounced us on their knees and given us baseball caps and bought us hotdogs. All of a sudden we were longhair freaks with homicidal drug-crazy bug-out eyes who frightened dogs and children. My Granddad threw me out of his house when he saw my hair. Hated the van, too. Don't know if it was the paint job or the make, though. He was a patriotic Ford man. Hated imports. Bad for the economy, he used to say. And that trip we took. People treated us bad. One morning we woke up and some farmer had smeared cow dung across the windshield. Most of the time we weren't even allowed to stop and get water . . .

GM: (*sarcastic*) Fascinating. I am sure you had it very bad. (*stands, closes engine hatch*)

MAN: Oh, don't get me wrong. We didn't care. Or if we did nobody ever showed it. But times have changed. Nobody takes that kind of shit anymore. Hell, you should see the guys now, the ones I still know about. One of 'em's a corporate lawyer. Does he kick ass! One guy turned out to be a cop. My ex-girlfriend at the time went out and made herself a million bucks in real estate . . .

GM: Too bad for you, eh?

MAN: Not really . . . Anyway, the point is we none of us take a beating anymore that we don't absolutely have to. We got memories. Good ones. There'll never be another time like that. But it's over. We all learned our lesson, we don't get kicked around anymore.

GM: You got hundred-fifty dollars?

MAN: What for?

GM: (*gestures at car*) Hundred-fifty.

MAN: Oh yeah? Long way from forty.

GM: Tough job. I do good work. Ask anybody.

MAN: (*digs in pocket*) True. You do good work. You come highly recommended. (*counts bills*) Say, I should put some of my friends onto you. One guy in particular. He's got a Rabbit.

GM: (*hand out*) Maybe. Pretty busy these days . . .

MAN: You'd really like this guy. He's as much a fanatic about these cars as I am . . .

GM: Then I know I don't want to work on it . . .

MAN: Great guy. Works for Revenue—

GM: What?

MAN: Got a nice little Rabbit, almost new.

GM: No.

MAN: A hundred-fifty bucks?

GM: Uh . . .

MAN: (*hands over a wad of bills*) There you go.

GM: No.

MAN: What do you mean?

GM: Nein. Here. (*hands back money*)

MAN: Well, hey, you do good work.

GM: Forty dollars.

MAN: What?

GM: You win. Forty dollars.

MAN: Sure?

The GM *nods, turns away, wipes hands on rag. The* MAN *peels a couple of bills from the wad in his hand and drops them on the workbench. They both sip their beers.*

GM: (*gesturing with bottle*) Good car.

MAN: I know.

GM: Good for then. Good for now.

MAN: Right.

Pause.

GM: (*brightening*) You know, what was good about when I was young and we had nothing, people were all so friendly. Laughing and singing. We had a sense of humour about it. Nobody protested. We wouldn't have dared. Protest against ourselves? Stupid! No one had time. We were all so busy. Working all the time. My father, how proud he was, he worked and worked. His hands would bleed at the end of the day. Barely time to say hello to all of us. But we all shared. We worked and shared. By themselves, people had almost nothing. Things are better nowadays.

MAN: (*thoughtful*) I don't know. Sounds okay as long as nobody went hungry.

GM: Okay? Funny word. Okay? Maybe . . .

MAN: Just what we were going for, way back then. (*drinks*) Didn't work.

GM: Ha, ha.

MAN: What's funny?

GM: The way you say it. "Didn't work!" Ha, ha.

MAN: That's funny?

The GM laughs some more. The MAN joins in, laughing more at the GM's laughter than anything else.

MAN: You got one weird sense of humour, there, pal.

GM: Ha, ha. You don't see it? You, who are strong. (*makes a comic, stern expression and thumps his chest*) The man who does not get kicked around anymore. You work for something . . . "Didn't work." You give up. Just like that. Hah!

MAN: I don't get it . . .

GM: Where I am from, a man works, he tries to do something, he does not give up.

MAN: Yeah? And the results are plain to see.

GM: Huh?

MAN: Look at the mess you guys made.

GM: Mess? Maybe. Maybe not. But the spirit has never died.

MAN: Oh yeah? That's bad news.

GM: Bad. Good. All in the perception.

MAN: I perceive it as bad.

GM: You don't like your car?

MAN: Huh?

GM: Your car is the living proof of our spirit. You drive it around every day. You advertise our ingenuity, pride, our work and sweat . . .

MAN: Lot of other things, too . . .

GM: Whatever you see in it.

MAN: No. You've got a point. A lot of people see different things. Maybe Granddad was right . . .

GM: Ah, but stick with your beliefs! Don't get kicked around! Drive it and to hell with what people think.

MAN: I don't know . . . That's how trouble like that gets started.

GM: Whatever. It's your car. It's what you can afford.

MAN: You got that right . . .

GM: By the way, you need a new wheel bearing. That squeaking . . .

MAN: In the back?

GM: The rear driver's side. Water got in there somehow.

MAN: Great. Just great.

GM: Don't worry. I'll do it next weekend.

MAN: Ah, maybe I should take it to the shop.

GM: It will cost you.

MAN: How much?

GM: Maybe two hundred.

MAN: Oh, man . . .

GM: I do it for eighty. Next Saturday.

MAN: Damn, two hundred dollars.

GM: That's the breaks . . .

MAN: Any other time... I could afford it.

GM: Relax. I will take care of you. (*gets bottle from beer case*) Have a beer.

MAN: No thanks. Haven't finished this one.

GM: Suit yourself. (*twists cap, drinks*) Don't worry. It will run until next weekend.

MAN: You sure? It's been squeaking pretty bad.

GM: (*puts hand on* **MAN***'s shoulder*) Trust your faithful mechanic.

MAN: (*walks around*) Hmm . . . Let me think.

GM: It comes down to one thing, my friend. Do you want to change the world or do you want to fix your car?

The **MAN** *looks at the mechanic sourly, finishes his beer, puts the bottle in the case and walks to the car. He pats a front fender. He turns to the* **GM**, *smiling.*

MAN: This thing gonna run?

GM: Are you kidding? (*puts beer on workbench, peels off coveralls*) Like new. You wouldn't believe it.

The **MAN** *gets behind the wheel, waits for the* **GM**. *The* **GM** *throws his coveralls over the stool and takes a deep swallow from his beer. He climbs in the passenger side and slams the door.*

GM: Give it lots of gas before you turn the key.

The **MAN** *pumps the gas pedal and turns the key. The engine turns over several times but fails to catch. The* **MAN** *stops and tries again. The engine does not start. The* **MAN** *stops winding the engine and turns to the* **GM**.

MAN: Try it once more?
GM: Ja wohl . . .

The **MAN** *tries once more, to no avail.*

GM: Must be flooded. (*getting out*) Take off the brake. We push it.
MAN: Okay . . .

They both get out, close the doors and begin pushing the car.

GM: (*pushing*) Brake is off?
MAN: Yes.
GM: Key is on? Make sure the key is on!
MAN: Ja wohl, mein invincible mechanic! (*laughs*)

They push the car off stage.

[End]

To Undo a Wrong

BY

TSERING LAMA

To Undo a Wrong was produced for the Brave New Play
Rites Festival in Vancouver in 2005 with the
following cast and crew:

NIRMAL: Edward Fong
CUSTOMER: Maurice Leblanc
SHARMA & PATAR: Duncan Mao
RAMU & SCHOOLBOY: Kuei-ming Lin
ANJU: Holly Ho
MADAM LAKSHIMI: Joy Castro

Directed by Lena Huggett
Costume Design: Marjika Brusse

CHARACTERS

(*in order of appearance*)

    SHARMA, *forties, tough chief inspector.*
    NIRMAL, *fifties, kind, naïve man.*
    RAMU, *young newspaper seller.*
    CUSTOMER, *late thirties, an obese, rude, and nervous man.*
    ANJU, **NIRMAL**'s *sweet twelve-year-old daughter, long black hair.*
    PATAR, *fifites, authoratative, prominent man in* **NIRMAL**'s *village.*
    SCHOOLBOY, *ten, runny-nosed letter writer dressed in school uniform.*
    MADAM LAKSHMI, *voluptuous brothel owner in her forties.*

    SETTING: *The play is set mostly on a New Delhi road and in a hut in a Nepali village in modern time.*

SCENE ONE

The stage is unlit. A **RADIO** *plays. (In the production, the two languages were overlapped.)*

RADIO: Aaj sham, Yamuna nadi ke matti bari that ek aurat ki la-ash payi gayi. Darya meh kam karne walleh baccho ne yey aurat dekha tha. Unki mouth ka karan pani mey drhub ney ki dhughatney sey huwa. Yeh bi dekah gaya ki ek cycle rickshaw be Yamuna key kali mitti mey phasa dekha tha.

    A female corpse was discovered in the mudflats of the Yamuna River earlier this evening. She was found facedown in water by local children picking up garbage. The cause of death is believed to be drowning due to an accident. Further into the dark water, a bicycle rickshaw was found wedged into the muddy floor of the river.

Lights come on to reveal the scene. In the background is the New Delhi skyline; it is sunrise. The setting is a police investigation at the Yamuna River, a garbage-filled swamp. There are bicycle tires

and parts of a rickshaw carriage popping out of the river.
SHARMA *addresses reporters off stage.*

SHARMA: The deceased woman was riding a rickshaw, which you see scattered in pieces behind us, when the vehicle lost control and dove into the river. (*sighs irritably*). Most likely, this was just a mishap, not a homicide. (*pointing off stage*) If you look at the poorly lit bend in the road, (*carrying the point behind him to the river*) and the tracks of the rickshaw's dive into the river, (*dropping arm*) you can see why we've concluded this. No other bodies have been found. (*pause, then coldly*) A thorough search of this vast, black, sewage and garbage ridden river would be very difficult. And unfruitful.

SCENE TWO

A roadside in New Delhi. It is sunset. **NIRMAL** *and* **RAMU** *are lounging on a rickshaw;* **NIRMAL** *on the bicycle seat and* **RAMU** *is sitting in the carriage with a stack of newspapers.* **NIRMAL** *is counting his earnings: some bills and coins.*

NIRMAL: Ramu, I won't get a customer if you sit there.

RAMU: If only recounting and reliving your hopes made the stack a little fatter, eh Nirmal? (**NIRMAL** *looks irritably at* **RAMU** *and begins to recount. Pause.*) Your boss isn't gonna let you rent the rickshaw anymore. Three weeks is as long as you'll get in the city.

NIRMAL: (*not looking up*) Why do you always pester me here? (*fanning*) Go! Sell your newspapers.

RAMU: (*surprised, then boisterously*) Oh look at you! You know, you came to my city. And too late, think you should know. Can't really expect to make any money here in your age. (*pause*) Some advice: go back to your village in Nepal. Die peacefully in the hills.

NIRMAL: (*puts his money away, then quizzically*) What do you know about dying peacefully? Haven't seen you fend for anyone but yourself. What worries could you have?

RAMU: (*sternly, though not offended*) Take that back! Didn't I fend for you? 'member when you wandered up to me? Who showed you where to buy the best butter chicken and aloo gobi? (*pause, then quieter.*) And you can die in peace . . . if you'll just give up looking for the little girl of yours. What's her name again? A-nnu? A-nnee?

NIRMAL: Anju.

RAMU: (*quieter*) Right. Well. If she's even still here, Nirmal . . . you'll probably never find her again. This city's just big; People just fade away . . . probably a person here to match every roach.

Enter **CUSTOMER**, *wiping his forehead from the heat with a hanky and walking leaning back because of his stomach.*

CUSTOMER: (*to offstage, yelling*) Yeah, yeah! I'll give you that much. Then I'll add in my wife, as well. Bastard rickshaw drivers, always trying to gouge me!

RAMU: (*cheerfully, hopping off the rickshaw*) See! I'm good luck! Whenever I sit here you get a customer.

NIRMAL: (*to* **RAMU**) Alright, go away now. (*gets off the rickshaw, then to* **CUSTOMER**, *smiling*) Where do you want to go? I'll take you—

CUSTOMER: (*impatiently*). I'll give you five to take me to GB Road.

RAMU: (*to* **CUSTOMER**, *jumps to the ground*) What?! That's way too low!

NIRMAL: (*to* **RAMU** *sternly*) Ramu!

RAMU: (*to* **NIRMAL**) Old man, you should get at least double, no triple that. Trust me, I know the vultures in this city. (*looking at* **CUSTOMER**) This fart is just duping you.

CUSTOMER: (*to* **RAMU**, *angrily*) Huh?! What'd you say?

NIRMAL: (*to* **CUSTOMER**) He's just a kid, sir. (*ushers* **CUSTOMER** *to rickshaw*)

SCENE THREE

NIRMAL's *hut. Night-time—very dark but for a candle.* **NIRMAL** *is sitting on the ground, sleeping against an empty, messy bed. From outside come sounds of people murmuring and feet shuffling.*

Enter **ANJU**. **NIRMAL** *awakes.*

NIRMAL: Anju . . .

ANJU: How do you know when . . . someone will pass away?

NIRMAL: (*pause.*) I don't know . . .

ANJU: I heard someone say . . . that when mom was—there was a black mark (*pointing to her forehead*) collecting there.

NIRMAL: Who said that?

ANJU: Everyone. All they're saying outside is "Ram, Ram, Ram," I could tell she was going soon.

NIRMAL: (*to himself*) In their minds, they cremated her as soon as she fell ill.

ANJU: Because of that black mark. Everyone saw it but me. What was it? Was it from her illness?

NIRMAL: Just one of those things people see when someone's dying.

ANJU: But how did they know? (*to herself*) I didn't see the mark. I stared a long time at her forehead before she went away and sometimes I thought I could see it, but I don't think I ever did.

NIRMAL: (*to himself*) Neither did I, Anju. I didn't see any of this.

SCENE FOUR

NIRMAL's *hut. Midday, though the hut is dark at first because the window and doors are shut.* **NIRMAL** *sits on the bed, drinking from a bottle. He looks unkempt and depressed. There is a knock at the door.*

NIRMAL: (*drunk, head slung low*) No one's here. (*knock again*)

PATAR: (*kindly but sternly*) Nirmal? It's Patar. Let me in, my friend. (**NIRMAL** *fumbles from the bed and opens the door, which is left open. Enter* **PATAR**, *surprised to see* **NIRMAL** *in this state.* **NIRMAL** *grabs a chair and wipes it with his hand for* **PATAR**. **PATAR** *sits down. They look at each other then* **NIRMAL** *lowers his head.*) It's gone on long enough now. Your wonderful wife (*to himself, shaking his head*) . . . her passing is a great loss to everyone in our village. She was a very good woman, very good. But you need to start thinking about your situation now.

NIRMAL: (*looking down embarrassed, respectfully*) Oh, this is true. Thank you, Patar jee.

PATAR: (*sighs*) My poor friend, so much grief in the world. Times are bad. But look at your situation carefully now. You cannot raise these two daughters on your own, not with a single rice patty wage, not without their wonderful mother. (*pause*) Priya, your eldest, is grown up now. Now you need to marry her, to a good family of course. And the little one, Anju; she's growing up too. Young women need things, my friend. Things you cannot provide. Do you understand, my friend?

NIRMAL: Patar jee, the thought of the future—it's very difficult. (*pause, then reflectively*) Of course, you are right. Priya will need to be wedded soon.

PATAR: Now . . . you don't have any money for such a thing right now. (*pause*) So I'm willing to lend you some of my own, on low interest.

NIRMAL: (*surprised, then gratefully*) Oh, that is very kind of you, Patar jee. But I could never take such money from you without knowing first how I could repay you. Such an amount, many years would pass before I could—no, I'll go to the capital myself. I can find some work in Kathmandu. There I have a cousin who works at a wool factory. If not, I can sell goods in the bazaar. My wife always said—

PATAR: (*shaking his head*) No, no a man in your state would be eaten alive there these days. It's not like before; there's nothing there for us lowly villagers. Even I face terrible hardships on my regular travels there. Times are bad. (*He pauses staring intently at the floor.* NIRMAL *stares at* PATAR *in awe of his generosity and empathy.*) Teektsa! I have a solution. I know a woman in New Delhi; her name is Lakshmi. She is a very good person, very good. And I happen to be privy to the fact that she is looking for a nice, gentle girl to do some housework. Light work: dishes, sweeping, laundry. Now, the pay is very good and any girl from our village would be lucky to have this opportunity . . . but in this situation, I think it will be best to send your youngest, Anju. She's what? Fourteen?

NIRMAL: My Anju is twelve, Patar jee.

PATAR: Oh, very good. If you send her to work there, she'll enjoy a good life full of things we ignorant villagers only dream of. And she'll easily spare the money to pay me back for Priya's wedding and a respectable dowry. *Claps his hand once, keeping them firmly clasped.*

NIRMAL: (*agreeing solemnly*) Oh . . . this is a good prospect, indeed. (*pause*) But Patar jee, I can't help thinking, my little girl is still just a child. I hear our cities are bird droppings compared to Indian cities. (*shakes his head*) She would not fare so well, not at all.

PATAR: (*slightly annoyed*) You insult me slightly, though I forgive you. You forget in your frail condition, but I've helped many young girls, younger than dear Anju, from many villages, find affable jobs in India. And I can say with some degree of pride that they all lead very good lives there now. After a few years pass, certainly Anju can return, mature with adventures, pockets fat with cash. My poor friend, think how her life will be improved, not to mention your older daughter's.

SCENCE FIVE

New Delhi road. Sunset. **NIRMAL** *is peddling the rickshaw.*
CUSTOMER *sits behind him, wiping his face constantly from the heat and tapping his toes with impatience.*

NIRMAL: (*talking over his shoulder, finding it difficult to start peddling because of* **CUSTOMER**'s *weight*) Where would you like to go, sir?

CUSTOMER: (*irritably*) GB Road. I already said.

NIRMAL: What part?

CUSTOMER: Just take me to the road.

NIRMAL: Oh, that's going to make things difficult.

CUSTOMER: (*perplexed*) What is?

NIRMAL: There's so many ways to get there.

CUSTOMER: Huh?! Just take a road.

NIRMAL: Would help if you knew where on GB Road.

CUSTOMER: (*irritably*) The red-light district. Just go to the red-light district.

NIRMAL: (*hiding surprise*) Oh. Was only asking so I could get you there faster. (*pause, then looking up at the sky, to himself*) Barely any stars out, again.

CUSTOMER: What?

NIRMAL: The skies are very dark here.

CUSTOMER: (*looking up, quizzically*) They're dark?

NIRMAL: Well, there aren't stars out here.

CUSTOMER: (*looking up*) Hmm. Never noticed that. (*pointing*) Well, what's that over there? That's a star.

NIRMAL: (*looking back*) Back home, at night the sky looked like it was dusted with salt.

CUSTOMER: (*authoritatively*) Huh?! What? Where is this?

NIRMAL: Near Gorkha. In Nepal.

CUSTOMER: In a village?

NIRMAL: Yes, a small one. On a hill between two rivers. One side of the hill never gets any sun. It's a high cliff so no one owns it. That's where I get the animal feed—

CUSTOMER: (*pedantically*) Well, of course you get all those stars in a village. You don't have any of the bright city lights. Here, everywhere you look it's dazzling lights from industry, entertainment— no one needs stars. (**NIRMAL** *shrugs and looks up at the sky again.* **CUSTOMER** *notices something ahead and slaps* **NIRMAL***'s bare shoulder with his hanky, panicking.*) WATCH OUT! (**NIRMAL** *swerves the rickshaw and keeps peddling.* **CUSTOMER** *realizing that his hanky is now dirty from touching* **NIRMAL***, tosses it off the rickshaw with disgust.*) You almost killed that cow! Bastard brainless rickshaw driver. Keep your eyes on the road, not the stupid sky.

NIRMAL: (*laughing nervously, jittery*) Not to worry, sir. If anything, the cow would've killed us.

SCENE SIX

> **NIRMAL***'s hut.* **ANJU** *is sitting, solemnly on the bed with an open suitcase of her clothes beside her.* **NIRMAL** *is standing beside her, holding a red travel clock.*

NIRMAL: (*wiping the clock*) I bought this a long time ago, when your

mother and I married. It needs a new battery. You can get someone to look at it in New Delhi. But it's a good clock. If you ever
need money, you sell it. (*He wraps it in a shiny scarf and passes it to
her. She takes it and examines it. He watches her lovingly for a moment*).
Where is the money? (**ANJU** *pulls out a bundled scarf.* **NIRMAL**
*unwraps the scarf and takes out the money, separating it, putting them in
different sections of the suitcase and handing a few bills to* **ANJU**.) Keep
your money separate all the time. When I get some more loans,
I'll send you more. (**ANJU** *nods. Pause.*) I'll come visit you soon.
Maybe in the winter.

Enter **PATAR**.

PATAR: We should get going soon.

> **ANJU** *closes the suitcase.* **NIRMAL** *rushes to grab a metal tiffin
> box and hands it to* **ANJU** *as she begins to get up from the bed.*

NIRMAL: Don't skip any meals.
PATAR: Nirmal, you are truly blessed to have such a daughter.
NIRMAL: I'm blessed to have your friendship, Patar jee.
PATAR: Truly, I feel your troubles are over. (*Motions to* **ANJU**, *kindly*)
Come.
Exit **ANJU** *and* **PATAR**.

SCENE SEVEN

> **NIRMAL**'s *hut, daytime, door and window open.* **NIRMAL** *is
> standing with a letter and* **SCHOOLBOY** *is sitting on the bed
> with a notebook.*

NIRMAL: (*handing the letter to* **SCHOOLBOY**, *beaming*) Will you read it to
me?
SCHOOLBOY: (*annoyed*) Again? I thought you just wanted me to write
the letter to Anju. (*takes the letter, reading loudly with a runny nose*)
Dear father and Priya, how are you doing? I am so happy to hear

that Priya has made a match. If you ever go to Gorkha bazaar, please take a photo of you two with the new groom and send it to me. I don't know when I will get to come home but I will treasure a photo if I can have one of my new brother-in-law. I hope he is handsome. Madam Lakshmi has me watching many babies. She says she will upgrade me soon, though I don't know to what. I live with many girls in a smelly part of the city. I hope to see the whole city soon. It seems to be very big. Some of the girls are Nepali like me and ask about their villages, but of course, I can never tell them much. I am lucky and happy so don't worry about me. I am enclosing my earnings minus what I spent on a new hairband and sweets. (*puts the letter down on the bed*) There, that's it.

NIRMAL: (*smiling*) How's her penmanship?

SCHOOLBOY: (*boastfully*) It's okay.

NIRMAL: (*smiling*) She'll go back to school when she comes back.

SCHOOLBOY: How much does she send each time, Nirmal jee? I see you walking around the village looking really happy these last weeks. And you're always coming back from Gorkha bazaar with rose-colored candy boxes . . . which you don't share.

NIRMAL: Those were for Priya's in-laws. Okay, so start writing. (**SCHOOLBOY** *scribbles frantically into the notebook while wiping his runny nose on his sleeve.*) My dear daughter, I am sending you a photo of your sister's groom. I am happy to hear that you're doing well. It was very smart of you to wrap your earnings in a plastic bag inside the envelope. (*to* **SCHOOLBOY**) Write legibly, okay? Anju, make sure you eat often. Buy food when you need to, don't worry about saving money all the time . . . be obedient to Madam Lakshmi. It's good to hear that she will be getting you a better position, though there's nothing wrong with taking care of children. My dear, your earnings have afforded your older sister a bright future as a head of a good family. As well, though I haven't told anyone else yet, I want to tell you my dear that one day we could buy a small patch of land, maybe start a rice field like the ones your mother and I worked for so many years. (*pause*) Well, how's that? Read it back to me.

SCHOOLBOY *picks up the letter to begin reading.*

SCENE EIGHT

NIRMAL's *hut.* NIRMAL *sits on the bed. Enter* PATAR.

PATAR: Well, what's the matter?

NIRMAL: It's Anju.

PATAR: (*dismissive*) She's in a big city now, Nirmal—

NIRMAL: She should write. It's been months.

PATAR: (*halfhearted*) There's so much to do there. The cinemas—

NIRMAL: She must be watching flicks all day and night in that case.

PATAR: (*shrugs impatiently, looking out door.*) Must be.

NIRMAL: No. (*pause*) Something might've happened. Would you contact Lakshmi jee? Maybe you could track her down . . . or I have to do something—

PATAR: (*firm*) Nirmal . . . as I said a while back, your daughter is very very young, is this right or not? When they're that young, they're easily distracted, am I right or what? Alright then, your daughter is probably enjoying herself in the city and has forgotten to write recently. It happens often. I'm telling you the truth. Now, does this do it or what?

NIRMAL: Patar jee—

PATAR: I know Lakshmi jee very well; you have nothing to worry about. Girls Anju's age do this often when they go off.

NIRMAL: (*to himself*) But Anju would write to me . . .

PATAR: (*looking out the door, getting up*) I have to get going now, my friend. You are worrying needlessly.

NIRMAL *gets up to show* PATAR *to the door, then packs his things.*

SCENE NINE

GB *Road, nighttime; a regular street but with red lights through some windows.* NIRMAL *is peddling the rickshaw with* CUS-TOMER *in the back.*

NIRMAL: All these red lights . . .

CUSTOMER: That's the industry, old man, GB Road. Here's your stars.

(*pause, motioning to stop*) Stop here. (**NIRMAL** *stops the rickshaw.* **CUSTOMER** *gets off, shaking the rickshaw violently. He pays* **NIRMAL**.) Look, you stay here and wait for me to come back, okay?

NIRMAL: Oh . . . that's not going to work—

CUSTOMER: Huh?! Of course it is. I'll only be gone a few minutes. It'll be easier for the both of us.

Exit **CUSTOMER** *into a building. A shriek is heard close by.* **NIRMAL** *sits up and looks around.* **ANJU** *enters into view from a window in the building the* **CUSTOMER** *entered. She stands, face obstructed by hair, under a dangling red light bulb that isn't turned on. Enter* **MADAM LAKSHMI** *into view and smacks* **ANJU**, *who falls to the floor out of view. She proceeds to beat* **ANJU**. **NIRMAL** *looks around the street, unsure of what to do. Finding no one else, he falls into a quick despair. He watches the scene in the window.*

ANJU: Please! Madam Lakshmi!

Upon hearing the name "Lakshmi," **NIRMAL** *becomes more agitated and paces the street, looking up all the time.*

NIRMAL: (*to himself*) Lakshmi jee?

LAKSHMI: (*while beating* **ANJU**) You—shut up! Shut—up! Ungrateful waste!

Silence.

ANJU: (*in pain, unable to speak*) Forgive—me. Please—stop. I'll do— what you want.

NIRMAL: (*to himself*) Lakshmi jee? Of all the Lakshmis I've encountered . . . riding in the rickshaw, at the teashop, at the markets . . . could that be her? Here? (*the red lightbulb comes on*) The red light! Lakshmi is leaving the room. I should act now. I have to speak to her, now! (**NIRMAL** *goes to the door. It is locked. He knocks.*) Lhakshmi jee, is it you? Open this door. I'm Anju's father. Please open the door. Where can I find Anju? Who was that little girl? Lakshmi jee! Open the door!

CUSTOMER *opens the door, zipping up his pants.*

CUSTOMER: What are you shouting about? Aye, old man . . . come for your go at it?

Inside the room is ANJU *lying motionless on the bed, face covered with hair.* NIRMAL *shoves past the* CUSTOMER. *Exit* CUSTOMER *with a shrug.* NIRMAL *walks towards the girl slowly. He kneels down beside and looks at her emaciated, bruised body. He slowly wipes away her hair and realizes it's* ANJU. ANJU *is immobile, good as dead.*

NIRMAL: (*barely able to speak*) Anju? What? (*silence, then looks around in desperation and shock*) What is this? What's happened to you? Anju? (*takes her off the bed and holds her limp body in his arms*) Wake up, it's father.

Enter LAKSHMI.

LAKSHMI: (*standing at the door authoritatively*) Who are you? The girl's taken. Come back later. Do you hear me? Well?

NIRMAL *turns his head. Silence.*

SCENE TEN
The stage is unlit; a RADIO *voice plays.*

RADIO: Jo la-ash local larkey ney Yamuna Nadi meh kal rath dekha tha unki shanagti Madam Lakshi hey aur yeh Red Light District ka ek randighar ki maliken tha.

We have now identified the woman found last night in Yamuna River by local children as the Red Light District's Madam Lakshmi.

Lights come on to reveal NIRMAL *sitting on a bench with his bag.*

RADIO: Police is natijey par ah-yey hai ki Madam Lakshmi ke mouth ka karan ek hasstha sey huwa hey aur police ney is case bandh kar-dhiya. Dusura samachar meh . . .

The police maintain that Madam Lakshmi's death was caused by an accident and they have now closed their investigation. In other news . . .

NIRMAL *turns off the* RADIO. *Enter* RAMU.

RAMU: Eh! The busses are leaving. Didn't you say you were going to Gorkha?

NIRMAL: Yes. That's me.

NIRMAL *grabs his bag and the radio and exits.*

[End]

Reunion

BY

TIM KENNALEY

Reunion was produced for the Brave New Play Rites
Festival in Vancouver in 2002 with the
following cast and crew:

PATRICK/CRAIG: Ryan Bell
BEN: Aaron Bell
OSGOOD: Christopher Scissons

Directed by Adam Cowart
Costumes: Kathy Kibble

SETTING: *A restaurant.* PATRICK *enters, looking around. He sits at a table, produces an envelope from his pocket, drops it on the table. Brief pause.* BEN *and* OSGOOD *enter.*

OSGOOD: There he is! That's him! I'm sure of it! (*approaches* PATRICK, *grabs his shoulder*) Can you believe it? It's me! Osgood! (*shakes* PATRICK) You scamp you. I knew you wouldn't let us down. (*turns to* BEN, *who has seized* PATRICK's *arm*) Doesn't he look good, Ben? Like a prince, like a prince.

PATRICK *regards the two men apprehensively.*

BEN: You've aged well. Your hair's as thick as ever.
PATRICK: What are you doing? (*stands up, backs away*) Why are you touching me?
OSGOOD: Why?
PATRICK: Yes! Yes! You can't go around grabbing people you don't know.
BEN: He's a kidder. A real jokester.
OSGOOD: (*takes* PATRICK *by the arm, leads him toward a seat*) Not another word, you prankster. Come. Sit. Sit. (*pushes him down*)
PATRICK: Hey!
OSGOOD: Enough of your rib tickling.
BEN: Wisecracking.
OSGOOD: Fill us in. Tell us what you've been up to, you old scamp you. (*grabs hold of* BEN) Can you believe this guy? He's really grown up, hasn't he? A little ugly if you ask me. (BEN *laughs heartily.*) But he hasn't turned out all that bad.
BEN: I'm a dentist. Isn't that great? Isn't that fantastic?
OSGOOD: Come on, Craig. You're holding out on us.
BEN: Yes, Craig. Fill us in.
OSGOOD: Let us in on what you've been up to for all these years.

PATRICK *rises to his feet.*

PATRICK: I'm sorry. You must be mistaken. My name isn't Craig. I'm Patrick Daniels. (*holds out the letter*) I came here out of the goodness of my heart to let you know that you mailed this letter to the wrong address.

OSGOOD: Such a joker. You prankster you. You pecker.

BEN: He hasn't changed at all. Once a jokester, always a jokester.

PATRICK: I'm not who you think I am.

OSGOOD: I love you. I love you. (*shoves* **PATRICK** *into his seat*) Now get down on your ass. We have so much to talk about.

PATRICK: What do you think you're doing? You can't touch me.

BEN *applauds excitedly.*

BEN: Such an actor. Such a wonderful actor.

OSGOOD: (*calms* **BEN** *down*) Okay. Okay. Enough joking around. Let's be serious for a moment.

PATRICK: (*tries to stand*) I'm leaving.

OSGOOD: Ah! Ah! Not so fast, buster. (*forces* **PATRICK** *back onto his seat*) We need to address some things.

BEN: There're so many things we need to discuss.

OSGOOD: Tell me about that girl you were dating way back when . . . . that one you'd just look at and you'd keel over, sick with desire. Now she was a beauty. Her face, her hair, her you know whats. She was damn near perfect.

PATRICK: Please. Let me go. I want to leave.

BEN: (*places his hand on* **PATRICK**'s *shoulder to keep him down*) Oh, yes. I remember her. I would have forfeited my life to see her naked.

OSGOOD: I heard you lost her, and now you live with all the "what ifs" and "what might have beens."

PATRICK: What?

BEN: It's okay, Craig. It's okay. This is what we learned when we were searching for you.

OSGOOD: Take my advice, Craig. Forget about her. Leave it alone. You can kill yourself thinking about the one that got away.

BEN: It's true. He's right.

PATRICK: I don't know what you're talking about.

BEN: (*to* **OSGOOD**) He's in denial. He won't let go.

OSGOOD: Come on, Craig. You're too romantic, too soft. You think she thinks about you?

PATRICK: (*tries to stand*) I insist that you let me leave.

BEN: (*pushes him back down*) She doesn't.

OSGOOD: You're old news.

BEN: Of little significance.

PATRICK *looks around disconcertedly.*

PATRICK: Hello? Can someone help me?

OSGOOD: That's it buddy. It's over. Kaput. She'll never love you the way we love you.

BEN: Always.

OSGOOD: Forever.

BEN: Without end.

OSGOOD *regards an invisible waitress.*

OSGOOD: Ah. Here's our waitress.

BEN: Hello, Jennifer. Will you be our waitress today?

PATRICK: (*to the waitress*) These men are harassing me.

OSGOOD: He's a jokester, Jennifer. Just smile. Just smile. Don't take offense.

BEN: How about three beef dips, Jennifer? Craig loves his beef dips.

PATRICK: They won't let me leave.

OSGOOD: (*to the waitress*) We'll begin with something to drink, Jennifer. But nothing with alcohol in it for Craig here. He's a wild one when he drinks.

BEN: How about some coffee, Jennifer? Craig likes coffee.

PATRICK: (*holding his hand out to the waitress*) No. Don't go.

OSGOOD: Now. Where were we?

PATRICK: (*he stands*) Listen to me. You've made a mistake. I'm not who you think I am.

BEN: Craig's at it again.

PATRICK: My name isn't Craig.

OSGOOD: You used to write things down. Do you still do that type of thing?

BEN: (*eases **PATRICK** back onto his seat*) Sit down, Craig. The food'll be out before you know it.

PATRICK *swats* BEN*'s hands away.*

PATRICK: Let go of me.

OSGOOD: I remember a poem you once wrote. How does it go?

BEN: "Once, when the sky was a swarm of green grapes."

OSGOOD: Yes! Yes! That's it.

PATRICK: I didn't write that.

OSGOOD: (*continues reciting*) "And the trees were the dotted 'i's in live, give, and infinite."

PATRICK: Waitress? Waitress?

BEN: When odours smelled like aromatic scents."

OSGOOD: "And mermaids lazed naked in the shallow surf."

PATRICK: Stop it. Stop it.

OSGOOD: "When shadows were washed and thrown over the line to dry."

BEN: "And the wind rose foaming and fierce."

OSGOOD: "The newborn day."

BEN: "Went back to sleep."

OSGOOD: "And dreamt of you."

BEN: "Daydreaming."

PATRICK: You're crazy. Both of you.

OSGOOD: You've a soft heart, Craig.

BEN: A little girl's heart.

OSGOOD: Do you still do that type of thing? I hope you haven't given it up.

PATRICK: You've mistaken me for someone else. I don't write. I never have.

BEN: Ah, yes. His own worst critic.

OSGOOD: Artists are too hard on themselves.

BEN: They are silly people.

PATRICK: (*stands*) Enough. Enough of this.

OSGOOD *plants his hands on* PATRICK*'s chest and shoves him onto his seat.*

OSGOOD: Oh no you don't. Come on you jokester. Sit down you pecker.

PATRICK: How dare you!

BEN: That's better. One must sit once in a while.

PATRICK: That was assault. Brutality.

OSGOOD: Oh. Come on, Craig. We still have lots to talk about.

BEN: So many things we haven't discussed.

OSGOOD: Now. I know this can be a touchy subject, but we were told that you're unemployed.

PATRICK: (*flustered, angry*) I have a job. A good job.

BEN: You do?

OSGOOD: What do you do?

PATRICK: That's none of your business.

BEN: I bet he's a playwright. Or a poet.

PATRICK: I'm neither.

OSGOOD: Either or?

PATRICK: What?

BEN: One or the other?

PATRICK: What are you talking about?

OSGOOD *slams his fist on the table.*

OSGOOD: Let's reminisce. Why don't we talk about old times?

BEN: An excellent idea. A superb idea.

PATRICK: Waitress!

OSGOOD: What should we start with? There're so many good memories to talk about.

BEN: Excellent memories. Superb memories.

PATRICK: Enough. Stop it.

OSGOOD: Why don't we talk about university? We had lots of fun at university.

BEN: We were so young.

PATRICK: I told you, I'm not who you think I am.

BEN: (*shakes his head in disbelief*) What a sense of humour.

PATRICK: I'm not joking!

OSGOOD: Do you remember that night when we got drunk at a party and tore our clothes off and piled into a bathtub?

PATRICK: That didn't happen,

BEN: We sang some lovely songs.

OSGOOD: And people came in, one after the other, to listen to us?

BEN: To take a little peak.

PATRICK: No.

OSGOOD: And you got out of the tub and walked right into the party and said, "Here I am. Feast your eyes on this."

BEN: And a nice young lady made a derogatory remark about the size of your penis.

OSGOOD: I shat my pants.

BEN: But we weren't wearing pants.

OSGOOD: So I shat on the floor.

PATRICK: (*stands*) You're mad! The both of you are mad!

OSGOOD: Oh, come on Craig. Come on. Sit for a while. You keep standing up. What would happen if Ben were to take offense?

BEN: I'd cry.

OSGOOD: Have they been working you too hard, Craig? You look a little tired. Are you tired?

PATRICK: I'm fine. Just please let me leave.

BEN: They don't let you writers sleep, do they? Eyes open or it's the whip.

OSGOOD: We worry about you, Craig. You seem a little out of sorts.

BEN: A little flustered.

OSGOOD: Bagged.

BEN: Beaten.

OSGOOD: Drained.

BEN: Devitalized.

OSGOOD: Tell us about it, Craig.

PATRICK: It's Patrick. My name is Patrick.

OSGOOD: Mmm. Yes. I know how it feels, Craig. It's like you've got your very own storm cloud overhead.

BEN: It's like you've tripped and fallen and a child kicks dust into your eyes.

OSGOOD: It's like a woman spitting in your face.

BEN: And the woman is your mother.

OSGOOD: It's unlike happiness.

BEN: Peace and comfort.

OSGOOD: Ejaculation.

PATRICK: (*attempts to escape, distressed*) Out of my way. Out of my way.

BEN *and* OSGOOD *chase him, stand in his way.*

OSGOOD: Well, well. It looks like we've struck a chord.

PATRICK: Stand aside.

BEN: He's hiding something.

OSGOOD: You're unhappy. Aren't you, Craig?

PATRICK: No.

BEN: You've forgotten who you are.

PATRICK: Just let me pass.

OSGOOD: Something in your life has made you forget.

BEN: The good times.

OSGOOD: The happy times.

BEN: The peaches and plums.

OSGOOD: The evenings on the beach, stargazing.

BEN: Looking up at the heavens.

OSGOOD: Saying, "It's fine to be alive."

BEN: "It's keen to be alive."

OSGOOD: "When you've got good friends."

BEN: "And a little bit of whiskey."

OSGOOD: Have you forgotten all that, Craig?

PATRICK: (*reaches into his pocket, produces his wallet*) Here. Look. Look for yourself. My identification says I'm Patrick Daniels. Look!

OSGOOD: What's this?

BEN: He's made himself phony ID.

OSGOOD: Why on earth did you do that, Craig?

PATRICK: It's not fake. That's my name.

OSGOOD: What do you think we are? Crazy?

BEN: We know who you really are, Craig.

OSGOOD: Come on, Craig. Come on back and sit down for a minute.

PATRICK: No. I'm leaving.

BEN: Won't you just hear us out?

OSGOOD: Come on. What harm will it do? Just one more minute. And if you don't like what we have to say, then by all means, go ahead and leave.

Beat.

PATRICK: You'll let me go?

OSGOOD: Of course, Craig. Of course. Anything you desire.

> BEN *brings a chair, places it behind* PATRICK. OSGOOD *eases him down.*

BEN: (*softly*) Thaaaat's a boy. Thaaaat's a boy. You're such a gentleman, Craig. I knew you would listen to what we have to say.

> *Beat.*

OSGOOD: Now. Isn't it possible that we're right? That you've lost your mind and convinced yourself that you're Patrick Whoseitsname?

PATRICK: (*shakes his head adamantly*) That's who I am.

OSGOOD: But how can you be sure? If you've lost your mind, I think it's safe to say that you can't be sure of anything.

BEN: Why would we make something like this up, Craig? Why?

PATRICK: I don't know.

OSGOOD: Something might have happened along the way, Craig. Something may have snapped.

BEN: Cracked.

OSGOOD: And you constructed this new persona to get by.

PATRICK: (*again, shaking his head*) Mmm-mmm.

OSGOOD: Oh, come on Craig. Come on. Something must have happened.

BEN: What is it, Craig? What is it that happened to you?

OSGOOD: Was it a woman? Did she ransack your heart?

PATRICK: No. It isn't a woman. There was never a woman.

BEN: Was it the stress then? Did you collapse under the pressure?

> PATRICK *shakes his head.*

OSGOOD: Was it the world itself? Is it too big? Too hairy?

PATRICK: No.

BEN: Did you not like who you were?

OSGOOD: It's a tough world. A horrible world.

PATRICK: (*stands*) I've listened to you. Now let me go.

They block him.

BEN: Oooh. But Craig, we're trying to bring you back. We love you.

OSGOOD: Do you admit that it's possible, Craig? Do you?

PATRICK: I . . .

BEN: Yes?

OSGOOD: What, Craig? What is it?

PATRICK: (*almost defeated*) I wish you would let me go.

BEN: Oh, Craig. Just admit it's possible. That's the first step toward recovery.

PATRICK: (*with less conviction*) You're mad. Both of you are mad.

OSGOOD: Isn't it more likely that it's you?

BEN: There's two of us, Craig.

OSGOOD: If we're mad . . . it's unlikely that we'd both share the same delusion.

BEN: It's you, Craig. Admit it.

OSGOOD: You must admit it's possible.

PATRICK: (*subdued*) No.

BEN: (*touching* **PATRICK**'s *shoulder*) Don't be afraid, Craig.

OSGOOD: Don't fret.

BEN: Don't fear.

OSGOOD: Don't worry.

BEN: We'll take you to someone who can fix this type of thing.

OSGOOD: A head shrinker.

BEN: Or a prostitute.

OSGOOD: And soon you'll be as happy as ever.

PATRICK: (*unhappily*) I am happy.

Beat. **BEN** guides **PATRICK** back to his seat.

BEN: Oh. Come now, Craig. Let's not fool ourselves. We all know that's not true.

OSGOOD: No. You're not the man you were.

BEN: You used to be such a chipper fella.

OSGOOD: You laughed and laughed *ad nauseam*.

BEN: You had all the girls.

OSGOOD: Big ones. Small ones.

BEN: Long hair. Short hair.

OSGOOD: Beautiful. Ugly.

BEN: Some with teeth. Some without.

OSGOOD: You were the life of the party.

BEN: The prince of the ball.

OSGOOD: Wouldn't you like to be that way again?

BEN: Wouldn't you like to be yourself?

OSGOOD: It's much better than what you are now, I'll tell you.

BEN: Way better.

Pause. **BEN** *and* **OSGOOD** *speak slowly, softly.*

OSGOOD: So what do you say, Craig? Are you ready to come back to us?

BEN: Come on, Craig. A paradise awaits you.

OSGOOD: There's no need to worry.

BEN: To fret.

OSGOOD: To fear.

BEN: We'll never leave you alone, Craig.

OSGOOD: We'll be with you, Craig. Every step of the way.

PATRICK *sits silently, as though he's contemplating it. Lights gradually fade.*

[End]

Necessary Comforts

BY

D.J. MITCHELL

Necessary Comforts was produced for the Brave New Play
Rites Festival in Vancouver in 1992 with
the following cast and crew:

JILL ZWICK: Beverly Bardal
EMMA SCHULTZ: Alison Jean Bell
ALAN PELLETIER: Greg Doerkson
FARMER: Michael O'Donnell
RCMP OFFICER: Robert Sapiecha
ROLAND HERTIG: Dean Way
TALK SHOW HOST: Jane MacFarlane

Directed by Gerald Van der Woude

CHARACTERS:

EMMA SCHULTZ: *Litigant*
NATASHA UBERT: *Talk Show Host*
CONSTABLE ORTOFILL: *First officer at the scene*
JILL ZWICK: *Friend of Emma's*
ROLAND HERTIG: *Former common-law husband of Emma Schultz, successful bee farmer*
ALLAN PELLETIER: *Emma's lawyer*
FARMER: *Paul Christiensen,* **EMMA**'s *employer*

SETTING: *Spot light on* **EMMA SCHULTZ**, *Stage Right. The rest of the stage is in darkness.* **EMMA** *is sitting upstage of a frame which represents a large video screen. Stage Left of the frame is a pewter urn on a pedestal. A velvet cord, supported on four stands, surrounds the urn.*

EMMA: My mother had a story she told me when I was a little girl. She told me I was in the medical history books. Somewhere, my case is written down. I had a stomach valve, it didn't close, and the doctors fed me through my big toe. The one on my left foot. Of course, in these books, they don't write your name. I would have to look for a listing under Baby E, or Infant S. Baby E grew up to be me. Emma Schultz. The very same Emma who once went away with a boy in a red pickup truck to live on a bee farm. Do you know the sound of bees in summer clover? Bees too many to count. A world of clover. And my very own life, it got so small I could not fit inside it. I left the bees, the farm, the man.

When she has finished speaking, **EMMA** *freezes. Talk show host* **NATASHA UBERT** *steps out of the shadows, crosses to a podium.*

NATASHA: Welcome, Good People of the Land. Welcome to "Let's Talk."

Lights up full, accompanied by upbeat talk show theme music. A line of four chairs is revealed. They are placed in a shallow curve,

facing Downstage. Above and upstage of the chairs, "Let's Talk"
is written in large flowing script.

NATASHA: Welcome to "Let's Talk." Today we are going to spend our
time together talking, really talking. Good People, please welcome my guests. First off, I'd like to introduce Constable Ortofill.

CONSTABLE ORTOFILL *enters from upstage, goes to a guest*
chair, sits. There is some confusion as **NATASHA** *indicates that the*
CONSTABLE *should choose a different seat.*

NATASHA: Next, we'll welcome Emma Schultz's best friend, Jill
Zwick.

JILL *enters, seats herself while* **NATASHA** *leads the audience*
applause.

NATASHA: Emma's common-law husband, Roland Hertig.

NATASHA *claps as* **ROLAND** *enters and sits down.*

NATASHA: Emma's lawyer, Allan Pelletier.

NATASHA *claps as* **PELLETIER** *enters and seats himself.*

NATASHA: Our guests today have a very compelling story to tell. The
story concerns Emma Schultz and her struggle with our country's legal system. Here is a story of hope . . . and of tragedy.

NATASHA *crosses upstage of* **JILL ZWICK**, *places a hand on* **JILL**'s
shoulder.

NATASHA: Jill, you were Emma's closest friend for many years. Tell us
why Emma was able to hang on for so long. After all, the battle
in the courts went on for years. Many many years.
JILL: She could be very stubborn. Very careful about getting things
just right. Ever since we were little. She would take a ruler to

NECESSARY COMFORTS   ▸   275

measure the exact middle of a candy bar, so she could cut it exactly in half. So the pieces would be exactly equal. It's hard to cut a candy bar exactly in half, but Emma had to try.

JILL begins to sniffle. NATASHA crosses to her podium, retrieves a large box of tissues, hands it to JILL, who continues to sniffle off and on during the remainder of the show.

NATASHA: You see the legal battle as Emma's way of setting things straight, Jill?

JILL: The legal thing. It was a mess. A sticky mess. Her lawyer, you read what he said in the papers. As if he cared. As if Emma's troubles meant anything to him.

PELLETIER: My client was not the easiest person to deal with.

During the show, NATASHA paces about, working the guests and the audience.

NATASHA: You were Ms. Schultz's lawyer for many years, is that correct?

PELLETIER: Circumstances of the court action evolved over time.

JILL: The case dragged out for years. All he cared about was getting paid. When some land finally got sold last year, you can be sure the lawyers took every penny.

PELLETIER: Initially my client was charged a small retainer.

NATASHA: A small retainer?

PELLETIER: Something under two thousand.

JILL: He could have left a few dollars for Emma. Her living in that tiny basement suite, looking after old man Whatsit, his galunking sons, working for pennies.

PELLETIER: The situation soon became a pro bono matter, community service work.

NATASHA: Let's talk to the common-law husband. Roland Hertig. Emma left you. Why?

ROLAND: You tell me. The mental thing I was dealing with, her mental state, who knows? I mean, toe tubes. She went on and on about that. Give me a break here.

JILL: He never let her be. Never left her alone. She couldn't go off for ten minutes without him buzzing around. She couldn't even go to the grocery store by herself—well, she didn't drive. He made sure of that. Said she didn't have any road sense, she'd run into a tree, kill herself. Honestly.

ROLAND: Listen, the whole mess probably started with her crazy family. And the people she knew. Her so-called friends.

NATASHA: Conflict, passion, dreams gone wrong. A legal tangle, wouldn't you say Mr. Pelletier?

PELLETIER: I was aware of course from the start that we had a favorable case. Her common-law husband had treated her shabbily.

NATASHA: What kind of treatment are we talking about?

PELLETIER: Well, unfortunately, the abuse seemed to be chiefly, if not entirely, of a psychological nature rather than having a physical component.

ROLAND: I never laid a hand on her.

NATASHA: Unfortunately? Mr. Pelletier? Why do you say unfortunately?

PELLETIER: There's apt to be more sympathy generated in circumstances where the abuse is noticeable, where it is physical, rather than psychological. Also, in cases of physical abuse, there will be, more often than not, a paper trail, a series of doctor's reports, police reports . . .

NATASHA: This is the world we live in, Good People, where it is better to have a black eye than an argument. Makes you wonder, doesn't it? Let's talk to Constable Ortofill. Constable, in your opinion, was this case anything out of the ordinary?

CONSTABLE: It's not the usual thing out here.

NATASHA: Not the usual thing?

CONSTABLE: The housekeeper shot herself in the head. Used a .22 calibre rifle. A pea-shooter. Goes to show how anyone can accomplish what they put their mind to. Steady nerves, a little bit of know-how, and it's done.

NATASHA: A little bit of know-how.

CONSTABLE: One bullet through the centre of the forehead. (*indicates with a finger*) It went in neat and clean, came out at the base of the skull. About here. (*indicating with a head-turn, and a pointed finger*)

That's the angle of the barrel talking. A lot of them, you know, they like to set themselves up with real big fire power. They can barely lift this cannon, it covers nearly the entire face. When they squeeze the trigger, you've got pieces everywhere. They're going for the big show. Makes it hard on everyone. No, she did it nice and neat. Considerate.

NATASHA: Thank you, Constable, for that insider's look at the tragedy. Let's talk to our studio audience. What do you think of Emma's story?

NATASHA solicits opinions from audience members. A man seated in the first row raises his hand. NATASHA approaches him, points her mike.

FARMER: I knew her.

NATASHA: You knew her.

FARMER: She was a real steady worker.

NATASHA: Who might that be?

FARMER: The Schultz woman. Emma Schultz.

NATASHA: And who are you?

FARMER: Paul Christiensen. She worked for me. Yah. I didn't have any complaints. She lived in the basement. Yah. We got it fixed up down there. My wife, she did the decorating. She passed on three years ago this March.

NATASHA: I'm so sorry to hear that. How about a hand for Paul Christiensen?

NATASHA leads the applause.

NATASHA: Jill, you and Emma were friends for a long time. When did you first meet?

JILL: Third grade. Shilliman Elementary School. Mrs. Porter's class.

NATASHA: Tell us about your friend, Jill.

JILL: We went through everything together. Everything. We had some wonderful times. A lot of our dreams, the fairy tales, they came true. The end of junior high school, we were flowers. Emma and me. It seemed to happen overnight. All of a sudden. We blossomed. Like that. "This mantle of loveliness, descending." That was what we called it. Emma read that somewhere. Overnight, we were the most popular, the most talked about, the most copied girls in school. We walked in beauty. The sky was the limit.

NATASHA: Let's find out how Roland Hertig met Emma Schultz. I understand it was a high school romance. How about it, Roland?

ROLAND: Yah. We met in high school. Start of senior high. I couldn't get enough of her, she couldn't get enough of me. She looked like nothing I ever saw before. I'm talking heart-stopper.

CONSTABLE: Yah, a quick glance, she looked okay. In fact, she looked neat and tidy. The back of the head, you know, who sees it. I won that bet.

NATASHA: I thought betting was pretty well illegal, Constable Ortofill.

CONSTABLE: It was a friendly bet. Just between members of the force. No money involved. When the calls come in, we place our bets. Will this one be open, or will it be shut? It's something we do. To pass the time. Lighten things up. It can be a hard job. Anyway, I drive out there, walk out to the scene. Her employer found her. She was stretched out, staring straight up. A quick glance, she looked fine. Open casket, all the way. I won my bet.

NATASHA: (*crosses to the urn*) As it turned out, the family chose another option, Constable. Roland, I understand you gave Emma three thousand dollars when she left. You operate a successful business, Mr. Hertig. Was three thousand dollars an equitable division of assets?

ROLAND: I gave her what her Gram gave her. No more. I told her, "Walk out that door right now, Emma, that's it. That's all you're getting out of this place." She knew what she was doing.

JILL: Eight months after Emma left, that one got married.

ROLAND: I cut my losses. She wasn't coming back.

NATASHA: It sounds like a deal was being done here. Smart player unloads longtime investment, cuts losses. Paul, you found her.

FARMER: I found her on the other side of my number two dairy barn. My dogs found her. She went away. Gone for three days. From Sunday, until Tuesday. The dishes were piling up. We don't do a lot of cleaning, the boys and me.

ROLAND: She disappeared one day, with that friend of hers. I let her go, what the hell. I was planning some time off, some duck hunting, the like, didn't need her on the farm. She came back five days later with this thing on her backside. A bee. Tattooed right on her butt. That Zwick woman put her up to it. She was a bad influence. Full of stupid ideas concerning any topic you could name.

JILL: Look who's talking. Some prize, you, Roland Hertig. Oh my dear Emma.

ROLAND: It was a goddamn killer bee. Inked on permanent. Another one of those bad breeds come from who knows where. Like AIDS and those toads make you see things. We were supposed to be a team. Her and me. This was not team work, her going off, getting a tattoo on her butt. That was the day it all went to hell. I told her. "Tattoos are for sluts, they're nasty whore's tricks."

NATASHA: Very strong sentiments, Mr. Hertig.

ROLAND: She's the one killed herself.

*The **FARMER** raises his hands. **NATASHA** crosses to him with her microphone.*

FARMER: My wife, she went in her sleep. She was fine on the Tuesday. The next day, Wednesday, she was gone. She went in her sleep. The next day. It's a very big change to make. A very big change. It's hard when they go.

NATASHA: Yes. Of course. It is very difficult, when a loved one passes on. Let's give Paul a hand, for reminding us. No matter the circumstances, it's always going to hurt.

***NATASHA** leads the applause.*

CONSTABLE: She did it neat and clean. To her credit. A lot of suicides, they go for overkill. People see too many movies. They think they need the big guns, the heavy ammo. Wrong. You can do it like that. (*snaps his fingers*)

NATASHA: Thank you Constable Ortofill. Now Jill, what do you think was the connection between Roland and Emma? Why did they get together in the first place?

JILL: Well. Okay. He looked good, he had plans. It was a small town. We didn't have all that many options.

NATASHA: Roland. What kept you together, all those years? Fifteen years common-law, without benefit of legal ties. It's a long time.

ROLAND: Like nothing I ever saw before. She just walked into my world. Right from the get go, she put out for me. I could not believe my luck. That's when I knew it. I was going to make things happen, and this girl was going to be by my side. We moved out to the farm after graduation. Her Gram died, left a few bucks. I had some money. Land was cheap. I knew what to do with it. In no time at all we were rolling in clover.

NATASHA: Mr. Pelletier, what's your take on all this? Speaking as a lawyer.

PELLETIER: Ms Ubert, Natasha. I always speak as a lawyer. But seriously, the farm clearly was a profit making venture. The common-law husband's contribution to my client's material well-being was grossly inadequate. It was my sincere belief that terms of property and capital disbursement in such instances must be negotiated equitably. That's what we fought for. And I will tell you this. Public sentiment was in alignment with my client's hopes.

NATASHA: Are you sure there was all that much support, Mr. Pelletier? Where were Emma's defenders? Who took her in when she left her common-law husband of fifteen years?

JILL: I told her she could stay with us. We had the spare back bedroom. I told her, "Stay as long as you need to, Emma." She said no. She had her pride.

NATASHA *crosses upstage of the chairs to console* JILL.

CONSTABLE: It was only the third one, all year. And I'm covering a lot of territory. Number one shot himself in a cornfield. Number two hung himself under a tree, a willow, down by Pauper's Creek. Number two didn't have any money problems. Not that we were able to establish. They like to do it away from the house. They don't want the families stumbling over the body. They think they're safe too. Nobody's going to walk in and stop them when they're setting up the rope or the gun or what have you. Mind you, if they're planning on asphyxiation, it almost has to be an inside situation. They have to shut the windows tight, towels need to be stuffed under doors—

NATASHA: (*cuts off the* CONSTABLE) Yes, uh, thank you for that analysis.

NATASHA *crosses to the urn, picks it up, hands it to* PELLETIER, *who takes it reluctantly.*

NATASHA: Mr. Pelletier, many people would hold the then current legal system accountable for this tragedy.

PELLETIER: I explained to my client at the start that the situation might easily become quite protracted in nature. Five years after we began, we secured a favourable ruling, one which would have secured for my client the necessary comforts. It was a happy time. I took the legal team and Ms. Schultz to dinner. More than one bottle was dispatched that evening. Sad to say however, it was merely the beginning. We spent years attempting to dislodge a settlement from Mr. Hertig. Finally, one small section of the jointly assessed property was sold. Twenty-five thousand dollars was realized from the sale. And this was only the beginning, in my opinion. These funds went to the firm, in partial payment for services rendered. As you might imagine, this was a blow to Ms. Schultz's optimism. I felt the frustration very keenly myself.

ROLAND: Valerie walked in four months after she walked out. We made it legal right away. Why fool around? I mean, look at what happened with her and me. It's like we never got off the starting block. Hell, I could live without kids. It didn't matter to me. I told her that.

In a gesture of reconciliation, PELLETIER *hands the urn to* ROLAND.

JILL: I sent a message to her, at the service. I reminded her, everyone is young once in their life. Young and pretty like us. "Don't forget," I told her. "This mantle of loveliness, descending." I sent her a prayer.

The **FARMER** *rises in his seat while* **JILL** *is speaking.* **NATASHA** *crosses to him on* **JILL**'s *last words.*

FARMER: Yah. Emma Schultz. She shot herself with one of my .22s. Good for squirrels, rats. I miss her too. Not like my wife, but I do.

NATASHA: Thank you for those lovely sentiments, Paul Christiensen. I'm afraid we're out of time, Jill Zwick, Roland Hertig, Allan Pelletier, Constable Ortofill, thank you all for being our guests today on "Let's Talk."

NATASHA *and Guests freeze, backlit, with spot on* **EMMA** *inside video frame. Lights on others fade out as* **EMMA** *crosses Downstage.*

EMMA: Early this morning of May 17th, in the dairy farmer's house, I have a dream of bees. A blanket of bees all over me. Bees on my face, a thousand little tickles, with dusty feet from the flowers. I get out of bed, I dress, I water my pots of African violets. Now I am ready. I will put on my honey-coloured sweater with the yellow flowers across the shoulders, and my big black rubber boots. I will walk along to the end of their corn field past the old falling down white barn where they keep their rusty tools. What a day it is. The sky is so blue, so big. A day to go straight up into the sky.

[End]

The Cipher and the Beagle

BY

CRAIG BARRON

The Cipher and the Beagle was produced for the Brave New Play Rites Festival in Vancouver in 1998 with the following cast and crew:

BRENDA: Kerriann Cardinal
OLIVER: Andrew Macleod
MOTHER: Jean Bell
MARLON: Martin Blais
MARLON'S WIFE: Monica Szewczyk

Directed by Joven Lin

OLIVER: *in his twenties, unemployed*
BERTHE: *his mother*
MARLON: *fifty, a communications mogul*
BRENDA: *twenties, a security guard employed by* MARLON
DONNA: MARLON'*s wife, a recently deceased journalist*

ACT ONE

SETTING: *The east end of a large Canadian city. Lights up inside*
BERTHE'*s house.* OLIVER *sits on the floor reading a dictionary,*
an open newspaper on his lap. BERTHE *practices modern dance.*

SCENE ONE

OLIVER: . . . evict, evidence, evidently . . .
BERTHE: Oliver?
OLIVER: . . . evidently, evil, evil eye . . .
BERTHE: What are you doing?
OLIVER: Evil-minded, evince . . .
BERTHE: Are you making up a story?
OLIVER: . . . eviscerate . . . Disembowel . . . empty of vital contents. (*goes back to his newspaper*) That's what I thought. (*reads*) "The puppy was eviscerated."
BERTHE: Terrible.
OLIVER: True. Front page news.
BERTHE: Newspapers are only good for lining cages.
OLIVER: No cages here since you lost the store.
BERTHE: Yes, so we don't need papers in the house.
OLIVER: I like to know what's going on.
BERTHE: And look for reasons to stay inside. No, don't answer then. I should've pushed you out of the nest years ago.
OLIVER: I'm not a bird.
BERTHE: You know what I mean. I was too protective. Giving you a job in the pet store. How lucky you were.
OLIVER: Cleaning cages. Draining aquariums. Washing floors.

BERTHE: Feeding, hours playing with the animals, not so bad.

OLIVER: Saw how many generations of rodents come into the world.

BERTHE: Puppies too.

OLIVER: I don't want to talk about dogs.

BERTHE: Things don't always work out the way we want.

OLIVER: You were globalized.

BERTHE: What kind of word is that?

OLIVER: Read the papers. Supposed to be a good thing.

BERTHE: Speaking of good things, you know I could use a treat.

OLIVER: Everything's closed.

BERTHE: Not the donut shop, never the donut shop.

OLIVER: It's not a shop. It's a chain.

BERTHE: Raspberry, blueberry, lemon, strawberry. Twelve of whatever you want. It's not so bad the night.

> **BERTHE** *hands him some money.* **OLIVER** *exits.*

SCENE TWO

A "restored" downtown city square: a renovated sewer, a small fake stone bridge. **OLIVER** *enters holding a bag of donuts. He is uninspired by the night, but seems to recognize something about the locale.* **BRENDA** *enters quietly. She watches as* **OLIVER** *sniffs a donut, tastes it and spits. He chucks the donut into the sewer.*

BRENDA: Hello, sir!

OLIVER: Hello?

BRENDA: We don't allow that.

OLIVER: Excuse me?

BRENDA: The object that you disposed of.

OLIVER: It's only a sewer.

BRENDA: It's long been clean. And private property. There are laws

OLIVER: The river, the old stone bridge, wasn't this a historic square?

BRENDA: Long privatized.

OLIVER: I read the papers. Nothing about it being for sale.

BRENDA: Why in the world would one need to read about it? And private, as I said. And you are trespassing. Now would you please clean up your litter?

She extracts a plastic bag from her pocket, hands it to **OLIVER**. *He searches in the sewer.*

OLIVER: Sewer's dry. Not too clean.
BRENDA: Keep looking!
OLIVER: (*touches something in the sewer*) Garbage. A lady's shoe. Purple . . . A gown . . . black, smooth . . . a leg!

OLIVER *recoils.* **BRENDA** *approaches.*

BRENDA: You're a bit of a joker? Get out of here.

She sees **DONNA***'s body. After a deep pause she props it up.*

OLIVER: Dead?
BRENDA: Evidently . . .
OLIVER: She looks nice.
BRENDA: Nice?
OLIVER: Peaceful. I've seen that face before.
BRENDA: A criminal? Or someone in the entertainment industry. (**BRENDA** *sees the pill bottle beside the body and pockets it.*) Shall we make a report to the authorities you and I?
OLIVER: Nothing to do with me.
BRENDA: The process is quite straight forward.
OLIVER: I should be getting home.
BRENDA: Someone waiting for you?
OLIVER: My mother.
BRENDA: I was an orphan myself. (*gently indicates that* **OLIVER** *should follow her*) My name is Brenda.
OLIVER: (*follows*) I'm Oliver. Would you like a donut?

BRENDA *takes one. She bites and jam squirts into her mouth.*

SCENE THREE

MARLON's *penthouse office overlooking the city square. He looks at the pill bottle.* BRENDA *eats a donut.*

MARLON: Seconal.
BRENDA: Yes, it's excellently potent.
MARLON: And illegal. A last little adventure for Donna. The bitch. Could you dispose of that thing!

BRENDA *puts donut in a plastic bag and pockets it.*

BRENDA: If there's anything I can do.
MARLON: You found the body?
BRENDA: No, not at first.
MARLON: The boy? The one outside? His name again?
BRENDA: Oliver.
MARLON: Oliver. Odd. Archaic.
BRENDA: He is somewhat strange. Shall I bring him in?
MARLON: No, one moment. You understand the situation is—
BRENDA: Yes, it is.
MARLON: You found him wandering?
BRENDA: Standing. Stunned. Pretty stupid I think. He littered. Like . . .
MARLON: Like?
BRENDA: As if he were a dog.
MARLON: And before, anything suspicious?
BRENDA: No, I was checking the parking lodges, counting your cars. She must have slipped into the square quickly.
MARLON: Yes, she was good at that, could dart like an eel. How did the boy find the body, exactly?
BRENDA: When I asked him to clean up his mess in the sewer.
MARLON: Not sewer, channel. And what was obvious to you was not to him.
BRENDA: He seemed to recognize her face, but couldn't put a name.
MARLON: That was often the case. It annoyed her. How . . . how was her face?
BRENDA: Sort of white, but with a bit of shine.
MARLON: No bruises then?

BRENDA: Would it be better if . . . ?

MARLON: Don't touch her! We don't have much time, the presses for the morning edition roll in under an hour. Angle. We'll need an angle. The boy. Bring him in.

BRENDA *goes to the door and leads in* **OLIVER**, *still carrying his donut bag.*

OLIVER: Hello.

MARLON: What are you staring at?

OLIVER: I don't know. I think I've seen you before.

MARLON: Indeed. You express familiarity, but no knowledge. Interesting.

OLIVER: I thought we were reporting a body?

BRENDA: And so we are.

OLIVER: This isn't a police station.

MARLON: A highly inefficient way to report an event, wouldn't you say, Brenda?

OLIVER: I don't—

MARLON: Don't worry, young man. I assure you the story will be dispatched.

OLIVER: This is a newspaper?

BRENDA: The newspaper. Isn't it exciting?

MARLON: So, Oliver. Story.

OLIVER: Pardon?

MARLON: We need to construct our story.

OLIVER: Our story?

MARLON: We have a story. We have, a body, and? . . . a location. Yes the corpse's role is clear. Clear in its obscurity: a beautiful victim whose life was accidentally, or purposefully quelled. Oliver's part, however, is not so clear.

OLIVER: No, it isn't, because I don't have one. Can I go home now?

BRENDA *blocks the door.*

MARLON: So, you do have a home? Not peripatetic?

OLIVER: Excuse me?

MARLON: Homeless, a wanderer?

BRENDA: He lives with his mother. Not successful, obviously.

MARLON: And how does your mother get by? Some sort of government cheque?

OLIVER: She squeaks by.

MARLON: The persisting munificence of the state. Time to rework a feature on the public debt, "Donuts for the Idle" perhaps? Now our Oliver, it's unlikely he would have been an acquaintance of the victim?

BRENDA: Obviously.

MARLON: And an agenda of a political nature seems unlikely?

BRENDA: No, though I understand there were a few against the lady.

OLIVER: Hey, it sounds like you guys know who she was.

MARLON: Patience, lad, we'll find you a role in our story. Brenda, do you think Mr. Oliver passes as an attractive male?

BRENDA: As things go in that regard . . . hard to say, he might to some.

MARLON: Not too pale?

BRENDA: Pale is sometimes trendy.

MARLON: So, the victim could have been involved with Mr. Oliver, on a physical level. Sex. Does sex interest you, Oliver?

OLIVER: No, thank you.

MARLON: Sex. The steadfast angle. Simple. A love affair gone awry, perhaps. And the victim's subsequent suicide. Yes, that's good, an anchor in veracity.

OLIVER: Excuse me, What you're letting slip into the air here. You know the dead lady, and now you know how she died.

MARLON: But newsworthy? A person's death by their own hands: tired, tawdry, artless despair, it's so . . . it's what Brenda?

BRENDA: Boring.

MARLON: Precisely. Unless the victim had some stature, unattainable status; the rumour mill will churn, and those close could come out in an unfortunate light. Donna would have wished no such thing.

OLIVER: Donna? Who is Donna? Your wife? Okay, I get it. She got moody and bumped herself off.

MARLON: How sugar diminishes the language. (*paces, inspired*) Deadline! Our story. Passion in the new millennium. What paths does it take. What lover's potion befell my brooding bride.

BRENDA: That's beautiful.

MARLON: Yes, the old story reinvented. What shall we say? "Donna's exclusive, executive lifestyle led her to exotic, erotic encounters. Encounters with nameless souls. She became lost in a disaffecting world."

BRENDA: Ohhh! But isn't that too much? Too much poetry for the readership?

MARLON: Casting hooks. This story must live on. A movie, a teleseries.

OLIVER: You're going to lie. And then lie some more.

MARLON: What a simpleton. Shall we call you Simon?

OLIVER: I know things.

MARLON: Do you, Oliver? Tell us what you know. What knowledge have you gleaned from your vocationless life?

OLIVER: I worked in my Mom's pet shop . . . The gestation period for gerbils is twenty-five days.

BRENDA: Disgusting.

OLIVER: Puffer fish prefer bloodworms to shrimp. Tiger barbs peck at Angelfish, shred the fins and body, until they give up the ghost.

MARLON: Are you saying that you live in an aquarium, Oliver?

BRENDA: He's trying to make up a story.

OLIVER: Maybe I'm saying I have a rich inner life.

MARLON: Hardly marketable. Shall we find you a role? I say, Brenda, we really should go for the jugular here.

BRENDA *extracts a dog leash. She stands behind* **OLIVER**. *She strangles him.*

MARLON: "The lovely victim had developed a taste for . . . individuals, usually pale young men, who were into . . . ritual, romantic rites, psychodrama," how's it called . . . autoasphyxiation? . . .

BRENDA: Erotic asphyxia. Call it scarfing in some circles. Oxygen deprivation giving severe orgasm.

OLIVER: Ahhh! (*he collapses*)

MARLON: Could use some elaborative details. Will you call the research department when you're done there?

BRENDA: Call the research . . . ? My job description. Are you saying that I have a promotion?

MARLON: How does Communications Manager sound?
BRENDA: Yes!

> **MARLON** *picks up the pill bottle and hands it to* **BRENDA**. *She puts it in her pocket. As* **MARLON** *continues to speak* **BRENDA** *drags* **OLIVER**'s *body out the door. He still clutches the donuts.*

MARLON: A young man's death, "Death by misadventure. And her guilt was overpowering. She carried his body to an anonymous site, and took her own life."

SCENE FOUR

> *The moon journeys over the city square. As* **MARLON** *speaks* **BRENDA** *entwines* **OLIVER** *and* **DONNA**'s *bodies.*

MARLON'S VOICE: Front page, above the fold. A photo from a charity ball. Donna looked divine in black. And on her neck, a single strand of gray pearls. My mother's pearls. The circulation doubles. After several weeks of discreet mourning the victim's husband, the CEO of a communications empire, consents to an interview. The circulation doubles again.

> **BRENDA** *positions the pill bottle. She takes photos. She wrests the bag of donuts from* **OLIVER**'s *fist, takes two for herself, then dumps the remains onto the bodies.* **BRENDA** *leaves. The moon disappears.*

[End]

Recess

BY

CORRINA HODGSON

Recess was produced for the Brave New Play Rites
Festival in Vancouver in 2002 with
the following cast and crew:

ROSE: Tara Avery
VICTORIA: Ruth Brown
JESSICA: Sarah Henriques

Directed by Robin Bancroft-Wilson
Costumes: Kathy Kibble

OTHER PRODUCTIONS OF *Recess*:

FemmeFest, Sarasvati Productions,
Winnipeg, Manitoba, 2004

Hysteria Festival, Nightwood Theatre,
Toronto, Ontario, 2003

Off-off Broadway, manhattantheatresource,
Estrogenius Festival, New York, N.Y., 2002

CHARACTERS

JESSICA, *14*
ROSE, *14*
VICTORIA, *12*

SETTING: *Behind the coach house of St. Mary's Academy for girls. Each scene takes place after a major holiday in the academic year. The play spans the school year.*

SCENE ONE

Single spot on JESSICA. *She sits rocking herself, holding an X-acto blade. In a burst of energy, she carves into her thigh.*

JESSICA: Susan "Storm" Richards. AKA Double Malice. AKA The Invisible Girl. First meets Reed Richards when he is a boarder at her mother's house. She is twelve. He is twenty-three. She instantly falls in love. He does not.

Well, she's twelve.

But, through patience and careful, gentle persistence, Susan "Storm" Richards, AKA Double Malice, AKA The Invisible Girl, eventually convinces Reed to marry her—this is years and years later—and together they combine their powers to fight the rampant evil in our universe.

SCENE TWO

Outdoors. Behind the coach house of St. Mary's Academy for Girls.

Early September. Gray and threatening to rain.

JESSICA *rifles through her backpack. She is in full uniform—kilt, blazer, blouse, kneesocks and oxfords. She takes something from her bag and pockets it. She furtively looks about. She sees something and races back to her bag. She grabs a comic book, plops to the ground and pretends to be fully engrossed in reading it.*

Moments later, **ROSE** *and* **VICTORIA** *enter. They are engaged in a pinching contest. Each grabs the other, inflicting the maximum amount of pain they can. They are high energy and the game is flirting with not being so fun. Then, they spot* **JESSICA**.

Pause.

ROSE: Ignore her. She's not really there. (*to* **JESSICA**) Are you?

JESSICA *does not respond.*

ROSE: (*to* **VICTORIA**) See?

ROSE *pulls out a pack of cigarettes.* **VICTORIA** *does the same. They light up.* **JESSICA** *watches.*

ROSE: (*without looking at* **JESSICA**) What are you staring at?

JESSICA *goes back to reading.*

ROSE: That's what I thought.

VICTORIA *snickers.* **ROSE** *follows suit.*

ROSE: Fucking newbies.
VICTORIA: Yeah.
ROSE: (*to* **VICTORIA**) Baaaaaaa–aaaaaaaaaaaa.

VICTORIA *shoves* **ROSE**. **ROSE** *shoves back.*

VICTORIA: Hey.
ROSE: (*mimicking*) Hey.

VICTORIA *shoves harder.* **ROSE** *steps back and almost trips over* **JESSICA**, *who scrambles to her feet.* **ROSE** *and* **JESSICA** *stare at each other for whole, slow seconds.*

ROSE: (*to* JESSICA) You're in the way.

JESSICA: I was here first.

ROSE: Ooooooh. Well then.

> ROSE *makes a face at* VICTORIA, *who snickers, then stops as* JESSICA *takes her own pack of cigarettes from her blazer pocket and lights up.* ROSE *turns and stares.*

VICTORIA: You can get suspended for that, you know.

JESSICA: Duh.

VICTORIA: Just warning ya.

JESSICA: Doesn't seem to bother you.

VICTORIA: Whatever.

ROSE: Well, if you're gonna then you gotta stand over here.

JESSICA: Why would I do that?

ROSE: Cuz I said.

VICTORIA: Yeah. She said.

JESSICA: I don't even do what my mum says, okay?

ROSE: Well, you're gonna do what I say.

JESSICA: Make me.

VICTORIA: You don't really mean that.

> *Pause.*

VICTORIA: Look, she only wants you to stand with us cuz Father Paul can see you from where you are.

JESSICA: I'll take my chances.

ROSE: NO YOU FUCKING WON'T. Listen, newbie, I don't know where you're from and I don't care, but I've been here since grade four, and me and Vic have been smoking here since grade seven, and I'll be damned if I'm gonna get suspended my first year of high school cuz of some tight-assed fuck-for-brains who thinks she's too tough to listen to the way things go around here. So either put that thing out or get your sorry ass over here.

> *Pause.*

JESSICA: Fine.
ROSE: Fine.
VICTORIA: Fine.

The bell rings. JESSICA *stomps her cigarette out and looks pan-
icked.* VICTORIA *and* ROSE *don't react.*

ROSE: Chill.
VICTORIA: It's the warning bell. You still have ten minutes.
JESSICA: What do they ring that for?
ROSE: Cuz they like fucking with our heads.
  All three girls smile.

VICTORIA: (*to* JESSICA) You might wanna push your kneesocks down.
JESSICA: Down?
VICTORIA: Yeah. The only people who pull them up are newbies.
  You'll be marked. Everyone'll totally pick on you. Ask her you
  don't believe me.
ROSE: She's right. Not that I give a shit people pick on you or not.

JESSICA *pushes her kneesocks down.*

VICTORIA: Yeah, that's better. That's way better.

SCENE THREE
Echo of Scene One. JESSICA *sits alone, holding the X-acto blade.*

JESSICA: Once she has combined forces with Reed Richards, AKA
  Mr. Fantastic, Susan "Storm" Richards, AKA Double Malice, AKA
  The Invisible Girl assumes all traditional female duties. She
  designs their costumes and does the grocery shopping. She takes
  a secondary role in fighting bad guys, and often faints after exert-
  ing her powers.
  It doesn't take long for her to say FUCK THIS.
  But then she's gotta figure out what to do. Cuz there's gotta
  be something she can do.

SCENE FOUR

Behind the coach house of St. Mary's Academy. Hallowe'en.
VICTORIA *and* **ROSE** *are smoking.* **VICTORIA** *has angel wings and*
a halo. **ROSE** *is not in costume. Instead, she picks at* **VICTORIA**'s
costume. **VICTORIA** *tries to play along, but she obviously likes her*
costume and is protective of it. **ROSE** *can sense this and goes after*
her hard. **JESSICA** *comes in while this is going on. She lights a*
smoke but keeps her distance.

VICTORIA: (*punching at* **ROSE**) Stop it.
ROSE: Fucking lucky you missed.
VICTORIA: I said STOP.
ROSE: You're such a child.
JESSICA: Do you guys actually like this?
VICTORIA: Like what?
JESSICA: This. What you do to each other?
ROSE: What do we do to each other? (*to* **VICTORIA**) Wouldn't she like
to know.

ROSE *and* **VICTORIA** *smirk.*

JESSICA: You know what? Never mind.
ROSE: Oh, are you through with us, Saint Jessica?

VICTORIA *laughs.*

JESSICA: (*to* **VICTORIA**) You think she's funny?

VICTORIA *shrugs.* **ROSE** *looks to her.*

VICTORIA: (*to* **JESSICA**) You hear Sister Joan's a hermaphrodite?
JESSICA: What?
VICTORIA: Yeah. Linda Tomlinson said so. Said you were, too.
JESSICA: Who the fuck is Linda Tomlinson?
ROSE: So are you?
JESSICA: No.
ROSE: Prove it.

JESSICA: (*pause*) What?

VICTORIA: You heard her.

JESSICA: Why d'you guys hafta do this?

ROSE: Do what? (*to* VICTORIA) Are we doing something? I don't think we're doing something.

VICTORIA: (*to* JESSICA) You think we're doing something?

JESSICA: Whatever.

She stubs her smoke out and goes to leave. As she passes by ROSE, ROSE *snaps her bra strap. She turns around and* VICTORIA *does the same thing.*

JESSICA: Fuck you both.

ROSE: Ooooh.

ROSE and VICTORIA *laugh as* JESSICA *exits.*

SCENE FIVE

JESSICA *stands without her X-acto blade.*

JESSICA: Susan "Storm" Richards, AKA Double Malice, AKA The Invisible Girl sets to work on improving her powers of invisibility. Before long, she can sustain an invisible state for, like, hours.

She also begins to be able to turn other objects invisible. At first, these are just small objects, but as her powers grow, so do the size of the objects she can make disappear.

Although, she still has a bad habit of fainting after she has done this. Cuz she's a girl.

SCENE SIX

Behind the coach house of St. Mary's Academy for Girls. Early January. JESSICA *and* ROSE *stand smoking. They are bundled against a biting cold, although both girls are bare legged, with their kneesocks rolled down about their ankles. They smoke in an awkward silence.*

JESSICA: You see Victoria?

ROSE: Kinda hard to miss.

JESSICA: What happened?

ROSE: Like I would know.

JESSICA: Like you wouldn't.

ROSE: Well, I don't.

JESSICA: I thought she told you everything. I thought you two were, like, inseparable.

ROSE: She's alright. You get anything good for Christmas?

JESSICA: Mostly clothes. You?

ROSE: No. I never get shit.

JESSICA: Bummer.

ROSE: Well, except time off school. I always like getting that. You pass everything?

JESSICA: Yeah. You?

ROSE: Yeah. Well, except math.

JESSICA: You got what's-her-name.

ROSE: Sister Elizabeth.

JESSICA: Yeah. Sister Elizabeth.

ROSE: She's killer.

JESSICA: I heard.

ROSE: She better pass me, or my mum is gonna totally—

VICTORIA enters. She has her hair down, trying unsuccessfully to cover her face. She has a fat lip. ROSE looks at her, then looks away. JESSICA stares.

JESSICA: Hey Victoria.

VICTORIA half acknowledges JESSICA, but mostly stays focussed on ROSE, who still refuses to meet her eye.

JESSICA: So, what happened to you?

VICTORIA: I fell.

JESSICA: On your LIP?

ROSE: She said she fell, alright?

VICTORIA: Got totally wasted.

ROSE: What?

VICTORIA: Yeah. New Year's Eve. I got totally wasted. And fell. On my lip.

JESSICA: (*to* **VICTORIA**) I saw you made honour roll.

VICTORIA: No big deal. It's kinda mandatory at my house.

JESSICA: I think it's cool.

ROSE: Yeah, our Vic's real smart. Aren't ya?

VICTORIA: Whatever.

ROSE: (*to* **JESSICA**) She skipped two grades, you know that?

JESSICA: Fuck off.

ROSE: Ask her.

VICTORIA: It's true. So what?

JESSICA: So how old are you?

VICTORIA: Two years younger than you.

JESSICA: TWELVE?

ROSE: Uh-huh, she's twelve. Twelve in grade nine. Pretty fuckin' smart, hey?

VICTORIA: Rose.

ROSE: (*mimicking*) Rose.

VICTORIA: Cut it out, would ya?

ROSE: Fine.

VICTORIA: Fine. That a new jacket?

ROSE: Yeah. My dad gave it to me for Christmas.

VICTORIA: Nice.

> **ROSE** *looks to* **JESSICA**, *who refuses to react.* **VICTORIA** *lights a cigarette.*

JESSICA: (*to* **VICTORIA**) Does it hurt?

VICTORIA: (*staring at* **ROSE**) Nope.

> **ROSE** *blows a puff of smoke in* **VICTORIA**'s *face.*

VICTORIA: Grow up.

ROSE: Says the pre-teen.

> **VICTORIA** *shoves* **ROSE**. **ROSE** *puts her arms up.*

ROSE: You wanna start this?

> VICTORIA *looks away.* ROSE *comes up behind* VICTORIA *and in an overtly sexual move, traces her neck and collarbone.*

ROSE: You look real pretty today.
JESSICA: Rose. What the fuck.

> ROSE *laughs.*

ROSE: Later kids.

> ROSE *exits. Pause.*

VICTORIA: Don't.
JESSICA: Do you need help?
VICTORIA: No more than you do.

> JESSICA *backs up. She puts out her cigarette and starts kicking at the wall.*

VICTORIA: Oh yeah. That's good. What, forget your fucking blade today?
JESSICA: YOU DON'T HAFTA PICK ON ME JUST CUZ SHE'S AN ASSHOLE.
VICTORIA: Yeah, well. At least she's a friend.

> VICTORIA *puts out her cigarette and leaves.*

SCENE SEVEN

> JESSICA, *without her X-acto blade, addresses the audience. From the shadows,* VICTORIA *listens.*

JESSICA: The Invisible Girl learns to harness her powers. In addition to being able to turn herself and other objects invisible, she also learns to create these really awesome forcefields that she uses defensively or, even better, offensively. She can manipulate them, turning them into staircases or levitating devices.

Although, they still have one drawback. The larger the force-field, the more of a strain it puts on her. All of her good deeds always come with a personal price.

Which really kinda sucks.

SCENE EIGHT

Behind the coach house of St. Mary's Academy for Girls. February. Night. **ROSE** *sits against the wall of the coach house, doing homework with a flashlight. Music from the Valentine's Day dance at the school spills out.* **ROSE** *turns out the flashlight as* **JESSICA** *enters.* **JESSICA** *pulls out her X-acto blade.* **ROSE** *turns on her flashlight.*

JESSICA: Holyfuckinshit. Scare me, why don't you?
ROSE: Well don't lemme stop you.
JESSICA: From what?

ROSE *mimes* **JESSICA**'s *cutting.*

JESSICA: Why d'you hate me so much?
ROSE: Who said anything about hating you?
JESSICA: Like you don't.
ROSE: Your words, not mine.
JESSICA: Are you doing homework?
ROSE: That a problem?
JESSICA: It's the middle of the night. Valentine's Day dance. Freezing cold.
ROSE: I'm waiting for someone.
JESSICA: Victoria's inside.
ROSE: Yeah. And.
JESSICA: And she's dancing with Josh Bauer, you really wanna know.
ROSE: Never said I did, but thanks for the update. You hot for her?
JESSICA: What? Who?
ROSE: You're always, like, watching her.
JESSICA: Am not.

ROSE: You give these, like, updates. On what Victoria's doing. Every hour on the hour.

JESSICA: Right. I have the hots for Victoria and I'm a hermaphrodite.

ROSE *and* JESSICA *laugh.*

ROSE: It's algebra.

JESSICA: I figured. Did you know Victoria liked Josh?

ROSE: She doesn't.

JESSICA: Oh, I think she does. You haven't seen them. I mean, they're, like, all over each other in there. It's so obvious—

ROSE *laughs.*

JESSICA: What.

ROSE: (*mimicking*) It's so obvious, I'm sure.

JESSICA: Like you'd know.

ROSE: Why don't you explain it to me, Saint Jessica?

Pause.

JESSICA: Whatever. You talk and act like you know everything, but it's total bullshit.

ROSE: Is it?

JESSICA: Total. I see right through you, okay?

ROSE: Oh, okay.

JESSICA: You weren't even in there, so I don't know how you think you'd know.

ROSE: Listen you fucking little idiot. I don't HAVE to be in there. I KNOW what Victoria is doing, cuz it's what Victoria ALWAYS does. It's, like, her compulsion. She's a total skank, okay?

JESSICA: What d'you mean "compulsion"?

ROSE: Get a dictionary. What d'you think I mean?

JESSICA: You gonna stop her? Talk to her or something?

ROSE: Okay. Sure.

JESSICA: Why not?

ROSE: Wouldn't make a difference. Trust me.

Pause.

ROSE: Fucking cold out here.

ROSE *gathers her stuff and leaves.*

SCENE NINE

JESSICA *and* VICTORIA *stand in* JESSICA's *spotlight.* VICTORIA *stands behind* JESSICA, *but is still a presence.*

JESSICA: Despite Reed's growing realization of the Invisible Girl's powers, she is never allowed to assume a leadership role. Oh, except for a couple of issues when everyone thinks Reed is dead. Then she takes over, but it's more a figurehead position.

She thinks back to her days as a mere mortal, in her mother's boarding house, and she begins to wish that she'd stayed there. Begins to wish that she'd never met Reed Richards. That she'd never fallen in love with him. But she knows this kinda thinking doesn't lead anywhere. So she pretends she's happy with things the way they are. Pretends that's the way they're supposed to be.

VICTORIA: But it's not. It's not the way it's supposed to be.

JESSICA *realizes—for the first time—that* VICTORIA *is there.*

SCENE TEN

Behind the coach house of St. Mary's Academy for Girls. March. ROSE, VICTORIA *and* JESSICA *are fighting. Chaos.* JESSICA *has* ROSE's *new jacket.* ROSE *is dodging and jumping for it.* JESSICA *hands it to* VICTORIA, *who hands it back to* JESSICA, *all the while eluding* ROSE. ROSE *is growing more and more infuriated. All the girls are pumped on adrenaline.*

JESSICA: How do YOU like it?

VICTORIA: Yeah, how d'you like it? Different now the tables are turned, huh? Doesn't feel so good, huh?

ROSE: Shut up.

JESSICA: No, YOU shut up.

VICTORIA: You got nothing to say, Rose.

JESSICA: Rosie-Posie.

VICTORIA: Rosie-Posie puddin' and pie.

ROSE: Give it back.

JESSICA: Nobody's listening.

VICTORIA: Yeah, Rose. Nobody's listening to you.

JESSICA: Rosie-Posie puddin' and pie.

ROSE: *AAAAARRRRRRRRGGGGGGGHHHHHHHHHH.*

JESSICA: Shut up. Shut the fuck up.

VICTORIA: Shut up.

JESSICA: Shut up you fucken cow.

VICTORIA: You fucken bully.

JESSICA: Fucken nobody.

VICTORIA: Fucken pussy licker.

ROSE stops jumping about and stands still. She's been hurt. She stares at **VICTORIA***, disbelieving.*

ROSE: Yeah. YOURS.

All three girls freeze. It's as though someone has fired a rifle in the air.

VICTORIA: Don't listen to her, Jess. Don't listen to HER.

ROSE: (*to* JESSICA) What. This is news to you? (*to* VICTORIA) You never told her?

VICTORIA: Nobody's listening, Rose.

ROSE: (*to* JESSICA) Me and Vic go way back. *Waaaaaaay* back. To what? Grade Seven? Yeah, I'd say Grade Seven's about right. Long before you got here.

VICTORIA: C'mon, Jess.

ROSE: Uh-oh. Saint Jessica looks confused.

VICTORIA: Jess? Give it over.

ROSE: Or is she grossed out?

VICTORIA: Whatever.

ROSE: Not whatever to Jess. Guess you don't know EVERYTHING she does, hey?

> **JESSICA** *looks at the jacket in her hands, then looks at* **ROSE**.

VICTORIA: What the fuck? WHAT THE FUCK?

> **JESSICA** *hands the jacket to* **ROSE**. **VICTORIA** *tries to intercept it, but* **JESSICA** *hits her away.* **ROSE** *starts laughing. She takes her jacket from* **JESSICA** *and shrugs it on.*

ROSE: You better be quaking in your boots.

JESSICA: (*to* **ROSE**) Get out of here.

ROSE: (*glowering at* **VICTORIA**) I mean really REALLY scared shitless quaking.

JESSICA: (*to* **ROSE**) GET OUT OF HERE.

ROSE: I TOLD you she was a skank.

> **ROSE** *leaves, staring down* **VICTORIA** *the entire time.*

JESSICA: (*to* **VICTORIA**) You, too.

VICTORIA: Jess—

JESSICA: I MEAN IT.

VICTORIA: Great.

> **VICTORIA** *slumps against the wall and lights a cigarette.*

JESSICA: I said to LEAVE.

VICTORIA: I HEARD YOU.

> **JESSICA** *kicks the wall.*

VICTORIA: You gonna do this? You gonna believe her?

JESSICA: Is she lying?

VICTORIA: Fuck you.

JESSICA: You coulda told me.

VICTORIA: None of your business.

JESSICA: I'm supposed to be your friend.

VICTORIA: Right.

> **JESSICA** *approaches* **VICTORIA**. *She leans in real close and*
> *pushes her hair out of her face, revealing a livid purple bruise.*
> *She traces the bruise, gently.* **VICTORIA** *pulls away.*

VICTORIA: You think you're any better? At least I don't do it to myself.

> **JESSICA** *slumps against the wall beside* **VICTORIA** *and lights a*
> *cigarette.*

VICTORIA: You think just cuz you're rich and your mummy and
daddy are still together and you spend your summers swimming
at the Granite Club that you're better than anybody else. Well,
YOU'RE NOT.

JESSICA: You love her?

VICTORIA: Hardly.

JESSICA: Then why—?

VICTORIA: Cuz she's good with her hands.

JESSICA: Is that what . . . I mean, what do, how do you . . .

VICTORIA: Don't be ignorant.

> *Pause.*

VICTORIA: You ever?

JESSICA: Not with a girl.

VICTORIA: I didn't ask with a girl, did I?

> **JESSICA** *takes out her X-acto blade and starts cutting her thigh.*

VICTORIA: GOD. I hate it when you do that.

JESSICA: So don't watch.

VICTORIA: It's completely fucking stupid.

JESSICA: It helps me think.

VICTORIA: (*watching* JESSICA *cut*) Will you PLEASE stop that? Please, Jess. For me.

JESSICA *retracts the blade, but holds onto it.*

JESSICA: Why do you let her treat you like that?

VICTORIA: She doesn't need my permission.

JESSICA: You should tell on her.

VICTORIA: Who would I tell?

JESSICA: I don't know. Your Mum? Father Paul.

VICTORIA: Oh yeah, they'd both love to hear about me and Rose, wouldn't they? They'd be into knowing all the details. All the stuff we do. Yeah. Good one. Grow up.

JESSICA: There's gotta be—

VICTORIA: There's nobody, okay? Nobody gives a shit. Except Rose. Rose is the only one who cares. How's that for fucked?

JESSICA *puts her blade down and comforts* VICTORIA. VICTORIA *maneouvers herself so that she's in position to kiss* JESSICA. JESSICA *pulls back.*

JESSICA: You don't hafta, Vic. Not with me. You don't have to.

SCENE ELEVEN

Spot on JESSICA *and* VICTORIA. JESSICA *stands slightly in front of* VICTORIA.

JESSICA: In every issue, the Invisible Girl is given a new hairstyle. The size of her breasts grow with every adventure. In one, horrifying, low moment in the life of this superhero, she designs a completely revealing costume, not to fight the powers of evil, but to try and get her husband's attention.

VICTORIA *steps closer to* JESSICA, *whispers the words just after her.*

JESSICA & VICTORIA: Nobody ever pays attention.

JESSICA: She tries her best. She continues to drive herself to exhaustion, without ever letting on just how much of a personal toll these superhuman battles are taking on her life. She continues to battle evil, and everyone else continues to dissect and analyze her hair. She knows she is capable of great things, and she clings to this knowledge. She consoles herself with her powers of invisibility, her force fields, her levitating disks. And she continues to fight.

JESSICA & VICTORIA: She continues to fight.

VICTORIA *takes over the lead.* JESSICA *whispers under her.*

JESSICA & VICTORIA: She fights and fights and fights. She fights Dr. Doom, Galactus, Psychoman, and every other evil motherfucker that comes her way. She leaves Reed for awhile, but then she goes back to him. I don't know why. I don't think she knows why. She saves his life shortly thereafter. And the entire time, she is never permitted to assume her rightful place as equal.
VICTORIA: And she never will.

JESSICA *looks at* VICTORIA, *completely confused. This is not part of the story. She's got it wrong. But* VICTORIA *is adamant.*

VICTORIA: She never, ever will. She will always be secondary. An afterthought. With big boobs and a kid to raise. Cuz that's how it goes. Even for superheroes. That's how it goes.

JESSICA *backs out of the spotlight.*

VICTORIA: And so, Susan "Storm" Richards, AKA Double Malice, AKA The Invisible Girl, does the only thing that she can do.
JESSICA: (*off*) Which is what? What does she do, Victoria? WHAT DOES SHE DO?

SCENE TWELVE

Behind the coach house of St. Mary's Academy for Girls. June. Scorching heat. Bright sunshine. **ROSE** *and* **JESSICA** *stand smoking. They are obviously distraught.* **JESSICA** *goes to kick at the wall a couple of times, but stops herself. They finish their cigarettes and stand as though frozen. Not once do they make eye contact, let alone speak. The bell rings.*

Blackout.

[End]

ABOUT THE PLAYWRIGHTS

Since its production at the Brave New Play Rites Festival, **CRAIG BARRON**'s *The Cipher and the Beagle* became a full-length play and received a staged reading at the Vancouver Playwrights Theatre Centre. His most recent stage production was the *Sex Now Cabaret* at Centennial Square in Victoria. Craig is also a published short fiction and non-fiction writer.

DENNIS E. BOLEN, BA (UVic), MFA (UBC), taught in UBC's Creative Writing Department from 1995 to 1997. He served as Fiction Editor at *subTerrain* for ten years and has authored four novels and one collection of short stories.

STEPHANIE BOLSTER has published three collections of poetry: *White Stone: The Alice Poems* (1998), which won the Governor General's Award and the Gerald Lampert Award; *Two Bowls of Milk* (1999), which won the Archibald Lampman Award; and *Pavilion* (2002). Raised in Burnaby, she teaches creative writing at Concordia University in Montréal.

AARON BUSHKOWSKY's plays, which include the award-winning *Strangers Among Us*, and *The Dead Reckoning*, have been produced throughout Canada. Aaron is the author of two books of drama: *Strangers Among Us* (Playwrights Canada Press) and more recently, *The Waterhead and Other Plays* (Playwrights Canada Press). Aaron is also known as a poet and prose writer with two books of poetry and one book of prose published.

TIM CARLSON is co-founder and co-artistic director of Western Theatre Conspiracy. His most recent play, *Omniscience*, was nominated for six Jessie Richardson theatre awards in 2005, including best production. He is a contributing editor for the cultural quarterly *Vancouver Review* and writes regularly for the *Globe and Mail*.

KEVIN CHONG graduated from the UBC BFA Creative Writing Program in 1997 and later received an MFA from Columbia University. He's published a novel, *Baroque-a-Nova*, and a work of narrative non-fiction, *Neil Young Nation*. He lives in Vancouver.

ANNE FLEMING is a playwright manqué whose most recent book is *Anomaly*, a novel. Her first book, *Pool-Hopping and Other Stories*, was shortlisted for the Governor-General's Award, the Ethel Wilson Fiction Prize and the Danuta Gleed Award. After fifteen years in Vancouver, Anne recently moved to Kelowna, B.C.., to teach creative writing at UBC Okanagan.

KATHY FRIEDMAN was born in Durban, South Africa and moved to Canada at the age of five. She has lived in Toronto and Glasgow and is currently completing a degree in creative writing and English at the University of British Columbia. *I'd Like to Throw a Party* is her first play.

DAN HERSHFIELD graduated from UBC with an MFA in Creative Writing and Theatre in 2005. In addition to writing, he also dabbles as an actor and a director. Dan is also a seasoned improviser, who has been a cast member with Theatresports Toronto, UBC Improv, and Vancouver TheatreSports, and is a regular performer with Urban Improv.

CORRINA HODGSON is a graduate of UBC's MFA in Creative Writing. Her work has been produced across Canada (Vancouver, Kamloops, Edmonton, Calgary, Winnipeg, and Toronto), and in the United States (Seattle, Off-off Broadway in New York), as well as on CBC Radio One. Recent awards include: Jane Chambers, Solo Collective, and TheatreB.C. Corrina teaches a radical playwriting workshop in Toronto.

TIM KENNALEY completed a BA and an MFA in Creative Writing. He is currently teaching international students in Victoria, B.C.

JAAN KOLK is a Vancouver writer whose other plays include *Chew the Blade, The Duplex,* and monologues *Love and DNA* and *Office Party.* He is currently writing a screenplay titled *North Island Time Warp* and works as a systems analyst at the City of Vancouver.

TSERING LAMA is currently a BA student in Creative Writing and International Relations at the University of British Columbia. She was born in Kathmandu, Nepal and moved to Vancouver, Canada in 1996.

KUEI-MING LIN graduated from UBC in Theatre. Her greatest joy in life is sharing stories through dance and theatre. *The Last Prayer* was first read by Peter Loeffler who gave it a two thumbs up before he passed away. She wants to thank everyone, especially Bryan Wade for their support of her plays.

SHERRY MACDONALD is a playwright and filmmaker. Her plays include *The Stone Face, The Duchess of Alba, Till Death Do Us Part* and *Cowgirl Jane*. After the Brave New Play Rites Festival, *Iraqi Karaoke* was produced at the Walking Fish Festival and was subsequently adapted into a film.

Since graduating from UBC in 1990 with a BFA in Acting, DAVID MACKAY has been working as a professional actor/playwright. His plays include *Necropolis, Big Shoes to Fill, KillJoy,* and *Beyond the Night Café*. He was also a co-writer of the international hit comedy *The Number 14*.

MEAH MARTIN has a BA Theatre, MFA in Creative Writing from UBC, where she taught Creative Writing from 2001-2005, and produced the Brave New Play Rites Festival in 2004. An excerpt from her play *White Skates* was published in *Going it Alone* by Kit Brennan, and her play *Over the Moon* was published in *Canadian Theatre Review*. Her play, *Brown Wasp*, was a winner in the 2000 National Playwrights Awards. Her new play, *The Rose Café*, will preview later this spring.

MAUREEN MEDVED writes plays, screenplays and fiction. Her novel, *The Tracey Fragments*, was published by House of Anansi Press in 1998, and is currently being adapted to film by acclaimed award-winning director Bruce McDonald. *Spanish Fly* was selected for the Best of Brave New Play Rites in 1994 and has since been performed in Vancouver, Toronto and Waterloo.

D. J. MITCHELL has been working as a set and costume designer since graduating from UBC in 1993. In addition to her design work, she has continued to write and direct play scripts. Her first play was written as an entry in UBC's Brave New Play Rites Festival in 1992. In 2005, a very short play of hers was presented as one of six scenes of a collective script produced in Calgary by A.P. Downey and 8-0-8 Productions.

SARA O'LEARY reads books for a living. She still can't believe that such a thing is possible. Her own most recent book is *When You Were Small*, illustrated by Julie Morstad (Simply Read Books). Sara's full-length plays include *The Dahl Sisters* (historical drama) and *The Kitchen Sink* (hysterical drama).

JASON PATRICK ROTHERY is the author of the plays *Wedgie, The Drop,* and *Menace*, as well as the creator and co-producer of the Walking Fish Festival. He has served as in-house dramaturge for Playwrights Theatre Centre and is the co-creator and author of *Dead End Days*, the flagship production of Rocket Ace Motion Pictures.

TIFFANY STONE is a children's poet. Her book, *Floyd the Flamingo and His Flock of Friends*, was published by Tradewind Books in fall 2004. Tiffany lives in Coquitlam with her husband and three young children (who are relieved their mom's a vegetarian). For other tasty tidbits, visit www.tiffanystone.ca.

RUDY THAUBERGER holds an MFA in Creative Writing from the University of British Columbia. He has published short stories and articles, and wrote the screenplay for the feature film *The Rhino Brothers*. He currently works as an instructor at the Vancouver Film School.

ANDREW WESTOLL is a writer and biologist with no fixed address. He is currently writing a memoir based on his travels in Suriname, South America. His travel writing has been nominated for a National Magazine Award and has appeared in newspapers across Canada. Other projects include redrafting his first novel and a full-length stage play.

A retired actress, **MEREDITH BAIN WOODWARD** graduated from the MFA program in 1993. She has since written animated cartoons for television, published two travel books, one history book, and many magazine articles. Her current project is a children's book, *Salsa Goes Sailing*, featuring her dog Salsa, which she diligently researches every summer. She lives in Vancouver.

ACKNOWLEDGEMENTS

This book is dedicated to all the actors, costumers, ASMs, backstage crew, audition wranglers, front-of-house volunteers, graphic artists, lighting and SFX designers, directors and playwrights who have been involved in Brave New Play Rites over the years. Special mention also has to be made of all the stage managers, technical directors and producers who worked on the festival. You made the difference, year in, year out, and I wish I could list everyone by name.

Personal thank yous go to George, who always came to the shows; Tom, who volunteered for far too many kicks at the can; and Kate, who was always there for the directors and playwrights. And what can I say about Johane? She went beyond the call of duty in her patience and understanding as I disappeared for several days each year to witness a jammed program of plays in a dark theatre. A big heartfelt thank you goes to her.

—Bryan Wade

ABOUT THE EDITOR

BRYAN WADE has had numerous productions of his stage plays in various theatres across the country. Some of these include: Factory Theatre Lab (Toronto), Toronto Free Theatre, Tarragon Theatre (Toronto), the Blyth Festival, Playwrights Workshop (Montreal), Quinzaine Internationale du Theatre Festival (Quebec City), Theatre Calgary and Vancouver's New Play Centre. He has also been Playwright-in-Residence at Factory Theatre and the Blyth Festival along with being an invited artist at the Playwrights' Colony at the Banff School of Fine Arts and the Stratford Festival.

Some of the radio drama series he has written for include: *Nightfall, Morningside, Vanishing Point, Stereo Theatre* and *Sunday Showcase*, and have been broadcast nationally across Canada and internationally in Australia. Several of his plays have been published by Playwrights Canada Press, including an anthology of five plays called *Blitzkrieg and Other Plays*. He currently teaches in the Creative Writing Program at the University of British Columbia.